Harper's Illustrated Handbook of Dogs

.WN

Health Care Section
by Robert W. Kirk, DVM

Edited by Roger Caras

With photographs by John L. Ashbey

PERENNIAL LIBRARY

Harper & Row, Publishers

New York, Cambridge, Philadelphia,
San Francisco, London, Mexico City, São
Paulo, Singapore, Sydney

Harper's Illustrated Handbook of Dogs.
All rights reserved. No part of this
book may be used or reproduced in any
manner whatsoever without permission.

For information address Harper & Row,
Publishers, Inc., 10 East 53rd Street,
New York, N.Y. 10022. Published
simultaneously in Canada by Fitzhenry
& Whiteside Limited, Toronto.

Prepared and produced by
Chanticleer Press, Inc., New York.

Designed by Massimo Vignelli.

Color reproductions by Nievergelt Repro
AG, Zurich, Switzerland.
Printed and bound by Dai Nippon,
Tokyo, Japan.
Typeset in Garamond by Dix Type Inc.,
Syracuse, New York.

Published July 1985
Second Printing, December 1987

Library of Congress Cataloging in
Publication Data

Harper's illustrated handbook of dogs.

Includes index.
1. Dogs.   2. Dog breeds.   3. Dog
breeds—Pictorial works.
I. Caras, Roger A.
SF426.H37 1985 636.7   85-1330
ISBN 0-06-091198-0 (pbk.)

The illustrations of Poodle clips are
reproduced from *The Complete Dog Book,*
by permission of the American Kennel
Club.

Harper's Illustrated Handbook of Dogs

A Chanticleer Press Edition

Contents

Contributors

Roger Caras
is general editor and author of the essays
The Origin of the Dog, A Special
Relationship, Watchdog or Guard Dog?,
Grooming and Routine Care, and
Showing Your Dog. He is special
correspondent for ABC News in the field
of pets, wildlife, and the environment,
and a columnist for several national
publications. He has written over fifty
books, including *The Roger Caras Dog
Book, A Celebration of Dogs,* and *Yankee:
The Inside Story of a Champion Bloodhound.*
Mr. Caras and his wife own several
Bloodhounds, a Basset Hound, a Golden
Retriever, a Jack Russell Terrier, and a
random-bred dog.

Robert W. Kirk, DVM,
wrote the section Health Care, reviewed
the Potential Health Problems for each
breed, and evaluated the seriousness of
common disorders for the Key to
Potential Health Problems. He is author
of *First Aid for Pets,* coauthor of *The
Handbook of Veterinary Procedures and
Emergency Treatment* and *Small Animal
Dermatology,* and editor of *Current
Veterinary Therapy.* Dr. Kirk is professor
of medicine and director of the Veterinary
Medical Teaching Hospital, New York
State College of Veterinary Medicine,
Cornell University, and has been a
veterinarian for forty years.

John Ashbey
photographed all of the breeds illustrated
specially for this guide. He is an official
photographer for the American Kennel
Club and his work has been featured in
Pure-Bred Dogs/American Kennel Gazette as
well as in several other publications. Mr.
Ashbey's studio is Photography
Unlimited in Philipsburg, New Jersey.
He owns three Rottweilers.

**Anne Rogers Clark and James
Edward Clark**
coauthored the section Working Dogs.
Anne and James Clark have worked with

dogs practically all their lives as
breeders, AKC judges, and handlers.
They contributed the chapter on non-
sporting dogs to *AKC's World of the Pure-
Bred Dog;* Anne Clark wrote the chapter
"Understanding the Standard of the
Chesapeake Bay Retriever" in *The
Chesapeake Bay Retriever,* and both have
written numerous articles for such
publications as *Popular Dogs* and *Poodle
Review.* The Clarks are AKC multi-
license judges and owners of The
Kennels of Surrey-Rimskiptle. They
breed English Cocker Spaniels, all three
sizes of Poodles, Whippets, Norfolk
Terriers, and Smooth Fox Terriers. The
couple's pets include two Norfolk
Terriers, a Smooth Fox Terrier, and a
Standard Poodle.

Chet Collier
wrote the Herding Dogs section. He is
show chairman of the Westminster
Kennel Club, vice-president of the
Westchester Kennel Club, and a member
of the Show Committee of the Eastern
Dog Club in Boston. Since 1968 Mr.
Collier has judged and exhibited dogs
and has owned some of the top-winning
Bouviers des Flandres. Mr. Collier is
executive vice-president of Metromedia
Producers Corporation.

George Dwyer
contributed the essays Raising a Puppy,
Purebred or Random-bred?, The Dog
Registries, and Registering Your
Dog. He works with Roger Caras at
ABC Television and Radio News in the
area of pets and wildlife. He has owned a
variety of dogs over the years and has
coproduced television news reports on
dog show events.

Jane Forsyth and Robert Forsyth
are the authors of the Toys section. They
have been involved with dogs since
childhood. As professional handlers, they
have had experience with almost every
breed recognized by the American

Kennel Club and have bred Boxers, English Cocker Spaniels, Pointers, and Shih Tzus at their kennel, Grayarlin Kennels in Southbury, Connecticut. The couple wrote the *Guide to Successful Dog Showing* and are AKC multi-license judges specializing in herding dogs, sporting dogs, and junior showmanship.

Brian Kilcommons
contributed the essays Obedience Training and Problem Solving, Temperament Testing, and How to Select a Breed. He has been a professional dog trainer for fifteen years. Currently the Behavior and Training Coordinator to the ASPCA, he has served as head of the training departments at the Humane Society of New York City and Bide-A-Wee Home. Mr. Kilcommons is coauthor of *Your Dog: An Owner's Manual* He has worked with Barbara Woodhouse in her training program throughout North America. Additionally, Mr. Kilcommons serves as animal expert for CBS Morning News.

Fred T. Miller
wrote the United Kennel Club Breeds section. He is president of the UKC and publisher of their magazines *Bloodlines, Coonhound Bloodlines,* and *Hunting Retriever.* He was assisted by Sara A. Jonas, office manager, and Andy Johnson, manager of breed field operations.

Pamela C. Rupert
contributed the sections Sporting Dogs and Non-Sporting Dogs. She coauthored, with Roger Caras, *Dogs: Records, Stars, Feats, and Facts* and contributed to the *Dog Owner's Bible.* A resident of Baltimore, Mrs. Rupert is a professional obedience trainer and has lived with dogs, cats, and other animals all her life. She owns a Golden Retriever, a Mastiff, and a Jack Russell Terrier.

Maxwell Riddle
wrote the section Hounds. He is author of over a dozen books, including *The Complete Book of Puppy Training, The Complete Brittany Spaniel, Dog People Are Crazy, The New Shetland Sheepdog,* and *Your Show Dog.* Mr. Riddle has judged dogs worldwide, from South America and South Africa to Japan. In this country he is an AKC all-breed judge and has been a UKC judge for hounds. Mr. Riddle has owned over thirty breeds, and currently has a Castro Laboreiro, a Portuguese breed that is not yet recognized in this country.

Seymour N. Weiss
prepared the Terriers section. He has been involved with dogs for over thirty years—he has bred Kerry Blue, Dandie Dinmont, and West Highland White terriers, and has successfully shown several breeds of terriers. Additionally, Mr. Weiss is approved to judge a number of terrier breeds in AKC shows. He has written numerous articles and books on dogs, is a member of the editorial staff of Howell Book House, which specializes in dog publications, and is an officer of the Dog Writers' Association of America. Mr. Weiss and his wife currently breed and own West Highland White Terriers.

Preface

The love of a dog is one of life's great rewards. To enjoy the company of a devoted, uncritical, and respectful friend, one who is eager to please and slow to feel resentment, is a pleasure that does not come often—but it is a pleasure that owning a dog is sure to bring.

The delight of a dog is accessible to everyone; all it really requires is time and a generous heart. Young people and old, large families and single people, experts and novices—all are able to give a dog the attention and care it requires, and to receive, in return, affection and companionship.

Whether you are an experienced owner with a dozen champions to your credit, or a newcomer in search of your first pet, selecting a dog that is right for you is a challenging and exciting experience. It also requires careful thought, for the dog that you take home with you now will be your companion and your responsibility for many years to come.

Presented here are photographs and full descriptions of 160 dogs, including the 129 breeds recognized by the American Kennel Club, 10 additional breeds recognized only by the United Kennel Club, plus more than 20 varieties. The accounts provide a clear and detailed profile of each breed, discussing its personality, appearance, and suitability for a particular environment. The history of every kind of dog is discussed as well, along with special hints for care and a warning about any health problems to which dogs may be susceptible.

This book will help you choose the dog that is best suited to your style of living. But whatever dog you select, whether a breed included here or a random-bred dog from the neighborhood shelter, browsing through these pages will give you a colorful and lively introduction to the world of dogs.

How to Use This Guide

Whether you are looking for a breed to buy, already have a pet, or simply love dogs, this book offers a new and fuller understanding of those wonderful animals—our first companions—dogs.

If You Are Trying to Choose a Pet
Are you thinking of buying your first dog? You will find that the lively color portraits of every breed recognized in America are particularly helpful. All of the dogs pictured were photographed specially for this book, and many are show champions. The essays on choosing the right dog give tips on what to look for, while the Key to Breed Characteristics provides a quick evaluation of each breed, rating its suitability for apartment life, children, or as a watchdog, as well as how much exercise and grooming time are required. Raising a Puppy offers advice for the early, often difficult, weeks of adjustment; Grooming and Routine Care provides hints on everyday requirements; and Registering Your Dog describes the registration procedure.

If a Dog Walks into Your Life
Has a lost dog suddenly arrived at your door? You will find guidelines on feeding, bedding, vaccinations, and even emergency first-aid treatment in the Health Care section. By looking through the color plates, you will be able to identify a purebred or find clues leading to a stray's purebred relatives—no matter how remote.

If You Are a Dog Owner
As a dog owner, you can discover more about your favorite breeds, learn about the origin of the dog as a companion, and trace the development of certain kinds of dogs, such as hounds, working dogs, terriers, toys, or any other of the official American Kennel Club groups. If you are having discipline problems with your pet, consult the essay Obedience Training and Problem Solving. Are you considering the show ring? Showing Your Dog offers pointers on how to prepare for a dog show.

If You Can't Have Your Own Dog
Have you always loved dogs but never been able to own one? You will be captivated by the striking photographs of America's finest purebreds and by the fascinating dog lore included here. The Pekingese, for example, is said to have been held in such esteem by the emperors of China that robbers were punished by death if they stole a royal pet, and the stately Saluki so impressed the ancient Egyptians that the pharaohs had their favorite dogs mummified and buried with them.

While not all breeds have an exalted or mysterious history, each dog has its own particular appeal. In these pages you will find every kind of purebred dog—each of them promising a lifetime of happiness.

The Origin of the Dog

An Ancient Lineage

The stories, legends, theories, and opinions about the origin of the domestic dog are seemingly without end. As a friend and helpmate of man, the dog has a long history. It is today believed that the dog's association with humans may trace back 25,000 years—perhaps somewhat less than that, but not much. All domestic dogs belong to a single species, *Canis familiaris*. Most people now seem to agree that the ancient ancestor of the dog was a small subspecies of wolf, *Canis lupus pallipes*, that is still found from Israel to India. While humans were leading a basic hunter-gatherer's existence, small wolves began to be part of the domestic picture; eventually, those animals were bred selectively. From that breeding has emerged every kind of dog we know today—over 400 breeds worldwide. Anthropological and historical investigations have demonstrated that certain distinct breeds of dogs have been known for a very long time. We know today that the Saluki probably goes back to Sumeria, 8000 or 9000 years ago; the Samoyed of Siberia may be nearly as old. The Greyhound predates Pharaonic Egypt; other breeds as well have their origins lost in the mist of time. Findings in Germany, Switzerland, and the British Isles show that before people had fully developed an agricultural way of life, there were already three or four different breeds of dogs to be found in the same village or settlement.

Travel to Distant Lands

As mysterious as those early breeding experiments are, the movement of dogs in prehistoric times are still more confounding. One of the oldest dog skeletons ever found was unearthed in a cave in what is now Idaho. Yet there is simply no way of knowing how the dog made that trip from the Middle East. In the eighteenth century, dogs were found on Pacific islands by Captain Cook, and the earliest settlers of Australia brought the dingo, a true dog, with them. Many of today's dogs are descended from a mastiff line and appear to have evolved in Tibet. How, in very ancient times, did these early descendants of wolves travel to Tibet from what is now Israel, Iran, and Iraq? The answer is probably that these animals were used as trade goods or cattle drovers and camp guards attached to caravans; but if this is so, then the early movements of traders across these lands must have taken place far earlier than many historians have calculated.

Lines of Descent

Until not very many years ago, it was assumed that there were two lines of descent leading to our modern dog, with one line descended from the small Middle Eastern wolf and the other from the African jackal. In recent years, the theory involving the jackal has been ruled out; nonetheless, there is evidence that a few breeds, at least, have had an additional ancestor. There is a line of dogs, known as the Northern Spitz, that includes the Siberian Husky, the Malamute, the Samoyed, the Keeshond, the Chow Chow, the Norwegian Elkhound, the Akita, and the original Pomeranian. It seems certain that the large timber wolf of the North has contributed to the evolution of these breeds. And in fact, modern Eskimos allow sled dogs to breed with wild wolves from time to time, presumably to add strength and stamina to the dog's blood lines.

Long before people kept cows or horses, they had dogs that would guard the home, protect the children, and help in the hunt. The earliest people even had dogs as pets—as lapdogs and fireside companions. Thus it is apparent that the dog is one of man's oldest friends—as well as one of his best.

A Special Relationship

The Test of Time

It seems that human history has never known a time when dogs were not a part of life—as workmates, playmates, or companions. In fact, our pets are such natural adjuncts to our lives that we often take them for granted. A quick glance through any family photograph album will reveal a Boston Terrier, a German Shepherd, or an indefinable random-bred gazing contentedly back at the camera. Titian, the famous Venetian painter and contemporary of Michelangelo, often included the family lapdog in his sumptuous portraits of Italian nobility. And Homer tells us that Odysseus had a dog who waited twenty years for his master's return.

An understanding such as this one between people and dogs cannot persist for centuries if it is not worthwhile for both parties. Countless social institutions have come and gone in society since dog-keeping became natural to the human condition. But through all the changes and upheavals of history, the intimate link between man and dog has persisted.

An Industrious Worker

In this century, especially in recent years, much research and investigation has taken place into the human-canine bond. What is at the basis of such a friendship? Clearly, dogs have just as strong a desire to be useful and to be part of a family as we have a notion to make use of them and include them in our lives.

Although the modern farm is almost completely mechanized, dogs still nip at the heels of cattle and keep the sheep in line. They kill rodents and deter unwelcome strangers. Dogs sniff out illegal drugs and other contraband at airports. And at home, dogs patrol endlessly, keeping tabs on windows and doors, and scrutinizing visitors.

But the single most important job of a dog is to offer love. This is the key element in a bond that has existed, perhaps unchanged, for many centuries —and a duty that is cheerfully performed.

The affection that a dog offers is nonjudgmental. A dog doesn't care what else you may do, what mistakes you make in your career, or if you lose at your tennis game, as long as you return its affection.

The Medical Benefits of Friendship

Medical studies demonstrate that pets, and dogs in particular, help us keep our blood pressure down and our heart rate steady. In fact, it seems almost certain that those people who have pets are likely to live longer than those who do not. People who keep pets are less likely to become ill, and those who do get ill seem to have a shorter recovery period. The many such cases on record, and the many studies now under way in leading universities and hospitals confirm these findings again and again. And in recent years, homes for geriatric residents have begun to include regular visits by volunteers with pets.

Something for Everyone

But it is not just those who are old or ill that benefit from the companionship of an uncritical and relentlessly affectionate friend. We all need to be listened to without interruption—which is something our human friends may not be able to do for us.

The bottom line is that dogs are wonderful. They make us feel good. So for that reason, perhaps more than any other, dogs have been around longer than the pyramids, longer than any religion, longer than cloth, metal tools, marriage, or art. There is no doubt that dogs will be with us when we colonize other planets. People and dogs were meant for each other, and there is no argument known that can suggest otherwise.

Purebred or Random-bred?

The Common Denominator

Call them mongrels, mixed-breeds, mutts, or random-breds—they are dogs, as surely as the most meticulously bred canines. And despite the sometimes exclusionary attitudes assumed by people who just don't know any better, random-breds can offer the same measure of joy to their owners as purebred animals. The differences are slight compared to the one overriding similarity: As dogs, they exist to love and be loved. Beyond that, when showing your dog is not an issue, choosing a specific breed or none at all is a question of personal preference.

Bred to a Purpose

Throughout many centuries, using increasingly refined methods of genetic manipulation, breeders have built on the physical and temperamental qualities of antecedent breeds to design animals that would fit their needs. Many purebreds are happiest and at their best when they have a chance to perform the services to which they were bred; thus one great advantage to owning purebreds is the predictability they offer. They can usually be depended upon to exhibit behavioral patterns peculiar to their breeds. For this reason, if you are considering a purebred, it is important to keep in mind the inherited character traits that a breed will have, and to select a dog whose breeding is compatible with your way of life. Naturally, in the case of random-breds, making such a determination will be somewhat more difficult. Traits become overridden and muddled, and even the best guesses in such cases are based on the assumption that you know what has gone into your random-bred animal—which is unlikely. Nonetheless, the purity of a dog's breeding does not always matter, and the initial cost of a random-bred is usually much less. Purebred dogs of less than fine show quality can also be had for

limited funds, and rather easily at that. Virtually every pound and shelter has such animals who are desperate for homes. Occasionally we hear of people who visit a pound or shelter and carry away the sorriest, saddest-looking dog in the place. They know that they can offer that animal the gift of life and that their own lives will be made better in turn.

A Matter of Taste

Just as some people enjoy fine examples of certain styles in art or architecture, many others take pleasure in the finest examples of specific breeds of dog. Such people are willing to expend time and money to promote the breed they fancy because it gives them pleasure. A certain benevolent snob appeal is at work here. Let it be noted, however, that, while show competition is exclusive with respect to dogs, all sorts of people are welcome. What is more, owning a show-quality animal is not necessarily an expensive venture. It certainly can be, but—as with most canine-related affairs—this is the owner's choice.
The fact that owners of fine show animals may spend more time or money on their animals than is strictly necessary does not mean that owners of mixed-breeds can't or don't do the same. Difference in breed, or lack of one, has no bearing at all.

Equals in Affection

Today, more often than not, the purpose our dogs are called upon to fulfill is that of companion. In that capacity, random-breds can stand proudly alongside purebreds in their ability to perform. So, whether your dog is a champion-caliber Affenpinscher or a slightly jumbled-looking no-name, be assured of this: It merely asks for all the love you can give, and is intent on returning it with interest.

Watchdog or Guard Dog?

Protection in the Home
In the minds of a great many prospective pet owners, an important factor in selecting a breed of dog is its suitability as a watchdog or a guard dog. There is ample reason to believe in dogs as effective deterrents to crime; deterrence, however, needs careful consideration, for human lives may be at stake.

Watchdogs
By definition, a watchdog is an animal that warns of the approach of strangers and the breach of territory. Many dogs are sensitive enough to distinguish the furtive behavior of a burglar from the legitimate bustle of a friendly visitor. You do not need a monster by the door to alert you to the presence of strangers. Numerous breeds are suited to the task, including some of the smallest dogs— toy Poodles, for instance—virtually all of the terriers, and many of the medium-size working and herding dogs.

Guard Dogs
Bred to a different purpose, guard dogs are animals whose already aggressive nature has been encouraged and expanded upon for defending territory and, often, attacking strangers. The purchase of such an animal is not something that should be decided upon without a great deal of careful reflection, for guard dogs can be dangerous.

If a watchdog barks inappropriately at your aunt or the paperboy, it may prove to be a mild annoyance; you must spend some time telling the dog to be still, to stop being silly. What has happened, of course, is that your watchdog has misjudged the nature and the intentions of the stranger.

But let us assume that you have a guard dog, trained to attack or allowed to become truly aggressive. What then of an inappropriate response? Every time a stranger enters a room or approaches you, your dog must make a split-second judgment call: Friend or foe? Attack or hold? And just as it is impossible to meet a human being who is incapable of error or poor judgment, so is it with guard dogs. It is simple nonsense to believe that well-trained guard dogs never make a mistake.

Professional criminals know how to elude alarm systems, by-pass locks, and otherwise avoid equipment that is designed to stop them. They also know how to make short work of guard dogs. No guard dog will ever stop a criminal who is intent on gaining entry. Dogs are easy to shoot (with a silent crossbow as well as a silencer-equipped gun); they are easy to poison (even if they are trained not to take food from strangers); and tear gas or mace will stop them in their tracks. There are a number of methods for effectively stopping any guard dog's attack; most professional criminals know these methods, but delivery boys, neighborhood children, and elderly relatives do not. Before you buy a guard dog, think long and carefully about the potential for tragic error.

Security and Peace of Mind
Choosing a watchdog is an excellent idea. Along with the sense of security such dogs give you—which is in large part justified—the breeds that make good watchdogs are also wonderful pets, bringing many fine qualities to their homes.

Buying an aggressive, attack-trained guard dog, on the other hand, is a terrible idea. These animals may be suitable escorts for uniformed police, or have a place on a military base where munitions are stored. But they do not belong in an apartment, on a farm, or in a suburban neighborhood. Dogs are meant to be helpful companions to human beings—not to make hasty judgments with their teeth.

Temperament Testing

Observing Behavior
Just as children from the same family have unique personalities, no two dogs are exactly the same either. Even two puppies of the same breed, from a single litter, can be quite different in temperament. A dog's personality is generally determined by inherited characteristics, its early environment, and its health. Observing the behavior of a puppy will often make it possible to predict what the animal will be like as an adult. The following guidelines will help you judge whether a puppy is right for you.

Assessing Inherited Personality Traits
First, if at all feasible, watch the behavior of the puppy's parents. Are they friendly or shy? Do they have an aggressive disposition? The chances are that the personality of the adults will turn up in their offspring. To have an overview of the breed, read the Personality section of the breed account carefully. This profile presents common personality traits that you may expect to find in the healthy adult dog.

Interaction Among Puppies
Some puppies are inclined to bite their littermates in play or mock aggression. Shy puppies may flinch and yelp excessively. Watch how puppies interact to determine which one is dominant. An assertive puppy is likely to behave with you just as it does with its littermates.

Responses to Touch
Dogs differ in their response to being touched. Cradle a puppy as if it were a baby. If the puppy has a calm disposition, it will settle down comfortably and quietly. The puppy that yelps and tries to right itself is showing anxiety. The yelper may have behavior problems as an adult.

Some dogs have overly sensitive skin and consequently a low tolerance for pain. A good way to test for skin sensitivity is to apply light pressure between the puppy's toes. Some animals will show pain or discomfort with even the slightest pressure. A puppy who reacts in this way may not be a good choice for a family with children, since children tend to hug and squeeze their puppy a lot and a sensitive puppy may overreact or be defensive when touched or caressed.

Sensitivity to Noise
Find out if a dog is overly sensitive to noise by taking a key ring and throwing it on the floor. A puppy should run up to see what that noise is all about; hanging back or hiding in a corner suggests timidity. The noise-sensitive puppy would do well with older, quieter people, but not in a noisy household or child-filled environment.

Knowing Your Own Temperament
When choosing a puppy it is important to remember that the dog's temperament should in some ways correspond to your own. Are you assertive, relaxed, or doting? A dog with an aggressive personality needs an owner who can direct this assertiveness properly. If a dog can adjust to your way of life, and if you can understand your dog's needs, your pet will provide you with years of pleasurable companionship.

How to Select a Breed

Starting Off Right

Whether your dog comes from a professional breeder, a friend whose female has had puppies, or a shelter, it is essential to select your new pet carefully. Remember that you are embarking on a long-term relationship that carries with it responsibility as well as enjoyment. Your dog will be totally dependent on you throughout its lifetime of ten or fifteen years.

The most serious problems in owning a dog arise because the initial selection of a pet was made thoughtlessly or in haste. Such an error is also easy to avoid, because there is a dog to fit almost every life-style. There are 131 breeds and varieties of purebred dogs currently recognized by the American Kennel Club, and an additional ten breeds recognized only by the United Kennel Club. In addition, of course, there is an unlimited variety of random-bred dogs. Breeds of dogs, like other things that people buy and sell, come in and out of vogue. The Cocker Spaniel has recently dethroned the Poodle as the most popular dog in the United States. And in recent years, breeds such as the Old English Sheepdog, Siberian Husky, Irish Setter, Golden Retriever, and Akita have experienced booms in popularity. Aesthetics and popularity will inevitably be considerations when you select a dog, but do not assume that the breed you find so attractive or compelling is necessarily the one to suit your style of living.

What Do You Want from Your Dog?

When people decide to buy a dog, they usually have in mind a few traits that they consider desirable in a pet. A prospective owner may want a male or female; a large dog or a small one; a playmate or a watchdog; a dog to take hunting or one for show; a popular breed; or simply a beautiful animal with a furry coat. Whatever you are looking for, it is important to bear in mind that different breeds have distinctive characters, which are the result of many years—sometimes centuries—of breeding for specific purposes. Study the breeds that interest you most, and learn the pros and cons of the choice you may be about to make.

What Can Your Dog Expect from You?

Many factors go into the selection of a dog. First ask yourself what kind of a dog will fit with your life-style. Consider four important points: how much you can afford to spend on a dog; where you live; whether you have children; and how much time you will devote to your pet. If you have reserved a small sum for the purchase of a dog, it might be wise to choose a random-bred shelter dog or one of the less expensive purebreds. Keep in mind that dogs are generally priced according to rarity and popularity. Remember, too, that the purchase price of a dog is just the initial outlay; you must be willing and able to pay for veterinary bills, dog food, and many miscellaneous items for the life of your dog.

Where you live will determine the amount and kind of exercise you can give your dog. Is your home in the city, the suburbs, or the country? Do you divide your time between two residences? Do you have fenced-in yard or live in a fifth-floor walk-up? Dogs that can be paper trained—such as any of the toys, or even some small breeds like the Dachshund—might be a good choice for owners who are away for much of the day or do not care to walk their dogs late at night. If you live in the country, you can more easily give a proper home to one of the larger sporting dogs, such as the Irish Setter or the Pointer, or a working dog, like a Great Dane or Mastiff, all of which require a prodigious amount of real exercise.

Do you have children, or are you planning to have children? If so, you should rule out selecting many of the miniature or toy breeds. These dogs are generally not pleased with the rough-and-tumble play of children. But many other, more robust, breeds—including the retrievers and terriers—thrive on the activity that living with children provides.

Large dogs—especially working dogs—were bred to protect their owners' property. These animals are powerful and intelligent, but they need firm training and a great deal of exercise. Their natural instincts can be a liability if they are not given proper direction. To live in harmony with such a dog, an owner must be assertive, confident, and experienced. On the other hand, small breeds often make excellent watchdogs—possibly even the best watchdogs of all.

Dogs with a full coat, such as the Old English Sheepdog, require extensive grooming to maintain their appearance. Double-coated dogs, such as the Siberian Husky, Rough Collie, and Chow Chow, shed far more than other breeds; this factor must be taken into consideration if you want to love your dog as much in April as you did in December. Shedding can be a constant annoyance, and there has been more than one dog banned from the house because of its unmanageable coat. But no dog grows its long, thick coat as a surprise. There is no excuse for being unprepared for the length of a dog's coat, or for being unwilling to spend time maintaining it. If someone in your family has allergies, it would be wise to choose a breed that does not shed, such as the Poodle or Schnauzer. (It is dog dander, rather than dog hair, that causes allergies; only shed hair has dander.)

Buying with Care

If you choose a dog that is currently in vogue, remember that breeds vary in popularity from decade to decade. It is well to remember that the more popular the breed, the greater the possibility of problems in temperament or behavior, or of inherited diseases. Mass commercial breeders engage in intensive inbreeding to capitalize on the large, unknowledgeable market for popular dogs. If you encounter sellers who point out only the positive and not the negative traits of a breed, beware. Such people are not interested in matching a dog and prospective owner. No good breeder ever appears anxious to sell a dog. On the contrary, careful breeders show great concern for the match they are about to make, and may be far less willing to close a sale than their customers are.

When you have narrowed your choices down to a few breeds, it might be a good idea to attend a dog show. It will provide an opportunity to see many different breeds in one day. You can talk to the people who breed and show dogs and learn about the dogs that appeal to you. Also, there are fine books available that describe individual breeds in detail and give the requirements for the proper care of each one. Call either the American Kennel Club or United Kennel Club for a listing of breed clubs and breeders near you. The knowledge and advice you will receive from a reputable breeder can be invaluable in helping you select exactly the right dog.

When you choose the right dog, you have chosen a friend. It is worth your time and trouble to do it right.

The Right Dog for You

Evaluating Your Choices
Choosing a pet is an important decision. Not only will your dog be a faithful companion for years to come, but it will also become a member of your family. A pet is a pleasure and a responsibility. You must meet its needs for proper care —from exercise, grooming, and training, to good nutrition and plenty of love—in order to make it a welcome and happy member of your household. Not everyone, however, can devote the same amount of time to a pet; nor does everyone seek the same temperament, personality, or appearance in a dog.

A Key to Breed Characteristics
To help you select the right dog, the Key to Breed Characteristics establishes five categories, according to which every breed and variety recognized in America is evaluated. These categories tell you if a dog is suitable to urban life, good with children, or a good watchdog; how much exercise is advisable; and how much grooming care is needed. For most categories, a breed is rated high, moderate, low, or unsuited; suitability for families with children and performance as a watchdog are only indicated if the breed is outstanding (high). On the chart, the breeds are divided into four size groups—tiny, small, medium-size, and large—in the same way that the color plates are divided.

Key to Breed Characteristics

	Suited to Urban Life	Good with Children	Good Watchdog	Exercise Advisable	Grooming Care
Tiny Dogs (Plates 1-20)					
Affenpinscher	●		●	◐	●
Brussels Griffon, rough	●			◐	●
Brussels Griffon, smooth	●			◐	●
Chihuahua, long coat	●			◐	●
Chihuahua, smooth coat	●			◐	●
Dachshund, longhaired	●	●		◐	●
Dachshund, smooth	●	●		◐	●
Dachshund, wirehaired	●	●		◐	●
English Toy Spaniel	●		●	◐	●
Japanese Chin	●			◐	●
Small Dogs (Plates 21-52)					
American Eskimo, miniature	●		●	●	●
Australian Terrier	●	●	●	●	●
Beagle	●	●	●	●	◐
Bichon Frise	●	●		◐	●
Border Terrier	●	●		●	◐
Cairn Terrier	●	●		●	●
Cocker Spaniel	●	●		●	●
Dachshund, longhaired	●	●		◐	●
Dachshund, smooth	●	●		◐	●
Dachshund, wirehaired	●	●		◐	●
Dandie Dinmont Terrier	●			●	●
English Cocker Spaniel	●	●		●	●
Italian Greyhound	●			◐	◐
Lakeland Terrier	●	●	●	●	●
Lhasa Apso	●			●	●

Color Key
● High
● Moderate
● Low
○ Unsuited

	Suited to Urban Life	Good with Children	Good Watchdog	Exercise Advisable	Grooming Care
Maltese	High			Low	High
Miniature Pinscher	High	High	High	Low	Moderate
Papillon	High			Moderate	Moderate
Pekingese	High			Low	High
Pomeranian	High		High	Low	Moderate
Poodle, toy	High	High		High	High
Silky Terrier	High		High	High	High
Tibetan Spaniel	High			Moderate	Moderate
Toy Fox Terrier	High			Moderate	Low
Yorkshire Terrier	High		High	Low	High
Manchester Terrier, toy	High		High	High	Low
Miniature Schnauzer	High	High	High	High	High
Norfolk Terrier	High	High		High	Low
Norwich Terrier	High	High		High	Low
Poodle, miniature	High			High	High
Pug	High	High		High	High
Schipperke	High	High	High	High	Low
Scottish Terrier	High			High	High
Sealyham Terrier	High	High		High	High
Shetland Sheepdog	High	High		High	High
Shih Tzu	High			Low	High
Skye Terrier	High		High	High	High
Smooth Fox Terrier	High	High	High	High	Moderate
West Highland White Terrier	High		High	High	High
Wire Fox Terrier	High	High	High	High	High

	Suited to Urban Life	Good with Children	Good Watchdog	Exercise Advisable	Grooming Care
Medium-size Dogs (Plates 53-108)					
Airedale Terrier	●	●	●	●	●
American Eskimo, standard	●		●	●	●
American Foxhound	●			●	●
American Staffordshire Terrier	●			●	●
American Water Spaniel	●	●	●	●	●
Australian Cattle Dog	●		●	●	●
Australian Shepherd	●			●	●
Basenji	●			●	●
Basset Hound	●	●		●	●
Bearded Collie	●			●	●
Bedlington Terrier	●			●	●
Belgian Malinois	●		●	●	●
Belgian Sheepdog	●		●	●	●
Belgian Tervuren	●		●	●	●
Bluetick Coonhound	●			●	●
Border Collie	●		●	●	●
Boston Terrier	●	●		●	●
Brittany	●	●	●	●	●
Bulldog	●	●		●	●
Bull Terrier	●			●	●
Cardigan Welsh Corgi	●		●	●	●
Clumber Spaniel	●	●		●	●
Dalmatian	●			●	●
English Coonhound	●			●	●
English Foxhound	●			●	●
English Shepherd	●		●	●	●
English Springer Spaniel	●	●		●	●

Color Key
- ● High
- ● Moderate
- ● Low
- ○ Unsuited

	Suited to Urban Life	Good with Children	Good Watchdog	Exercise Advisable	Grooming Care
Field Spaniel	Moderate	High	High	High	Moderate
French Bulldog	High		High	Moderate	Low
Harrier	Unsuited			High	Moderate
Irish Terrier	High	High	High	High	Moderate
Keeshond	High	High	High	Moderate	High
Kerry Blue Terrier	High		High	High	Moderate
Manchester Terrier, standard	High	High	High	High	Low
Norwegian Elkhound	High	High	High	High	Moderate
Pembroke Welsh Corgi	High		High	High	Moderate
Pharaoh Hound	Low	High		High	Moderate
Plott Hound	Unsuited			High	Low
Poodle, standard	High		High	High	High
Portugese Water Dog	Low			High	Moderate
Puli	Low		High	High	High
Redbone Coonhound	Unsuited			High	Low
Samoyed	Low	High	High	High	High
Siberian Husky	Low	High		High	Moderate
Soft-Coated Wheaten Terrier	High	High	High	High	Moderate
Staffordshire Bull Terrier	High		High	High	Low
Standard Schnauzer	High		High	High	High
Sussex Spaniel	High	High	High	Moderate	Moderate
Tibetan Terrier	High		High	High	High
Treeing Walker Coonhound	Low			High	Low
Welsh Springer Spaniel	High	High	High	High	Moderate
Welsh Terrier	High	High	High	Moderate	Moderate
Whippet	High	High		High	Low
Wirehaired Pointing Griffon	Low	High	High	High	Low

	Suited to Urban Life	Good with Children	Good Watchdog	Exercise Advisable	Grooming Care
Large Dogs (Plates 109-144)					
Afghan Hound	●		●	●	●
Alaskan Malamute	●	●		●	●
Bernese Mountain Dog	●			●	●
Black and Tan Coonhound	●			●	●
Bouvier des Flandres	●	●	●	●	●
Boxer	●		●	●	●
Briard	●		●	●	●
Chow Chow	●		●	●	●
Chesapeake Bay Retriever	●	●	●	●	●
Collie, rough	●	●	●	●	●
Collie, smooth	●	●	●	●	●
Curly-Coated Retriever	●		●	●	●
Doberman Pinscher	●		●	●	●
English Setter	●	●		●	●
Flat-Coated Retriever	●	●		●	●
German Shepherd	●		●	●	●
German Shorthaired Pointer	●			●	●
Giant Dogs (Plates 145-160)					
Akita	●		●	●	●
Bloodhound	●	●		●	●
Borzoi	●	●		●	●
Bullmastiff	●		●	●	●
Great Dane	●	●	●	●	●
Great Pyrenees	●		●	●	●
Irish Wolfhound	●			●	●
Komondor	●		●	●	●

Color Key
- ● High
- ● Moderate
- ● Low
- ○ Unsuited

	Suited to Urban Life	Good with Children	Good Watchdog	Exercise Advisable	Grooming Care
German Wirehaired Pointer	●		●	●	●
Giant Schnauzer	●	●	●	●	●
Golden Retriever	●	●		●	●
Gordon Setter	●	●		●	●
Greyhound	●			●	●
Ibizan Hound	●			●	●
Irish Setter	●	●		●	●
Irish Water Spaniel	●			●	●
Labrador Retriever	●	●		●	●
Old English Sheepdog	●		●	●	●
Otter Hound	●	●	●	●	●
Pointer	●			●	●
Rhodesian Ridgeback	●			●	●
Saluki	●			●	●
Vizsla	●		●	●	●
Weimaraner	●		●	●	●

	Suited to Urban Life	Good with Children	Good Watchdog	Exercise Advisable	Grooming Care
Kuvasz	●		●	●	●
Mastiff	●	●	●	●	●
Newfoundland	●	●		●	●
Rottweiler	●		●	●	●
Saint Bernard, longhaired	●		●	●	●
Saint Bernard, shorthaired	●		●	●	●
Scottish Deerhound	●	●		●	●

The Dog's Anatomy

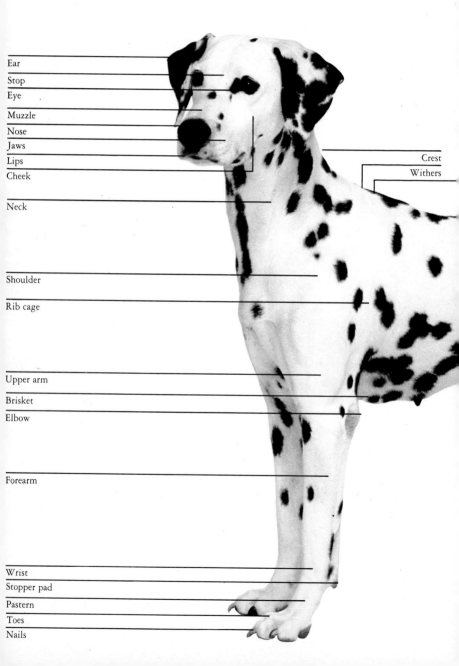

Ear

Stop

Eye

Muzzle

Nose

Jaws

Lips

Cheek

Crest

Withers

Neck

Shoulder

Rib cage

Upper arm

Brisket

Elbow

Forearm

Wrist

Stopper pad

Pastern

Toes

Nails

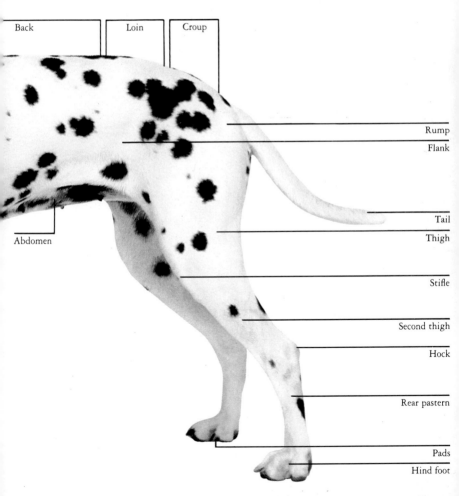

Wrinkles

Flews

Dewlap

Measure height from the withers to the ground.

Back

Loin

Croup

Rump

Flank

Tail

Thigh

Abdomen

Stifle

Second thigh

Hock

Rear pastern

Pads

Hind foot

Coat Types

The length, texture, style, and thickness of dogs' coats vary considerably among breeds and varieties. Dogs with short, smooth coats usually require only routine grooming. Although some wiry coats, such as that of the German Wirehaired Pointer, need little extra care, many

Short, Smooth Coat

Basset Hound

Wiry Coat

Wirehaired Dachshund

Miniature Schnauzer

Wavy, Curly, or Corded Coat

Chesapeake Bay Retriever

Long or Well-feathered Coat

Shih Tzu

Thick, Double Coat

Chow Chow

wirehaired breeds, such as the Miniature Schnauzer, require a fair amount of trimming to appear presentable. Some wavy or curly coats are relatively easy to groom, but other curly or corded coats may need extensive attention. Dogs with long or well-feathered coats generally demand more than average grooming. Breeds with thick, double coats tend to shed a lot. When selecting a dog, you should consider the amount of grooming required.

Dalmatian

Boxer

Wirehaired Pointing Griffon

Airedale Terrier

Irish Water Spaniel

Komondor

Cocker Spaniel

Afghan Hound

Rough Collie

Siberian Husky

Key to the Color Plates

This visual key is designed to help you find dog breeds easily. In the color plates on the following pages, the dogs have been arranged according to five sizes—tiny, small, medium-size, large, and giant. Within each category, the various breeds and varieties are grouped by

Tiny Dogs

Known as lapdogs, most of these breeds are toys. Several weigh 7 pounds or less.
Long, low build, 1–4
Fluffy ears and tail, 5–7
Spaniels, 8–12
Whiskers or mane, 13–16
Chihuahua-like build, 17–20

1–4

5–7

Small Dogs

These breeds range from about 9 to 15 inches tall and weigh between 10 and 25 pounds.
Long, low build, 21–24
Stylish coat, 25–28
Scottie-like build, 29–36
Fox Terrier-like build, 37–40
Beagle-like build, 41–44
Cocker Spaniels, 45–48
Collie-like build, 49–50
Greyhound-like build, 51–52

21–24

25–28

49–50

51–52

Medium-size Dogs

The selection of medium-size dogs includes every type except toy breeds. Most range from 15 to 27 inches tall and weigh between 26 and 60 pounds.
Long, low build, 53–56
Bull Terrier-like build, 57–64
Greyhound-like build, 65–68
Hounds, 69–76
Spaniel-like build, 77–83
Shaggy coat, 84–86
Poodle-like coat, 87–89
Airedale-like build, 90–96
Shepherd-type build, 97–100
Husky-like build, 101–108

53–56

57–64

87–89

90–96

similarities in build or appearance. Each category is described on the left; photographs of the representative dogs in that group are shown at right with corresponding plate numbers above them. By turning to the color plates, you will learn the breed name, ideal height and weight, coat characteristics and colors, and the page number of the text description.

Most of the breeds are recognized by the American Kennel Club, except for eleven breeds recognized only by the United Kennel Club.

8–12 13–16 17–20

29–36 37–40 41–44 45–48

65–68 69–76 77–83 84–86

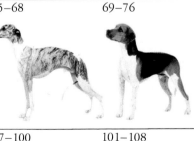

97–100 101–108

Large Dogs

Most of the breeds included here are strong and muscular. They range from 21 to 27 inches tall and weigh between 65 and 86 pounds.

Shaggy coat, 109–112
Schnauzer-like build, 113–114
Pointer-like build, 115–117, 119–120
Black and Tan Coonhound, 118
Retriever-like build, 121–129
Setters, 130–132
Greyhound-like build, 133–137
Boxer and other powerful builds, 138–140
Collie-like build, 141–144

109–112

113–114

133–137 138–140

Giant Dogs

Distinguished by enormous height or bulk, most of theses dogs measure from 27 to 34 inches tall or more and often weigh well over 100 pounds.

Hairy look, 145–148
Great Danes, 149–150
Akita, 151
Rottweiler, 152
Mastiffs and Saint Bernards, 153–156
Bloodhound, 157
Great Pyrenees and similar builds, 158–160

145–148 149–150

158–160

115–117, 119, 120   118   121–129   130–132

141–144

151   152   153–156   157

1 Miniature Dachshund

Height: about 5". Weight: under 10 lbs. Smooth, longhaired, or wirehaired coat. Red or tan; black; chocolate; gray or gray and white, both with tan markings; or dappled gray or brown. Brown to brownish-black eyes. Page 147.

3 Yorkshire Terrier

Height: 6–7". Weight: 2–7 lbs. Glossy, fine, silky, straight coat hangs evenly to the ground. Hair parted on face and down back. Steel-blue on back and tail; golden tan on head, chest, and legs. Dark eyes with dark rims. Page 223.

2 Pekingese

Height: 8–9″ Weight: to 14 lbs.
Long, flat coat with thick undercoat and
feathering on ears, neck, legs, tail, and
toes. All colors, including parti-colored.
Black mask desirable. Dark eyes.
Page 217.

4 Silky Terrier

Height: 9–10″. Weight: 8–10 lbs.
Long, fine, silky, flat coat; profuse on top
of head. Hair parted down back to tail.
Tan and various shades of blue. Dark
eyes.
Page 222.

5 Papillon

Height: 8–11″. Weight: 8–10 lbs. Long, flowing, silky coat, especially abundant on chest and tail. Long hair forms breeches on hind legs. Always parti-colored: white with patches of any color over ears and eyes. Dark eyes. Page 216.

7 Japanese Chin

Height: about 9″. Weight: under or over 7 lbs. Long, straight, silky coat with a ruff around neck and feathering on ears, thighs, and tail. Black and white or red and white. Dark eyes. Page 212.

6 Maltese

Height: about 5″. Weight: under 7 lbs. Extremely long, silky, white coat reaches almost to the ground. Very long hair on head and tail. Dark eyes with black rims.
Page 213.

8 Tibetan Spaniel

Height: about 10″. Weight: 9–15 lbs. Moderately long, silky coat with feathering on ears, forelegs, tail, and rear. All colors allowed. Dark brown eyes with black rims.
Page 235.

9 Prince Charles English Toy Spaniel

Height: 9–10″. Weight: 9–12 lbs. Long, soft, wavy coat with profuse mane and feathering on ears, legs, and tail. Tricolor: white with large black markings and tan over eyes, and on chest and legs. Dark eyes.
Page 210.

11 King Charles English Toy Spaniel

Height: 9–10″. Weight: 9–12 lbs. Long, soft, wavy coat with profuse mane and feathering on ears, legs, and tail. Black with tan markings over eyes, and on muzzle, chest, and legs. Dark eyes.
Page 210.

10 Blenheim English Toy Spaniel

Height: 9–10″. Weight: 9–12 lbs.
Long, soft, wavy coat with profuse mane
and feathering on ears, legs, and tail.
White with red on ears and cheeks, and
dime-size red blaze on forehead. Dark
eyes.
Page 210.

12 Ruby English Toy Spaniel

Height: 9–10″. Weight: 9–12 lbs.
Long, soft, wavy coat with profuse mane
and feathering on ears, legs, and tail.
Solid chestnut-red. Dark eyes.
Page 210.

13 Brussels Griffon

Height: about 8″. Weight: 8–12 lbs. Smooth, straight coat or rough, wiry, longer coat as shown. Reddish brown or black and reddish brown. Solid black in rough coat only. Black eyes with black rims.
Page 208.

15 Toy Poodle

Height: to 10″. Weight: 5–7 lbs. Harsh, dense coat may be curly or corded, with feathered ears. Many stylish clips. Solid colors only: cream as shown, black, white, apricot, café au lait, brown, silver, gray, or blue. Dark eyes.
Page 219.

14 Affenpinscher

Height: under 10¼". Weight: to 8 lbs. Harsh, wiry coat with a mustache and a tuft of hair on chin. Black or black with tan, red, gray, or another mixture. Black eyes.
Page 207.

16 Pomeranian

Height: 6½–7". Weight: 3–7 lbs. Soft undercoat, harsh outer coat, with feathering on forelegs, rear, and tail. Any solid color with or without shading; white and any solid; sable; or black and tan. Dark eyes.
Page 218.

17 Long Coat Chihuahua

Height: about 5″. Weight: 2–6 lbs. Soft coat with fringe on ears and feathering on legs and tail. May have undercoat. Any color in any combination. Usually dark eyes, light eyes acceptable for light coats. Page 209.

19 Toy Fox Terrier

Height: to 10″. Weight: 3½–7 lbs. Short, satiny, full-textured coat, slightly longer at ruff. Black and white with tan trim, or tan and white. Dark eyes. Page 263.

18 Smooth Coat Chihuahua

Height: about 5″. Weight: 2–6 lbs. Smooth, close-fitting coat with ruff around neck. May have undercoat. Any color in any combination. Usually dark eyes, light eyes acceptable for light coats.
Page 209.

20 Miniature Pinscher

Height: 10–12½″. Weight: 9–10 lbs. Smooth coat. Solid red, black with tan markings, or chocolate with rust markings. Dark brown or black eyes.
Page 215.

21 Smooth Dachshund

Height: about 9". Weight: 10–20 lbs. Short, smooth coat. Solid red or tan; black, chocolate, gray, or white, each with tan markings; or dappled gray or brown with darker patches. Dark reddish-brown to brownish-black eyes. Page 147.

23 Wirehaired Dachshund

Height: about 9". Weight: 10–20 lbs. Short, wiry outer coat with finer undercoat. Bushy eyebrows and beard. All colors allowed. Dark reddish-brown to brownish-black eyes. Page 147.

22 Longhaired Dachshund

Height: about 9". Weight: 10–20 lbs. Long, smooth, slightly wavy coat. Solid red or tan; black, chocolate, gray, or white, each with tan markings; or dappled gray or brown with darker patches. Dark brown eyes.
Page 147.

24 Dandie Dinmont Terrier

Height: 8–11". Weight: 18–24 lbs. Crisp outer coat and soft undercoat. Soft topknot and tasseled ears. Pepper colors, silver to blue-black; or mustard hues, pale fawn to dark red. Head may be cream-white. Hazel eyes.
Page 189.

25 Miniature Poodle

Height: 10–15″. Weight: 15–16 lbs. Harsh, dense coat may be curly or corded, with feathered ears. Many stylish clips. Solid colors only: silver as shown, black, white, cream, apricot, café au lait, brown, gray, or blue. Dark eyes. Page 233.

27 Lhasa Apso

Height: 10–11″. Weight: 14–15 lbs. Long, straight, heavy, dense coat. Long hair covers head, body, legs, and feet and forms whiskers and beard. Any color allowed, lionlike hues preferred. Dark brown eyes. Page 232.

26 Bichon Frise

Height: 9–12″. Weight: 7–12 lbs. Profuse, loosely curled outer coat and short, soft undercoat. Topknot and long hair on ears and tail. White or white with buff, cream, apricot, or gray. Dark brown or black eyes.
Page 225.

28 Shih Tzu

Height: 8–11″. Weight: 9–18 lbs. Luxurious, long, flowing coat may be wavy, but not curly. Woolly undercoat. Appears to have long mustache. All colors permissible. Dark eyes with black rims.
Page 221.

29 Norfolk Terrier

Height: 10″. Weight: 11–12 lbs. Harsh, straight, wiry outer coat; softer undercoat. Slight whiskers and eyebrows and the suggestion of a mane. Drop ears. Wheaten as shown, red, black and tan, or grizzle. Dark eyes with black rims. Page 195.

31 Australian Terrier

Height: 10″. Weight: 12–14 lbs. Straight, harsh outer coat; soft undercoat. Topknot on head and ruff around throat. Blue-black or silver-black, with tan markings; or solid red or sandy color. Dark eyes. Page 184.

30 Norwich Terrier

Height: 10″. Weight: 11–12 lbs.
Harsh, straight, wiry outer coat; softer
undercoat. Slight whiskers and beard and
the suggestion of a mane. Erect ears.
Red, wheaten, black and tan, or grizzle.
Dark eyes with black rims.
Page 196.

32 Cairn Terrier

Height: 9½–10″. Weight: 13–14 lbs.
Shaggy, harsh outer coat; short, soft
undercoat. Any color but white;
typically brindle as shown, or wheaten,
tan, or silver. Hazel or dark eyes.
Page 188.

33 West Highland White Terrier

Height: 10–11″. Weight: 17–19 lbs.
Harsh, dense, straight outer coat; soft
undercoat. Hair abundant on head and
face, shorter on neck and shoulders.
White only. Dark eyes with black rims.
Page 204.

35 Skye Terrier

Height: 9½–10″. Weight: 23–25 lbs.
Long coat covers face, ears, and body to
the ground. Hard, straight outer coat;
soft, woolly undercoat. Black, blue,
cream, fawn, gray, or silver-platinum.
Brown eyes.
Page 199.

34 Sealyham Terrier

Height: about 10½". Weight: 23–24 lbs. Hard, wiry outer coat, soft undercoat. Shaggy eyebrows and long whiskers. All white, or with tan, lemon, or badger markings on head and ears. Dark eyes. Page 198.

36 Scottish Terrier

Height: 10". Weight: 18–22 lbs. Hard, wiry outer coat; soft undercoat. Thick eyebrows and whiskers. Usually brindle as shown; also black, steel- or iron-gray, grizzle, sandy, or wheaten. Dark brown or almost black eyes. Page 197.

37 Miniature Schnauzer

Height: 12–14″. Weight: 14–15 lbs. Harsh, wiry outer coat; close undercoat. Bushy eyebrows and whiskers. Abundant hair on legs and feet. Salt-and-pepper, black and silver, or solid black; tan shading allowed. Dark brown eyes. Page 194.

39 Lakeland Terrier

Height: 14–15″. Weight: about 17 lbs. Dense, wiry outer coat; soft undercoat. Long hair on muzzle and legs. Blue, black, liver, black and tan, blue and tan, red, red grizzle, grizzle and tan, or wheaten. Dark brown or black eyes. Page 192.

38 Wire Fox Terrier

Height: to 15½". Weight: 16–18 lbs. Hard, wiry, slightly wavy coat with longer hair over eyes, muzzle, legs, and under body. White with random black and/or tan markings. Dark eyes and rims.
Page 205.

40 Smooth Fox Terrier

Height: to 15". Weight: 16–18 lbs. Close, sleek, but hard and abundant coat. White with random black and/or tan markings. Dark eyes and rims.
Page 200.

41 Border Terrier

Height: 12–13″. Weight: 11½–15½ lbs.
Harsh, wiry, close outer coat; soft, dense
undercoat. Short whiskers. Red, grizzle
and tan, blue and tan, or wheaten. Dark
hazel eyes.
Page 186.

43 Beagle

Height: 13″ or less. Weight: 18 lbs.
Short, hard, dense coat. Black, tan, and
white in any combination and with any
hound markings. Brown or hazel eyes.
Page 143.

42 Pug

Height: 10–11″. Weight: 14–18 lbs.
Short, soft, fine, glossy coat. Black,
silver-fawn, or apricot-fawn, with black
mask. Dark eyes.
Page 220.

44 Beagle

Height: 13–15″. Weight: about 20 lbs.
Short, hard, dense coat. Black, tan, and
white in any combination and with any
hound markings. Brown or hazel eyes.
Page 143.

45 English Cocker Spaniel

Height: 15–17″. Weight: 26–34 lbs. Silky, flat or slightly wavy coat with feathering on ears, chest, belly, and legs. White, black, black and tan, or roan pattern in blue, liver, red, lemon, or orange as shown. Dark or hazel eyes. Page 130.

47 Cocker Spaniel

Height: 14–15″. Weight: 26–28 lbs. Silky coat, flat or slightly wavy. Feathering on ears, chest, belly, and legs. Parti-color variety: 2 or more colors such as black and white or roan patterns. Dark brown eyes. Page 129.

46 Cocker Spaniel

Height: 14–15″. Weight: 26–28 lbs. Silky coat, flat or slightly wavy. Feathering on ears, chest, belly, and legs. ASCOB variety: white, tan, liver, or any other solid color except black. Dark brown eyes. Page 129.

48 Cocker Spaniel

Height: 14–15″. Weight: 26–28 lbs. Silky coat, flat or slightly wavy. Feathering on ears, chest, belly, and legs. Black variety: entirely black or with tan points. Dark brown eyes. Page 129.

49 Shetland Sheepdog

Height: 13–16". Weight: about 20 lbs. Long, straight, harsh outer coat with short, dense, furry undercoat. Profuse hair on tail. Black, blue merle, or sable, marked with white and/or tan. Dark eyes.
Page 249.

51 Toy Manchester Terrier

Height: 6–7". Weight: under 7 lbs. to 12 lbs. Short, shiny, smooth coat. Jet-black with mahogany and tan markings. Dark eyes.
Page 214.

50 Schipperke

Height: 12–13″. Weight: 16–18 lbs.
Abundant double coat: slightly harsh
outer coat, short, dense undercoat; ruff
around neck. Solid black only. Dark
brown eyes.
Page 234.

52 Italian Greyhound

Height: 13–15″. Weight: 5–15 lbs.
Short, glossy coat. All colors and
markings acceptable except brindle or
tan markings. Bronze-blue with white
trim shown. Dark eyes.
Page 211.

53 Basset Hound

Height: to 14″. Weight: about 60 lbs. Short, smooth, dense coat. Typical colors are combinations of black, tan, and white, but all hound colors and markings are acceptable. Brown eyes. Page 142.

55 Pembroke Welsh Corgi

Height: 10–12″. Weight: 25–30 lbs. Short, thick undercoat with longer, coarser, straight or slightly wavy outer coat. Red, sable, fawn, black, or tan, with or without white markings. Brown eyes with dark or black rims. Page 251.

54 Clumber Spaniel

Height: 17–20″. Weight: 55–58 lbs. Straight, silky, dense coat with ruff and feathering on legs and belly. White with lemon or orange markings. Amber eyes. Page 128.

56 Cardigan Welsh Corgi

Height: 10½–12½″. Weight: 25–38 lbs. Dense, slightly harsh but not wiry coat. Red, sable, brindle, black or blue merle, with or without tan or brindle points; white markings. Blue merle shown. Dark eyes. Page 250.

57 Bulldog

Height: 14½–15". Weight: 40–50 lbs.
Short, smooth, fine coat lies flat.
Brindle, preferably red; piebald; solid
white, red, or fawn, but not black. Dark
eyes.
Page 227.

59 Boston Terrier

Height: 16–17". Weight: under 15 lbs.
to 25 lbs. Smooth, short, shiny coat.
Brindle and white preferable; also black
and white. Should have white muzzle
and blaze. Dark eyes.
Page 226.

58 French Bulldog

Height: 12″. Weight: under 22 lbs. to 28 lbs. Short, fine, smooth coat. All brindles, as well as white, fawn, and brindle and white. Dark eyes.
Page 230.

60 American Staffordshire Terrier

Height: 17–19″. Weight: 45–50 lbs. Short, stiff, glossy coat. Any color except all white; liver, black and tan, or more than 80 percent white are not desirable. Dark eyes.
Page 183.

61 Staffordshire Bull Terrier

Height: 14–16". Weight: 24–38 lbs. Smooth, short coat. Red, fawn, white, black, or blue, or any of these colors with white; any shade of brindle, with or without white. Dark eyes.
Page 202.

63 Bull Terrier

Height: 21–22". Weight: 50–60 lbs. Smooth, close-lying coat. Colored variety: preferably brindle or red, with some white markings permitted. Dark eyes.
Page 187.

62 American Pit Bull Terrier

Height: 17–20″. Weight: 35–90 lbs. Smooth, stiff, glossy, short coat. Any color coat or eyes acceptable. Page 183.

64 Bull Terrier

Height: 21–22″. Weight: 50–60 lbs. Short, flat, harsh, glossy coat. White variety: all white or white with some markings on head only. Dark eyes. Page 187.

65 Basenji

Height: 16–17″. Weight: 22–24 lbs.
Short, silky coat. Chestnut-red, pure
black, or black and tan, with white on
feet, chest, and tail tip; white legs,
blaze, and collar allowed. Dark hazel
eyes.
Page 141.

67 Pharaoh Hound

Height: 21–25″. Weight: 40–60 lbs.
Short, shiny coat. Rich tan with white
on tail tip, toes, star on chest, and
sometimes a slender blaze on centerline
of skull. Amber eyes.
Page 156.

66 Manchester Terrier

Height: 15–16″. Weight: 12–22 lbs.
Short, sleek, smooth, thick coat; dense,
never soft. Jet-black and mahogany-tan,
with divisions between colors well
defined. Almost black eyes.
Page 193.

68 Whippet

Height: 18–22″. Weight: 20–28 lbs.
Close, smooth, firm coat. Any color
acceptable; usually gray, tan, brindle, or
white. Dark eyes.
Page 160.

69 Plott Hound

Height: 20–27". Weight: 40–75 lbs.
Coarse, glossy coat of short or medium
length. Brindle or black with brindle
trim. No solids. Some white allowed on
chest and feet. Coat should look streaked
or striped. Dark eyes.
Page 260.

71 English Coonhound

Height: 22–27". Weight: 40–80 lbs.
Short, glossy coat. Any good hound
color, ticked color, or tricolor with black
saddle. Dark eyes.
Page 258.

70 Bluetick Coonhound

Height: 22–27". Weight: 55–80 lbs. Short, neat, glossy coat. Dark blue predominant, with black spots; tan dots on face, dark red ticking on feet and lower legs. Markings not required. Dark brown, black, or hazel eyes. Page 257.

72 Redbone Coonhound

Height: 22–27". Weight: 40–80 lbs. Hard, short, glossy coat. Solid red preferred; small amount of white allowed on brisket or feet. Brown to hazel eyes; dark eyes preferred. Page 261.

73 Harrier

Height: 19–21″. Weight: 45–50 lbs.
Hard, short, dense, glossy coat. All
hound colors and markings acceptable, as
well as a blue mottle color known only
in Harrier. Dark eyes.
Page 151.

75 English Foxhound

Height: 24–25″. Weight: 62–70 lbs.
Hard, short, dense, glossy coat. Any
hound colors and markings acceptable;
usually black, white, and tan, or
combined with yellow. Symmetry is
important. Brown or hazel eyes.
Page 149.

74 Treeing Walker Coonhound

Height: 22–27″. Weight: 40–80 lbs. Smooth, fine coat. Preferably tricolor: white, black, and tan, with white or black predominant. White with tan spots or white with black spots acceptable. Brown or black eyes. Page 262.

76 American Foxhound

Height: 21–25″. Weight: 65–70 lbs. Typical, hard hound coat. Any hound colors and markings; usually black, tan, and/or white, or sometimes piebald or hare color. Brown or hazel eyes. Page 148.

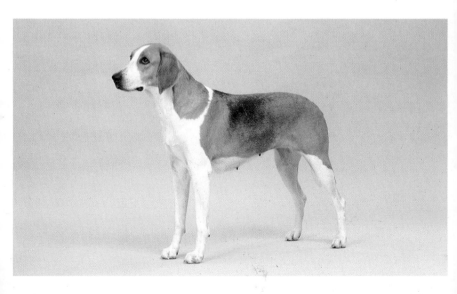

77 Dalmatian

Height: 19–23″. Weight: 55–65 lbs.
Short, hard, dense coat. Round, well-
defined spots on pure white ground.
With black spots: black, brown, or dark
blue eyes. With liver spots: light brown,
blue, or gold eyes.
Page 229.

79 English Springer Spaniel

Height: 19–20″. Weight: 49–55 lbs.
Flat or wavy coat with feathering.
Blue or liver roan; liver or black with
white markings; white with liver or
black markings; or liver or white with
tan markings. Dark eyes.
Page 131.

78 Brittany

Height: 17½–20½". Weight: 30–40 lbs. Dense, flat, wavy coat without curls. Dark orange and white or liver and white. Dark eyes preferred, amber acceptable.
Page 115.

80 Welsh Springer Spaniel

Height: 16½–17". Weight: 38–45 lbs. Flat, straight coat is thick and silky, not wiry or wavy. Feathering on ears, chest, belly, and legs. Dark, rich red and white. Dark or hazel eyes.
Page 135.

81 Sussex Spaniel

Height: 15–16″. Weight: 35–45 lbs. Abundant, flat or slightly wavy coat with moderate feathering on ears, legs, stern, and tail. Rich golden-liver. Hazel eyes. Page 134.

83 American Water Spaniel

Height: 15–18″. Weight: 25–45 lbs. Coat closely curled and dense but not coarse, with short, smooth hair on forehead and feathering on legs. Liver or dark chocolate with a bit of white. Hazel or brown to dark brown eyes. Page 127.

82 Field Spaniel

Height: about 18″. Weight: 35–50 lbs.
Silky, glossy, flat or slightly wavy coat
with abundant feathering. Black, liver,
golden-liver, roan, mahogany-red; solid
or with tan markings. Dark hazel,
brown, or nearly black eyes.
Page 132.

84 Tibetan Terrier

Height: 14–16″. Weight: 18–30 lbs.
Fine, woolly undercoat; long, profuse,
fine outer coat, not silky or woolly;
straight or wavy. Small beard, feathered
ears. Any color or combination of colors.
Dark eyes with dark lids.
Page 236.

85 Bearded Collie

Height: 20–22″. Weight: about 50 lbs.
Shaggy, long, rough outer coat and soft
undercoat. Black, fawn, blue, chocolate-
brown to sandy, gray, silver, or slate,
with touches of white. Eyes harmonize
with coat color.
Page 239.

87 Standard Poodle

Height: 15″ or more. Weight: 50 lbs.
Harsh, dense coat may be curly or
corded, with feathered ears. Many stylish
clips. Solid colors only: black, white,
cream, apricot, café au lait, brown,
silver, gray, or blue. Dark eyes.
Page 233.

86 Puli

Height: 15–18″. Weight: about 30 lbs.
Unusual, natural corded coat reaches the
ground. Solid colors without markings;
usually black, rusty black, shades of
gray, or white. Dark brown eyes.
Page 248.

88 Portuguese Water Dog

Height: 17–23″. Weight: 35–60 lbs.
Coat is wavy, fairly long, with a slight
sheen and upright hair on head; or made
of compact, cylindrical, lusterless curls.
Brown, black, white, or brown or black
with white. Brown or black eyes.
Page 175.

89 Bedlington Terrier

Height: 15–17½". Weight: 17–23 lbs. Curly, crisp coat consists of both hard and soft hairs. Blue as shown, liver, or sandy, often combined with tan. Light hazel to dark eyes, depending on coat color.
Page 185.

91 Standard Schnauzer

Height: 17½–19½". Weight: 30–50 lbs. Tight, hard, wiry, thick coat composed of soft undercoat and harsh outer coat that does not lie smooth or flat. Pepper-and-salt or pure black. Dark brown eyes.
Page 180.

90 Wirehaired Pointing Griffon

Height: 19½–23½″. Weight: about 55–60 lbs. Harsh, stiff outer coat forms eyebrows, mustache, and beard. Soft undercoat. Steel-gray, gray-white, or dirty white with chestnut; or all chestnut. Yellowish or light brown eyes. Page 138.

92 Soft-Coated Wheaten Terrier

Height: 18–19″. Weight: 35–40 lbs. Soft, wavy coat. Wheaten color. Ears and muzzle may be shaded. Dark hazel or brown eyes with black rims. Page 201.

93 Kerry Blue Terrier

Height: 17½–19½″. Weight: 33–40 lbs. Soft, dense, wavy coat. Deep slate to light blue-gray, uniform but often with darker points about head, feet, and tail. Dark eyes.
Page 191.

95 Airedale Terrier

Height: about 23″. Weight: 45–60 lbs. Hard, dense, wiry double coat, straight or sometimes wavy. Light, soft undercoat. Tan, with black or dark grizzle sides and upper parts of body. Dark eyes.
Page 182.

94 Welsh Terrier

Height: 15″. Weight: about 20 lbs.
Thick, hard, wiry double coat. Black
and tan or black grizzle and tan. Dark
hazel eyes.
Page 203.

96 Irish Terrier

Height: about 18″. Weight: 25–27 lbs.
Dense, wiry double coat; undercoat is
softer and lighter. Solid colors from
bright red to wheaten. Small white patch
on chest allowed. Dark brown eyes.
Page 190.

97 Australian Shepherd

Height: 18–23″. Weight: 50–65 lbs. Medium-length coat. Blue merle; red merle; solid black, with or without white markings and/or tan points; or solid red. Brown, blue, or amber eyes, or any variation.
Page 255.

99 Border Collie

Height: 17–21″. Weight: 30–50 lbs. Dense, curly or wavy coat; harsh outer coat, soft undercoat, with feathering on legs and full mane. Black, gray, or blue merle with white points; or black, white, and tan. Dark eyes.
Page 256.

98 English Shepherd

Height: 18–22″. Weight: 35–50 lbs. Heavy, glossy coat is straight or curly. No mane. Black and white; black and tan; or black, white, and tan. White markings allowed; tan dots over eyes, sable feet. Dark eyes. Page 259.

100 Australian Cattle Dog

Height: 17–20″. Weight: 40–45 lbs. Moderately short, rough, double coat. Mottled blue as shown, with or without markings in black, blue, or tan; or speckled red, with or without darker red markings on head. Dark eyes. Page 238.

101 Norwegian Elkhound

Height: 19½–20½". Weight: about 48–55 lbs. Thick, hard, smooth outer coat and soft, woolly undercoat. Any shade of gray with black-tipped outer hairs and silver undercoat. Dark brown eyes. Page 154.

103 American Eskimo

Height: 16–20". Weight: 18–35 lbs. Long coat with mane. White or biscuit-cream. Dark brown or black eyes with white eyelashes. Page 254.

110 Otter Hound

Height: 22–27″. Weight: 65–115 lbs.
Coarse, crisp outer coat and short,
woolly, oily undercoat; mop of hair over
eyes. All colors; blue and white
combination preferred. Dark eyes.
Page 155.

112 Briard

Height: 22–27″. Weight: 75–90 lbs.
Long, coarse, slightly wavy coat, with
mustache and beard. All solid colors
except white; black and various shades
of gray or tawny as shown. Black or
black-brown eyes.
Page 244.

113 Bouvier des Flandres

Height: 23½–27½″. Weight: 75–95 lbs. Rough, tousled coat: very thick, harsh outer coat and soft, fine undercoat. Fawn to black; brindle, gray, and salt-and-pepper. Dark brown eyes. Page 243.

115 German Wirehaired Pointer

Height: 22–26″. Weight: 60–70 lbs. Harsh, straight, wiry outer coat; undercoat thick in winter, thin in summer. Solid liver or liver and white, with brown head and ears, occasionally with white blaze. Brown eyes. Page 118.

114 Giant Schnauzer

Height: 23½–27½". Weight: 75–95 lbs. Hard, wiry, dense coat: soft undercoat and harsh outer coat with harsh beard and eyebrows. Salt-and-pepper as shown or solid black. Dark brown eyes.
Page 168.

116 German Shorthaired Pointer

Height: 21–25". Weight: 45–70 lbs. Short, hard, thick coat. Solid liver or liver and white only. Dark brown eyes.
Page 117.

117 Pointer

Height: 23–28". Weight: 45–75 lbs. Short, dense, smooth, shiny coat. Solid liver, black, lemon, or orange, or any one of these combined with white. Dark eyes.
Page 116.

119 Weimaraner

Height: 23–27". Weight: 70–85 lbs. Short, smooth, sleek coat. Solid shades of gray from mouse to silver. Light amber, gray, or blue-gray eyes.
Page 137.

118 Black and Tan Coonhound

Height: 23–27". Weight: 80–85 lbs. Shiny, smooth, dense coat. Black with tan markings on muzzle, chest, legs, and typically a pumpkinseed-size tan spot over each eye. Hazel to dark brown eyes. Page 144.

120 Vizsla

Height: 21–24". Weight: 55–60 lbs. Short, smooth, close-lying coat. Solid shades from rusty gold to dark, sandy yellow. Eyes harmonize with coat. Page 136.

121 Rhodesian Ridgeback

Height: 24–27″. Weight: 65–75 lbs.
Short, sleek, glossy coat with
symmetrical ridge of stiff hair along
spine, widest at shoulder blades and
ending at hips. Wheaten or red-wheaten.
Dark amber eyes.
Page 157.

123 Labrador Retriever

Height: 21½–24½″. Weight: 55–
75 lbs. Short, dense, hard coat; no
waves. Yellow variety: solid yellow.
Brown, hazel, yellow, or black eyes.
Page 123.

122 Labrador Retriever

Height: 21½–24½″. Weight: 55–75 lbs. Short, dense, hard coat; no waves. Chocolate variety: solid chocolate. Light brown or yellow eyes with dark brown or liver rims.
Page 123.

124 Labrador Retriever

Height: 21½–24½″. Weight: 55–75 lbs. Short, dense, hard coat; no waves. Black variety: solid black. Brown, hazel, yellow, or black eyes.
Page 123.

125 Golden Retriever

Height: 21½–24″. Weight: 55–75 lbs. Dense, firm, flat outer coat and good undercoat. Straight or wavy, with feathering on forelegs, neck, thighs, and tail. Solid, lustrous shades of gold. Dark brown eyes.
Page 122.

127 Chesapeake Bay Retriever

Height: 21–26″. Weight: 55–80 lbs. Thick, short outer coat and fine, woolly undercoat, wavy in places but not curly. Dark brown to tan. Solid colors preferred. Yellowish or amber eyes.
Page 119.

126 Flat-Coated Retriever

Height: 22–24½". Weight: 60–70 lbs. Moderately long, dense, flat, lustrous coat with feathering on chest, backs of legs, belly, and tail. Solid black or liver. Dark brown or hazel eyes.
Page 121.

128 Curly-Coated Retriever

Height: about 24". Weight: 65–70 lbs. Mass of crisp curls, including tail. Black or liver; only a few white hairs allowed. Black or brown eyes.
Page 120.

129 Irish Water Spaniel

Height: 21–24″. Weight: 45–65 lbs. Tight, crisp ringlets on neck, back, and sides; curls or waves on ears and legs; short, smooth hair on tail; topknot of loose curls in peak over eyes. Solid liver. Dark hazel eyes.
Page 133.

131 Irish Setter

Height: 25–27″. Weight: 60–70 lbs. Straight, moderately long coat, with feathering and fringe; short, fine hair on head, forelegs, and ear tips. Mahogany to rich chestnut-red; some white allowed. Brown eyes.
Page 126.

130 Gordon Setter

Height: 23–27″. Weight: 45–80 lbs.
Soft, shiny coat, straight or wavy, with
feathering. Black with chestnut or red-
mahogany markings over eyes, on muzzle
and throat, chest, inside of hind legs,
under tail, and on feet. Dark eyes.
Page 125.

132 English Setter

Height: 24–25″. Weight: 65–66 lbs.
Flat, medium-length coat with
feathering. Solid white; black, white,
and tan; white with black, liver, orange,
or lemon; or belton in blue, lemon,
liver, or orange as shown. Brown eyes.
Page 124.

133 Afghan Hound

Height: 25–27". Weight: 50–60 lbs.
Long, thick, silky hair except on neck,
saddle, and back. Silky topknot.
Champagne to black, either solid or with
patterns. Dark eyes.
Page 140.

135 Greyhound

Height: 27–30". Weight: 40–80 lbs.
Short, firm, smooth coat. Any colors or
markings acceptable; usually white,
gray, or fawn. Dark eyes.
Page 150.

134 Saluki

Height: 23–28″. Weight: 55–60 lbs. Soft, silky coat: longhaired, with feathering on ears, legs, and tail; or smooth, without feathering. White to golden to red; black and tan, with or without white. Dark to hazel eyes. Page 158.

136 Ibizan Hound

Height: 22½–27½″. Weight: 42–50 lbs. Smooth or wiry coat. White and lion as shown, red and white, solid white, or solid red. Amber or caramel-colored eyes. Page 152.

137 Doberman Pinscher

Height: 24–28″. Weight: 60–75 lbs.
Smooth, short, hard, thick, and close-lying coat; invisible gray undercoat permitted on neck. Black, red, blue, or fawn; with sharply defined rust markings. Brown eyes.
Page 167.

139 Alaskan Malamute

Height: 23–25″. Weight: 75–85 lbs.
Thick, coarse outer coat; dense, oily, woolly undercoat; thick fur around neck. Light gray to black, with white belly and white markings on legs, feet, and face; or solid white. Dark brown eyes.
Page 163.

138 Boxer

Height: 21–25″. Weight: 60–70 lbs. Short, smooth, shiny, tight coat. Fawn, from light tan to mahogany; or brindle, which may be dark stripes on light ground, or light on dark. Black, white, or black and white mask. Dark eyes. Page 165.

140 German Shepherd

Height: 22–28″. Weight: 65–90 lbs. Medium-length double coat; straight, harsh, dense outer coat lies close to body. Short hair on head, legs, and paws; longer and thicker on neck. Black, tan, tan and black, or gray. Dark eyes. Page 246.

141 Smooth Collie

Height: 22–26″. Weight: 50–75 lbs. Short, hard, dense, flat coat with abundant undercoat. This dog is blue merle. Dark eyes
Page 245.

143 Rough Collie

Height: 22–26″. Weight: 50–75 lbs. Straight, harsh outer coat; full, soft undercoat. Sable and white as shown; black with white and tan; blue merle; or white with sable, tricolor, or blue merle markings. Dark eyes.
Page 245.

142 Smooth Collie

Height: 22–26″. Weight: 50–75 lbs. Short, flat coat with abundant undercoat. Tricolor shown: black with white and tan; also sable and white; blue merle; or white with sable, tricolor, or blue merle markings. Dark eyes.
Page 245.

144 Bernese Mountain Dog

Height: 22½–27½″. Weight: 75–105 lbs. Silky, moderately long coat with bright sheen, slightly wavy or straight. Tricolor: jet-black ground with rich rust and white markings. Dark eyes.
Page 164.

145 Komondor

Height: 23½–25½" or more. Weight: 80–95 lbs. Dense double coat: coarse, wavy or curly outer coat forms tassel-like cords with soft, woolly undercoat. White only. Dark brown eyes.
Page 171.

147 Borzoi

Height: 26–34" or more. Weight: 55–105 lbs. Long, silky coat; flat, wavy, or curly, with feathering on hindquarters, tail, and chest. Any color permissible, though mostly white. Dark eyes.
Page 146.

146 Irish Wolfhound

Height: 30–34" or more. Weight: 105–120 lbs. Rough, hard coat, particularly long and wiry over eyes and under jaw. Gray, brindle, red, black, fawn, or pure white. Dark eyes.
Page 153.

148 Scottish Deerhound

Height: 28–32" or more. Weight: 75–110 lbs. Harsh, wiry, thick, ragged coat with silky mustache and beard. Usually one color with lighter shadings; blue-gray preferred. Ears always blackish. Dark brown to hazel eyes.
Page 159.

149 Great Dane

Height: 28–32″ or more. Weight: 120–150 lbs. Short, thick, smooth, glossy coat. The black and white pattern on this dog is called harlequin. Dark eyes. Page 169.

151 Akita

Height: 24–28″. Weight: 75–100 lbs. Thick, soft, dense undercoat; straight, harsh, longer outer coat stands off body. Any color, including brindle and pinto, with or without mask or blaze. Dark brown eyes. Page 162.

150 Great Dane

Height: 28–32″ or more. Weight: 120–150 lbs. Short, thick, smooth, glossy coat. Fawn with black mask as shown; brindle, pure steel-blue, black, or harlequin pattern of pure white with black patches. Dark eyes.
Page 169.

152 Rottweiler

Height: 22–27″. Weight: 100–115 lbs. Short, straight, coarse outer coat lies flat; undercoat on neck and thighs. Black with tan to mahogany markings on cheeks, muzzle, chest, legs, and over eyes. Dark brown eyes.
Page 176.

153 Bullmastiff

Height: 24–27″. Weight: 100–130 lbs.
Short, dense coat. Red, fawn, or brindle;
very small white spot allowed on chest.
Dark eyes.
Page 166.

155 Shorthaired Saint Bernard

Height: 25½–27½″ or more. Weight:
145–165 lbs. Very dense, tough,
smooth-lying coat, not rough. White
with red or red with white; brindle
patches. Dark brown eyes.
Page 177.

154 Mastiff

Height: 27½–30″ or more. Weight: 170–180 lbs. Moderately coarse outer coat; dense, short, close-lying undercoat. Silver-fawn as shown, apricot, or dark fawn-brindle, with blackish muzzle, ears, and nose. Dark brown eyes. Page 173.

156 Longhaired Saint Bernard

Height: 25½–27½″ or more. Weight: 145–165 lbs. Medium length, straight to slightly wavy coat. Slightly feathered forelegs, bushy thighs and tail. White with red or red with white; brindle patches. Dark brown eyes. Page 177.

157 Bloodhound

Height: 23–27″. Weight: 80–140 lbs.
Short, dense coat. Black, tan, reddish
brown, or any combination of these.
Small amount of white allowed on chest.
Deep hazel or brown to yellow eyes,
corresponding with coat.
Page 145.

159 Kuvasz

Height: 26–30″. Weight: 70–115 lbs.
Wavy or straight, medium-coarse coat
with fine undercoat and feathering on
backs of forelegs. White without
markings. Dark brown eyes.
Page 172.

158 Newfoundland

Height: 26–28". Weight: 100–150 lbs. Coarse, flat, straight or wavy but not shaggy outer coat; soft, dense undercoat. Feathering on legs. Black or white and black; other solid colors acceptable. Dark brown eyes.
Page 174.

160 Great Pyrenees

Height: 25–32". Weight: 90–125 lbs. Heavy, fine, white undercoat; long, flat, thick, and coarser outer coat. All white or white with gray, tan, or badger markings as shown. Dark brown eyes.
Page 170.

American Kennel Club Breeds

Groups
Sporting Dogs
Hounds
Working Dogs
Terriers
Toys
Non-Sporting Dogs
Herding Dogs

Sporting Dogs

Specialized Hunters

The twenty-four breeds included in the sporting dog group are all gundogs used by hunters to locate game and then collect it once it has been shot down. These dogs are specialists, each devoted to a clearly defined task.

Forerunners

The pointers and the setters locate game by working ahead of the gun. Long before a hunter is able to see the quarry, these dogs find it and silently show the hunter its location. A pointer comes "to the point" by standing rigidly with one foot in mid-stride. Its tail stands out in a straight line, enabling the hunter to use the dog's body like the sight of a gun. Pointers often work in pairs, moving far apart in the same field. They act as coordinates, indicating the direction and distance to the game. Setters perform similarly, but sink down to the ground, or "set," after locating the target. Both pointers and setters remain still until given the command to retrieve.

Flushing Dogs

The spaniels are the flushing dogs. Their task is to move the game toward the hunter, working back and forth so that they do not drive it out of range. These dogs hunt a variety of quarries, including birds and ground game such as rabbits, hares, and woodchucks. Spaniels come in several sizes and abilities, and are chosen to match the circumstances under which they will be expected to work. The Cocker Spaniel is a specialist in hunting the snipelike woodcock; the Springer Spaniel "springs" on game; and the Brittany, really a cross between a spaniel and a pointer, both points and flushes out game.

Retrievers

The retrievers are large, strong dogs with good noses and keen eyesight. They stay next to the hunter, marking the fall of the bird after it has been shot, and then fetch it either on land or from the water. They are generally used as bird dogs, but will in fact retrieve just about anything, including newspapers and slippers.

All-Purpose Breeds

Some breeds perform two tasks well, while others are truly all-purpose dogs. Many are experts in the water, where they are undeterred by cold or icy conditions. Some breeds work only for their masters, while others thrive on kennel life and perform well for anyone. Intelligent, hardworking, and companionable, many sporting dogs make fine household pets. The most popular sporting breed in the United States, the Cocker Spaniel, is rarely used in the field and is kept almost exclusively as a companion. However, the larger and more active sporting breeds do require plenty of exercise. These dogs need to interact with people, and they also need to work, since they have been bred for that purpose for many centuries.

Brittany

Characteristics
Compact body
Long legs
Short hanging ears
Flat, wavy coat
Short tail
Minimal feathering

Personality
Highly intelligent, active, and easy to train. A hard working, loyal gundog, the Brittany is fearless and aggressive, and makes an alert watchdog. Pleasant with children and other pets.

Ideal Appearance
Appears more compact and long-legged than most spaniels. Males, 17½" to 20½" tall and 30 to 40 pounds; bitches are slightly smaller. Rounded, slightly wedge-shaped head with gently sloping stop. High-set ears lie close to head and appear short and leafy. Heavy, expressive eyebrows provide protection from briars. Body is as long as it is tall. Short, straight back with slight slope. Tail may be natural or docked, but should not exceed 4" in length. Dense, flat, wavy coat without curls; some feathering on legs. Fairly loose skin. Permissible colors: dark orange and white, or liver and white; no black allowed; and tricolored dogs are severely faulted. Nose should be fawn, tan, light brown, or pink; black is not accepted. Dark eyes preferred, amber accepted.

Potential Health Problems
Generally healthy. Poorly bred dogs can be high-strung and nervous. Possible hip dysplasia and glaucoma, as well as lens luxation.

Care and Exercise
Coat care requires only 5 minutes of brushing twice a week. To be a happy, well-adjusted pet, this breed needs a great deal of exercise. Although adaptable to urban life, too much time indoors and a lack of exercise will cause restlessness and even hyperactivity. Confinement may also cause excessive barking. Dogs tend to roam and should thus be kept in fenced yards.

Puppies
Average litter, 6 to 10 puppies. Like all puppies, Brittanys do best if accustomed to people at an early age.

Comment
The Brittany gets its name from the French province where it originated. Brittany-like dogs frequently appear in French and Dutch paintings and tapestries from the 17th century, which suggests that the breed was already quite common by that time. Traditionally the Brittany is shown with a short tail, and some are born with no tail at all. The first, tailless ancestor is said to have been bred around the mid-1800s.

The breed was imported into the United States in 1931, and was officially recognized by the American Kennel Club in 1934. Although French standards recognize a range of coat colors, only 2 are allowed in the United States: liver or orange, with white markings. The compact yet leggy build makes this breed a strong and agile worker on land and in water. Overall, it is highly intelligent and an affectionate companion.

Recommendation
This superb gundog is friendly, easy to train, and loves to work. It requires a great deal of exercise, and the Brittany that gets the chance to hunt is the happiest Brittany of all. This breed tends to be a one-person dog, but will adjust readily to living in a household. Today it is more a field dog than most of the smaller sporting breeds.

Plate 78

Pointer

Characteristics
Solid, strong build
Deep chest
Long muzzle
Hanging ears
Short, dense coat
Natural tail

Personality

An ideal field dog. Independent and competitive. Highly suitable for kennel life, as it requires less personal attention than many of its sporting cousins. Works willingly for almost anyone, since its primary objective is its job, which is pointing game in the field. It can make a good house pet, if handled and trained as a small puppy.

Ideal Appearance

First impression should be of power and agility. Males, 25" to 28" tall and 55 to 75 pounds; bitches, 23" to 26" and 45 to 65 pounds. Strong, solid body with deep chest. Muzzle as long as skull is wide. Large, round, dark eyes. Face appears clean and chiseled. Ears set at eye level, hanging naturally just below lower jaw. Natural tail. Short, dense coat has smooth sheen. Permissible colors: solid liver, lemon, black, or orange; or any of these combined with white. On dark-colored dogs, nose should be brown or black; otherwise it is lighter or pinkish.

Potential Health Problems

Healthy overall, although some dogs subject to hip dysplasia, progressive retinal atrophy, and cysts.

Care and Exercise

Short coat requires very little care; a quick rub with a rough cloth a few times a week is generally sufficient. The Pointer's eagerness to perform fills it with nervous energy; thus frequent, rigorous exercise is mandatory. Confinement may result in hyperactivity. Obedience training is strongly recommended.

Puppies

Average litter, 5 to 6 puppies. Newborns paler than adults, but darken as they mature. Puppies need to be handled by people daily.

Comment

The Pointer was developed in Europe in the Middle Ages, but its origins are a mystery. The breed probably existed in France, Belgium, Germany, Spain, and Portugal at about the same time, and surely contains traces of the Foxhound, the Greyhound, and the Bloodhound in its lineage. The first real record of Pointers indicates they were in England in about 1650, when, long before the practice of bird hunting was common, the Pointer was taken into the field to point hare, while the Greyhound ran it to ground. Around the early 18th century, bird hunting, called wing shooting, became popular, and the Pointer became exclusively a bird dog. Its speed, endurance, courage, and concentration make the breed superb in the field. The hunting instinct becomes evident very early, often as soon as 2 months of age. Moreover, the Pointer's poise and clean-limbed build have made this breed especially suitable as a show dog.

Recommendation

This breed is a superior gundog. The Pointer's energy and devotion to its profession make it an ideal member of the sporting family. Although generally congenial and eager to work, the Pointer may be quick-tempered, stubborn, or high-strung. It benefits greatly from obedience training. This breed is not designed for apartment life nor is it an ideal first dog.

Plate 117

German Shorthaired Pointer

Characteristics
Powerful build
Deep chest
Sloping shoulders
Large muzzle
Short, rough coat
Docked tail

Personality
An even-tempered and loving companion. Without proper exercise, however, this breed may become noisy and unmanageable. Tends to bark more than most sporting breeds. If allowed to roam free in rural settings, can cause problems with livestock. Should be kept under a watchful eye.

Ideal Appearance
Medium-size, well-balanced, and symmetrical build. Males, 23″ to 25″ tall and 55 to 70 pounds; bitches, 21″ to 23″ and 45 to 60 pounds. Clean-cut head in proportion to body. Large muzzle. Broad, hanging ears set at eye level. Shoulders should be sloping; chest, deep; and back and hindquarters, strong. Coat is short, thick, and rough to the touch. Tail is docked to 40 percent of original length. Permissible colors: solid liver or any combination of liver and white. Eyes are dark brown; nose is brown. Flesh-colored nose or areas of black, red, orange, tan, lemon, or solid white are not allowed.

Potential Health Problems
Generally robust. Subject to hip dysplasia, so should be X-rayed by a veterinarian before breeding.

Care and Exercise
Minimal coat care required: Give a quick rub with a rough cloth twice a week. This breed demands a lot of vigorous exercise in order to satisfy its endless energy. Should spend as much time as possible outdoors. Dog is a roamer. A large, fenced-in yard and obedience training are highly recommended. May be hard to housebreak.

Puppies
Average litter, about 8 puppies. Liver ticking on liver and white puppies darkens as puppies mature. House-training should begin at 6 weeks, with more serious obedience training following by the age of 6 months.

Comment
The German Shorthaired Pointer combines qualities found in several breeds of hunting dogs and probably descended from the German Bird Dog, the Spanish Pointer, and a variety of scent hounds. The result of such refined breeding is a truly all-purpose dog with style, aristocratic temperament, and a keenness for water. Its webbed feet and water-repellent coat make this breed equally valuable in water and on land. The German Shorthaired Pointer is a fine pointer, trailer, and retriever, as well as an excellent family dog and companion. This breed's versatility is apparent in its successful work in hunting a wide variety of game—from pheasant and quail to raccoons, opossums, rabbits, and even deer.

Recommendation
A favorite among hunters, the German Shorthaired Pointer is equally successful as an all-around family dog, given the proper environment. Since it demands to be on the move, this dog is generally unsuited for city life. With proper training and plenty of long walks and runs, the German Shorthaired Pointer is a great pet and a faithful companion for anyone willing to devote time to its exercise. Not an ideal first dog, however.

Plate 116

German Wirehaired Pointer

Characteristics
Wiry outer coat
Bushy eyebrows, mustache, and beard
Body slightly longer than high
Short, sloping back
Docked tail

Personality
Although not unfriendly, this breed is often aloof to strangers. Energetic, intelligent, and determined. At its best in a setting that allows a good deal of exercise; not really suited to close, restricted quarters or life styles.

Ideal Appearance
Males, 24" to 26"; bitches, smaller but not under 22". Although standard does not specify weight, males usually weigh about 70 pounds; bitches, around 60 pounds. Sturdy body is slightly longer than it is high, with a short back and a perceptible slope from withers to croup. Toes are webbed. Double coat: harsh, wiry outer coat; and an undercoat that is thick in winter and thin in summer. Bushy eyebrows, mustache, and beard. Tail docked to 40 percent of original length. Permissible colors: liver and white, or solid liver with brown head, occasionally with a white blaze; solid white or areas of black, red, orange, lemon, or tan not acceptable. Nose is dark brown. Eyes dark brown.

Potential Health Problems
Usually healthy, but subject to hip dysplasia. Should be X-rayed by a veterinarian before breeding.

Care and Exercise
Short, harsh coat is naturally clean and requires minimal care. Brushing will help keep it crisp and clean. Bathing usually not necessary. Undercoat should be combed out early in the spring. Needs extensive exercise in open areas. Tends to roam and thus should be carefully controlled. Can be a nuisance around livestock unless taught early on to leave these animals alone. A very active dog.

Puppies
Average litter, 6 to 10 puppies. Newborns are liver or liver and white, but attain full adult color at 5 months. Although not essential, obedience training is recommended at about 3 months. Should become accustomed to people when young.

Comment
Originally recognized as a breed in Germany in 1870, the German Wirehaired Pointer is a combination of German Shorthaired Pointer, Poodle, Foxhound, and terrier, and perhaps other breeds. The Germans, preferring an all-purpose dog, combined the distinctive traits of these specialized breeds and created one of the finest and most rugged of all hunting dogs. The German Wirehaired Pointer is an equally good scent dog, pointer, and retriever. These extremely courageous dogs have a coat that is appropriate for any place or weather. The water-repellent outer coat protects against rough conditions—both on land and in water—while the undercoat grows dense in winter to provide insulation and thins drastically in summer. The thick eyebrows protect the eyes from briars.

Recommendation
Naturally protective of its household, the German Wirehaired Pointer is an intelligent, sturdy, and lively dog that is highly suited to a family with the space and time for frequent and strenuous exercise. Strictly a one-family dog, it may be reserved with strangers and unpredictable with other dogs. Given its love of open country and its energy, this breed thrives in a country home. It should only be purchased from a fine specialty breeder.

Plate 115

Chesapeake Bay Retriever

Characteristics
Thick, short, wavy outer coat
Woolly undercoat
Broad head
Well-proportioned body
Natural tail

Personality
Courageous, intelligent, and even-tempered. Gets along well with other animals; is exceptionally good with children; and is cordial with strangers. Its good disposition gets high marks in the show ring. Above all, this breed loves the water. Can be somewhat sharper than Golden and Labrador retrievers.

Ideal Appearance
Males, 23" to 26" tall and 65 to 80 pounds; bitches, 21" to 24" and 55 to 70 pounds. This breed should appear bright, happy, and intelligent. Broad, round skull with medium-length muzzle; small, high-set ears; and large yellowish or amber eyes set wide apart. Well-proportioned body. Natural tail. Double coat: thick, short outer coat; and fine, woolly undercoat. Although coat is wavy in places, a curly coat is not allowed. Permissible colors: dark brown to tan, ideally as similar to working surroundings as possible, for camouflage; solid colors preferred, but white spots on chest, belly, and toes acceptable.

Potential Health Problems
Basically a healthy breed; subject to hip dysplasia and eczema. Check puppies for hereditary eye diseases. Possible skin disorders and cataracts.

Care and Exercise
Minimal coat care required, but some brushing strongly recommended to keep coat clean and skin healthy. Requires a great deal of exercise and, whenever possible, opportunities to retrieve in water. Long walks essential for pets. Should not be allowed to wander. Obedience training is recommended.

Puppies
Average litter of 7 to 8 puppies. Coat can become either lighter or darker as puppies get older; mature coat develops around 11 weeks. Needs to become accustomed to people at an early age.

Comment
In 1807 a pair of Newfoundland puppies were rescued from a sinking British ship off the coast of Maryland. Dubbed Sailor and Canton, the pups proved splendid duck retrievers. They were crossed with other unknown breeds in the region to eventually produce the Chesapeake Bay Retriever. Some people believe that the English Otter Hound played a substantial role in this evolution, but since the Chesapeake Bay Retriever does not have any hound characteristics, the Flat-Coated and Curly-Coated retrievers are more likely candidates. Remarkable water retrievers, the resultant breed was used on Chesapeake Bay around 1885 to retrieve up to 300 ducks daily, and it soon became known as the Chesapeake Bay Retriever.

One of the breed's most distinctive features is its coat, which resists water in the same way the feathers of a duck do. Oil in the harsh outer coat and a thick, woolly undercoat prevent the cold, icy water from reaching the dog's skin, and also help it dry quickly. In addition to its talents as a sporting dog, the Chesapeake Bay Retriever is one of the few American breeds that has been used successfully as a guide dog for the blind.

Recommendation
A good watchdog and companion, this breed craves personal attention. Although better suited to country life, it will adapt to the city if given plenty of exercise. Its love for the water makes occasional trips to the shore—where it can retrieve sticks—a must. The Chesapeake Bay Retriever can tolerate roughhousing from children.

Plate 127

Curly-Coated Retriever

Characteristics
Short, curly coat
Deep chest
Muscular
hindquarters
Low-set, curly ears
Natural tail

Personality

A good companion or family dog that is aloof with strangers. Highly intelligent, though perhaps stubborn, this breed makes a better watchdog than most sporting breeds.

Ideal Appearance

Strong build with distinctive, curly coat. Although standard does not specify size, males are usually about 24″ tall and 65 to 70 pounds; bitches, slightly smaller. Long, well-proportioned head with rather small, low-set ears and large eyes. Deep chest and muscular hindquarters. Masses of crisp curls all over, even on tail. A saddle or patch of uncurled hair past shoulders is severely penalized in the show ring. Permissible colors: black or liver; only a few white hairs allowed. Black or brown eyes.

Potential Health Problems

Generally healthy, but subject to hip dysplasia. Possible seborrheic skin disorders.

Care and Exercise

Despite abundant curls, coat actually requires minimal care. However, periodic brushing is suggested. Plenty of exercise is a must. This hardy breed loves the outdoors and the water. It can become hyperactive, even cranky, if kept in close confinement. Exercise is not a casual affair. When field work is not practical, then very long walks and plenty of opportunities to retrieve sticks will help. Early and lengthy obedience training is highly recommended, since this clever breed has a reputation for being somewhat harder to manage than most of its retrieving cousins.

Puppies

Average litter, about 8 puppies. Adult color at birth. Puppies should become accustomed to people from an early age.

Comment

The English Water Spaniel, the Irish Water Spaniel, the Poodle, and the Newfoundland are all said to be ancestors of the Curly-Coated Retriever. Despite its vague origin, this breed is considered one of the oldest of the dogs now classified as retrievers. The Curly-Coated Retriever first appeared in the show ring in England in 1860. Popular in Australia and New Zealand as duck retrievers, this dog arrived in the United States around 1907. Like the coats of other water dogs, the thick outer coat insulates the skin from wet and cold, enabling the dog to spend as much time as is necessary in the water. The Curly-Coated Retriever is known for its great stamina and strength, as well as its intelligence and occasional stubbornness.

Recommendation

The Curly-Coated Retriever is a faithful companion and a devoted worker. This sporting dog is made for action regardless of weather, and needs a setting that will allow an occasional swim, which is desirable even in icy waters. Short, leashed walks in the city are unsatisfactory.

Plate 128

Flat-Coated Retriever

Characteristics
Thick, flat coat
Long head
Small ears
Deep chest
Short, square back
Natural tail

Personality
Cheerful, loving, and loyal. A hard-working field dog and an equally ideal family pet. Gentle with children, but initially suspicious of strangers. Tends to be head-strong and needs obedience training, to which it responds well. Not possessive.

Ideal Appearance
Powerful and athletic. Males, 23″ to 24½″ tall; bitches, 22″ to 23½″. Although standard does not specify weight, males and bitches usually weigh 60 to 70 pounds. Short, square back; deep chest; and straight forelegs. Long, nicely molded head; broad, flat skull. Small ears hang close to the head. Fine, dense coat with feathering on chest, back of legs, and belly. Permissible colors: black coat with black nose; or liver coat with brown nose. Eyes are usually dark brown or hazel.

Potential Health Problems
Subject to hip dysplasia, although generally hardy.

Care and Exercise
Minimal coat care needed, but a good brushing helps keep the dog looking its best. Exercise frequently, taking regular trips to open areas where dog can run freely. Occasional swims are a must for a happy Flat-Coated Retriever. This active, athletic animal needs to be able to fetch and run like all retrievers.

Puppies
Average litter, 6 to 9 puppies. Adult coloring at birth. Puppies should become accustomed to people at an early age and be trained early.

Comment
Descended from the Labrador and the Newfoundland, the Flat-Coated Retriever is one of the few truly American breeds. Its popularity, however, comes from England, where the breed first appeared in the show ring in 1860. Favored by S. E. Shirley, the founder of the Kennel Club in England, the Flat-Coated Retriever became famous as a combination show dog and worker. Since the early 20th century, the breed's popularity has fallen dramatically as the Labrador and Golden retrievers have become more popular.

Recommendation
Handsome, happy, and eager to work, this admirable water dog's hallmark is its constant tail wagging. It likes everyone and everything, especially children. The Flat-Coated Retriever makes an ideal family pet, as well as a serious sporting dog. It thrives on attention. Adaptable to various environments, it deserves frequent trips to open spaces, and an occasional swim. It is not well-suited to urban life, as it is far too active and needs more time outdoors than just a few minutes a day. Pleasant to people and animals alike, it is surprising that the Flat-Coated Retriever is not more popular than it is.

Plate 126

Golden Retriever

Characteristics
Broad head
Short body
Dense coat with some
wave
Feathering
Natural tail

Personality
An enormously affectionate breed.
Friendly, willing, and devoted. Ideal
dog in a household with other animals
and children. This butterscotch-colored
dog is one of the most beloved
companion breeds of our time, as it well
deserves.

Ideal Appearance
Symmetrical, well-balanced, powerful
build. Males, 23" to 24" tall and 65 to
75 pounds; bitches, 21½" to 22½" and
55 to 65 pounds. Short back and a broad
skull. Rather short ears hang flat against
head and fall slightly below jaw. Dense,
water-repellent coat. Feathering on neck,
forelegs, thighs, belly and underside of
tail. Permissible colors: various shades of
lustrous gold; white hairs on chest
allowed but not desirable, and other
white markings are show faults. Dark
brown eyes with dark rims; black or
brown nose.

Potential Health Problems
Generally healthy breed. Subject to hip
dysplasia. Some dogs prone to skin
disorders: hot spots, allergic skin disease,
and bacterial skin disease. All are easily
treatable. Possibility of hypothyroidism,
von Willebrand's disease, and epilepsy.

Care and Exercise
Thick coat requires weekly brushings
and bathing is needed to keep it clean
and smelling nice. Do not allow thick
double coat to remain damp or wet; this
can cause hot spots or other skin
reactions. Exercise at least 2 hours per
day. Allow it frequent swims, regardless
of weather, and give it the opportunity
to fetch and carry.

Puppies
Average litter, 6 to 10 puppies. At
birth, coats are various shades of gold,
darkening to adult color by 10 to 14
months; some will continue to darken 1 4
or 5 years old. Puppies need to be
handled from the start; they respond well
to obedience training as early as 8 weeks.
Avoid overfeeding. Give puppies plenty
of room in which to play; a 3′ by 3′ pen
is ideal.

Comment
During the early 19th century, when
game hunting became an extremely
popular sport in England and Scotland,
the pursuit of game birds—on water as
well as land—created a demand for a
new, specialized sporting dog that could
retrieve game from icy waters. Setters
and water spaniels were crossed with the
St. John's Newfoundland to create the
Golden, Curly-Coated, Flat-Coated, and
Labrador retrievers.
At first lumped together with the Flat-
Coated Retriever, the Golden was
registered as a separate breed in 1913.
An outstanding hunting dog, the
Golden is equally superb in the field, in
obedience trials, and as a guide dog for
the blind. The first 3 dogs of any kind to
win the AKC Obedience Champion title,
available as of July 1977, were all
Golden Retrievers. Valued for its keen
intelligence and gentleness, the Golden
is one of the most popular family pets.

Recommendation
An all-around dog, ideal in homes with
children and other pets. This
affectionate, intelligent breed belongs
with owners that are willing to give it
the attention it deserves and, in fact,
requires. The Golden seems to crave a
sense of helping or participating. It
adjusts easily to city life as long as it gets
plenty of exercise. It is used as a guide
dog for the blind with great success.

Plate 125

Labrador Retriever

Characteristics
Wide head
Strong build
Muscular
hindquarters
Thick, rounded tail
Clean, athletic looks

Personality
Even-tempered and hardworking. Considered one of the very best all-around dogs in the world. This is a steadfast, affectionate, and adaptable dog, useful as a field dog, a house pet, or a guide for the blind. Outstanding in all categories.

Ideal Appearance
Males, 22½″ to 24½″ tall and 60 to 75 pounds; bitches, 21½″ to 23½″ and 55 to 70 pounds. Strong build, with wide chest, short back, and muscular hindquarters. Wide head has slight stop; powerful neck. Tail is very thick at base, tapers toward tip. Short, dense coat; no waves. Permissible colors: solid black, yellow, or chocolate; only small white spot on chest allowed. Eyes may be brown, hazel, yellow, or black.

Potential Health Problems
Basically a hardy breed. Subject to hip dysplasia. Possible allergic skin disease, ostrochondritis desicans, and congenital and acquired eye defects. Puppies should be checked by a veterinarian, because dwarfism with eye defects is known.

Care and Exercise
Coat care is minimal, though light daily brushing enhances sheen and helps cement bond between dog and owner. Needs vigorous exercise on a regular basis. Occasional swims should be included, for, like all Retrievers, the Lab was made for the water.

Puppies
Average litter, 7 to 8 puppies, which are easy to raise and train. Adult coloring at birth. Puppies should become accustomed to people at an early age.

Comment
First imported to England from Newfoundland in the early 19th century, the Labrador earned its popularity from the Earl of Malmesbury, who gave it the name Labrador and was one of the first to praise the breed. Not only did it excel in the field and in the water, but the Lab proved valuable in wartime, when its strong nose was used to detect mines buried at considerable depths.

The Lab has long been popular in the show ring, and is one of the most frequently used guide dogs for the blind. Slightly more dour than the Golden Retriever, the Labrador makes a faithful guard and companion. It is loving and always eager to work.

Recommendation
An adaptable animal, this steady breed will fit into almost any setting as long as it gets generous amounts of exercise. It is unfair to keep such a fine animal locked up. Ideal with other pets and children, the Lab is attached to its family and devoted to the task of pleasing them in every way possible. It is not a fighter by nature, but early training and socializing with other animals and people brings out the best in a Labrador.

Plates 122, 123, 124

English Setter

Characteristics
Long, lean head
Silky hair on ears
Moderate feathering
Natural tail
Athletic

Personality
Quiet and gentle with a sweet, mild disposition. Settles into home life easily. Exceptionally good with other animals and children. An aristocrat among dogs. May be slightly aloof with strangers until certain that they are worthy of attention.

Ideal Appearance
Graceful, well-balanced, refined-looking dog. Males, about 25″ tall; bitches, about 24″. Although standard does not specify weight, males usually weigh approximately 70 pounds; bitches, around 65 pounds. Long, lean head with well-defined stop and square muzzle. Ears set well back, low, and close to head, covered with silky hair. In overall evaluation, a handsome head is very important. Coat should be flat, of medium length, and without curl. Legs, belly, chest, and tail have moderately thin feathering. Permissible colors: black, white and tan, black and white, blue belton, orange and white, orange belton, liver and white, liver belton, or solid white. Flecks throughout are more desirable than heavy patches of colors. Dark brown eyes.

Potential Health Problems
Quite healthy. Subject to hip dysplasia, so should be checked by a veterinarian before breeding. Possible allergic skin disease and progressive retinal atrophy.

Care and Exercise
To keep dog looking stylish and healthy, brush daily. Some professional grooming or shaping is valuable occasionally, as on all well-feathered breeds. Exercise must be frequent and rigorous; the best dispositions may sour if this breed is cooped up indoors. English Setters may be hard to housebreak, but learn with consistent training. They tend to roam and should not be left in unfenced areas.

Puppies
Easy whelping. Average litter of 6 to 8 puppies. White at birth; color changes gradually from first week on. Puppies are easy to train and care for.

Comment
The old English Setter is believed to have derived from the Spanish Pointer, the Water Spaniel, and the Spanish Spaniel, and was used as a bird dog in England over 400 years ago. The modern English Setter developed in around 1825 with the beginning of the Laverack line, a strain named after its original breeder. In 1874 another type, known as the Llewellin line, was started in the United States by crossing Laverack dogs with other English strains.

Aristocratic in appearance, the English Setter is a hardy, sturdy breed. In the field, the English Setter's job is to locate game, and then to sit and remain motionless while the hunter shoots over its head. Its elegance is especially apparent in the show ring, where the dog moves easily and gracefully with its head held high. The English Setter is one of the great showmen of the dog show world; and in fact, if there is applause and cheering, it is a downright ham.

Recommendation
This mild-mannered breed is considered less exuberant than many of its sporting cousins. It is a loyal, affectionate family dog, although at times pleasantly stubborn. Because the English Setter requires an enormous amount of exercise, country life is far more suitable to this breed than the confines of the city.

Plate 132

Gordon Setter

Characteristics
Finely chiseled head
Short, strong back
Feathering
Natural tail
Sturdy build

Personality
An ideal family pet. Affectionate and even-tempered. Wary of strangers and occasionally aggressive with other dogs, the Gordon Setter is reluctant to share its family. Tends to be jealous and should be kept in check. Renowned for its gentleness with children, this breed thrives on love and attention. Very intelligent and knows how to manipulate its owners. An active dog.

Ideal Appearance
Stylish and sturdily built. Males, 24″ to 27″ tall and 55 to 80 pounds; bitches, 23″ to 26″ and 45 to 70 pounds. Fairly heavy and finely chiseled head. Rather short, strong back. Soft coat is either straight or slightly wavy. Feathering on ears, belly, chest, legs, and tail. Permissible colors: black with chestnut or red-mahogany markings over eyes, on muzzle, throat, chest, feet, inside of hind legs, and under tail; markings should not be mixed with black. Very small amount of white allowed on chest, and may have black pencil lines on toes. Dark brown eyes.

Potential Health Problems
Healthy overall. Some dogs subject to hip dysplasia and allergic skin disease. Possible progressive retinal atrophy, gait ataxia, and epilepsy.

Care and Exercise
Moderate coat care is necessary to keep this dog looking elegant. The Gordon Setter needs plenty of exercise or it will become tense and unmanageable. In the city, ongoing obedience training, long walks, and runs are imperative. Like other setters, it tends to roam and may be hard to housebreak. Sometimes a picky eater.

Puppies
Average litter of about 8 hearty puppies. Like all dogs, they should become used to different people and environments at an early age.

Comment
This breed dates back to the 1600s, but came into prominence only in the late 18th century, via the kennels of the fourth Duke of Gordon in Scotland. Its first American fancier is believed to have been Daniel Webster, the great 19th-century statesman, who imported the breed to the United States. Known for both its beauty and brains—but not speed—the Gordon Setter also has terrific endurance, scenting ability, and bird sense. It is a superb gundog, and its keen intelligence enables it to improve from season to season. It is equally successful in the field and the show ring. The AKC standard for this breed, unlike most others, allows for a considerable range in size and weight, because preferences of individual hunters vary greatly depending on the hunting terrain.

Recommendation
Aggressive and fearless, the Gordon Setter makes a loyal and protective pet. Abundant exercise and attention are essential for this breed's happiness. The Gordon Setter is eager to please and should be given the opportunity to do so in the field, the show ring, or obedience class. While it can adapt to the city, this beautiful, active breed deserves more than a couple of 1-mile walks each day. It is really a country dog suited to an appreciative, dog-oriented family.

Plate 130

Irish Setter

Characteristics
Long, lean head
Chiseled muzzle
Sloping shoulders
Long body
Long feathering
Natural tail

Personality
A true clown. Energetic, demonstrative, and excitable, the Irish Setter is often stubborn, but lovable. Seldom cranky. Excellent with children, and pleasant to other pets. A stunningly handsome aristocrat with a sense of humor.

Ideal Appearance
Elegant, substantial build. Males, 27" tall and about 70 pounds; bitches, 25" and 60 pounds. Variance of an inch either way is acceptable. Lean, long head with delicately chiseled muzzle. Almond-shaped eyes are set far apart. Long body has long, wide, sloping shoulders. Flat, moderately long coat without waves or curls. Short, fine hair on head, forelegs, and ear tips; long, silky feathering on ears, back of forelegs, and toes, and some on hind legs, belly, chest, and tail. Permissible colors: mahogany to rich chestnut-red; no black hair allowed; very little white on chest, throat, or toes acceptable. Brown eyes.

Potential Health Problems
Generally healthy, although some dogs subject to bloat, progressive retinal atrophy, and hip dysplasia. Possible allergic skin disease, congenital heart disease, bone problems, hypothyroidism, and epilepsy.

Care and Exercise
Moderate daily brushing of coat is necessary to keep this breed in proper shape. Although adaptable to city life, the Irish Setter is a bundle of energy and requires regular runs in open spaces. Lack of exercise may make dogs giddy and difficult or even impossible to manage. The Irish Setter tends to roam when off leash and needs a firm hand to housebreak and train.

Puppies
Litter of about 8 puppies. A light shade at birth; color darkens as puppies age. Puppies should not be overexercised. They need to get used to people.

Comment
Although dubbed the Irish Setter, this breed's origin is vague at best. It appeared in Ireland in the 19th century, probably as a result of crossing various spaniels and setters, and perhaps even some pointers. While the breed's early ancestors were red and white (often with white predominant), only solid red is acceptable today in the United States. In England and on the Continent, however, the two-colored dogs are still popular. A highly intelligent and trainable breed, the Irish Setter is a steadfast bird dog in the field. In the show ring, it is unequalled in color and graceful movement. The Irish Setter's reputation for being flighty and excitable is generally due to a lack of training and exercise. A gay and lively breed, this dog's energy must be channeled if it is to make a good house pet. It tends to be a thief and loves bringing treasures home to its owners.

Recommendation
Graceful, beautiful, loving, and clownish, the Irish Setter is a willing companion. Enormous amounts of exercise are a must. This is a special breed for the right owner, someone willing to take the time for training and exercise.

Plate 131

American Water Spaniel

Characteristics
Curly coat
Broad head
Muscular build
Long, wide ears
Slightly curved tail

Personality
Intelligent and adaptable to almost any situation. Extremely affectionate toward people, and gets along well with other animals. A superb hunting dog and a delightful family pet that is splendid with children. Alert watchdog, although pleasant to strangers that have been properly introduced. Barks a lot.

Ideal Appearance
Medium-size, muscular dog. Males and bitches 15″ to 18″ tall. Males weigh 28 to 45 pounds; bitches, 25 to 40 pounds. Moderately long, broad head with medium-length muzzle. Long, wide ears are set slightly above eyeline. Tail is moderately long and slightly curved. Coat should be very closely curled, and dense but not coarse. Short, smooth hair on forehead; close curls on ears; curly feathers on legs and tail. Permissible colors: liver or dark chocolate, with very small amount of white allowed on toes and chest. Hazel or light to dark brown eyes to match coat; yellow eyes not allowed.

Potential Health Problems
Generally robust. Possible skin problems.

Care and Exercise
Requires minimal coat care; brushing once or twice a week—to remove dead hair and prevent matting—is usually enough. Although the breed is easily adaptable to urban life, regular, vigorous exercise is essential. It is only fair to allow occasional swims and to provide opportunities for this talented sporting dog to retrieve sticks from the water.

Puppies
Average litter, 4 to 6 puppies. Adult coloring at birth. Puppies should be around people as early as possible.

Comment
This breed's curly coat, muscular build, and retrieving skills suggest that the Irish Water Spaniel and probably the Curly-Coated Retriever were its ancestors. Yet little is known about the American Water Spaniel, except that it was developed in the American Midwest. Not as handsome as other spaniels, the American Water Spaniel is certainly their equal in the field. It works well on land and in water, regardless of weather or water temperature. The dog does not point, but it has a strong nose, great intelligence, and a "soft" mouth that enables it to retrieve game without the slightest damage to feathers or fur. This excellent swimmer uses its tail as a rudder in rapidly flowing water. Registered by the American Kennel Club in 1940, the American Water Spaniel is still not popular in the show ring, but it is a superb hunting dog.

Recommendation
The American Water Spaniel makes an affectionate, sensible family pet, as it is exceptionally good with children. It is lively, obedient, and a willing companion. An easy dog to keep. As long as it is with its family, the American Water Spaniel accepts any living conditions—even apartments. But if confined to the city, frequent exercise is mandatory to prevent hyperactivity indoors. A breed whose time is yet to come. It is now quite rare in most parts of the country.

Plate 83

Clumber Spaniel

Characteristics
Massive head
Low-set ears
Long, low build
Feathering
Docked tail
Heavy looking

Personality
A steady, phlegmatic dog. Affectionate and gentle, but stubborn. The Clumber Spaniel is somewhat slow to learn, yet is a no-nonsense worker in the field. Tends to be a one-person dog.

Ideal Appearance
Long, low, heavy-looking, and somewhat jowly dog with great power. Males, 19″ to 20″ tall and 70 to 85 pounds; bitches, 17″ to 19″ and 55 to 70 pounds. Large, massive head is round above eyes and flat on top, with a marked stop. Upper lip overhangs lower lip. Large, deep-set eyes. Low-set ears are broad at top and slightly feathered on front edge. Long, thick ruff at neck. Deep chest. Long, broad back, and immensely strong and muscular shoulders. Docked tail. Straight, silky, and very dense coat; should not grow too long. Feathering on legs and belly. Permissible colors: white with lemon or orange markings; the fewer markings on the body, the better. Dark amber eyes.

Potential Health Problems
Generally robust, but subject to hip dysplasia, like many heavy dogs.

Care and Exercise
Requires moderate coat care, with some trimming at least monthly. Fairly inactive when indoors, this breed should get long walks to keep it from growing fat. Training should start as early as possible; learns somewhat slowly and requires patient repetition.

Puppies
Litters of 2 to 8 puppies. Whelping is usually normal, but occasionally a cesarean section is required. At 3 to 4 months, puppies can be taught to obey simple commands.

Comment
The Clumber Spaniel is unlike any of its spaniel cousins—in both appearance and name. Rather than being titled after a particular task—like the Cocker, Springer, or Field spaniel—the Clumber is named after a place: Clumber Park, the Nottingham estate of the Duke of Newcastle. It is said that during the mid-18th century, the French Duke de Noailles gave several spaniels to the English duke, who in turn developed the ancestors of the Clumber Spaniel. Generally regarded as English, the breed is probably a descendant of the Alpine Spaniel and the Basset Hound. Despite its stocky appearance, the Clumber Spaniel is an agile, strong sporting dog with enormous stamina. It has a powerful nose and a natural inclination to hunt. An able and willing retriever, it is an independent and deliberate worker.

Recommendation
Pleasant with other animals and children, although not always as demonstrative with its family as are other spaniels. A gentle, affectionate breed, the Clumber Spaniel is slow-moving and sedate, and lacks the social grace exhibited by many other sporting dogs. It is an interesting companion, and its owners quickly become devoted. Its unusual appearance is sure to attract attention.

Plate 54

Cocker Spaniel

Characteristics
Round, domed head
Broad, square muzzle
Long, hanging ears
Compact body
Long, silky coat with
feathering
Docked tail

Personality
A small, lively, stylish dog. The carefully bred Cocker Spaniel is a fast-learning, easygoing, affectionate, and gentle dog. Friendly and eager to please. Sparkling charm.

Ideal Appearance
Smallest sporting dog. Males, ideally 15″; bitches, 14″. Although standard does not specify weight, males usually weigh around 28 pounds; bitches, approximately 26 pounds. Head has pronounced stop and broad, square muzzle. Long, hanging, low-set ears. Short, sturdy body with deep chest and strong, sloping back. Docked tail. Silky, flat or slightly wavy coat. Abundant feathering on ears, chest, belly, and legs. Three color divisions compete against each other. Black varieties are either solid black or black with tan points; nose is black. ASCOB varieties (any solid color other than black) include white, tan, liver, or others; nose is brown, liver, or black. Parti-color varieties have 2 or more distinct colors; primary color must be less than 90 percent, and tan marking less than 10 percent; black and tan has black nose; noses of others may be any color. All varieties have dark brown eyes.

Potential Health Problems
Generally hardy, but problems are prevalent in puppy-mill dogs. Subject to progressive retinal atrophy, cataracts, and other eye problems, slipped stifle, ear trouble, multiple skin disorders, bleeding, and some other serious ailments.

Care and Exercise
Coat should be groomed for about 45 minutes twice a week. Some professional trimming is necessary to keep hair on head properly clipped, and to cut hair on neck and shoulders. Although breed is highly suited to city life, dogs need plenty of exercise. May be hard to housebreak. Should not get fat.

Puppies
Average litter, 4 to 6 puppies. Solid-colored dogs are born with their adult color, but parti-colored dogs are often born white and show color at about 2 weeks. Puppies need to be handled daily.

Comment
The descendant of a long line of setters and spaniels, the Cocker Spaniel is the smallest of today's sporting dogs. Prior to the 17th century, all spaniels were grouped together. Gradually they were separated into water and land spaniels, and later, the land dogs were divided into small and larger dogs. Eventually, very small spaniels were reclassified solely as companion dogs, or toys, but the Cocker Spaniel remained in the sporting group. Its name derived from its proficiency at stalking woodcock, a snipelike game bird. Introduced in the United States in the late 1870s and 1880s, the breed developed along different lines than in England. In recent years, the English Cocker Spaniel was made a separate breed.
Today the Cocker Spaniel is still an efficient gundog, rushing ahead of the hunter's gun to flush out game. More often, however, this breed is a show dog or family pet. The Cocker Spaniel was the number one AKC breed in 1984.

Recommendation
A delightful, handsome pet, the Cocker Spaniel is exceptionally good with children, is obedient, and is generally even-tempered. At one time, the tremendous demand for this breed made the Cocker a victim of careless, puppy-mill breeding, resulting in some high-strung, noisy dogs, as well as unhealthy animals. This breed must be purchased with great caution, from only the most reputable breeders.

Plates 46, 48

English Cocker Spaniel

Characteristics
Larger than American Cocker
Long, hanging ears
Large, square muzzle
Strong, compact body
Feathering
Docked tail

Personality
Exceptionally good with children, the English Cocker is gentle, obedient, and even-tempered. Thoroughly delightful, and adaptable to any environment. A fine field dog, but will do as well in an apartment.

Ideal Appearance
Larger than American Cocker. Males, 16" to 17" tall and 28 to 34 pounds; bitches, 15" to 16" and 26 to 32 pounds. Head is slightly flattened on top and has well-developed forehead, square muzzle, and definite stop. Long, low-set, hanging ears. Powerful, compact body is as tall as it is long. Sloping shoulders and deep chest. Docked tail carried even with back. Silky coat should be flat or slightly wavy, with abundant feathering on ears, chest, belly, and legs. Permissible colors: white, black, black and tan, or roan pattern in blue, liver red, orange, or lemon. Dark or hazel eyes.

Potential Health Problems
Healthy overall. Subject to progressive retinal atrophy and ear trouble.

Care and Exercise
Coat only requires moderate care, except for some professional trimming about once a month. These energetic dogs want lots of exercise—especially frequent romps in the country, after which they need a good brushing.

Puppies
Average litter, 3 to 8 puppies. Solid colors do not change; parti-colors acquire more patterning and ticking as they age; blue roan puppies appear black and white at birth—or sometimes very dark —but change color within days. Puppies benefit from early handling and training.

Comment
Among the oldest of the land spaniels, both the Cocker Spaniel and the English Cocker Spaniel descended from the original Spanish Spaniel. They were both considered a single breed and grouped with the larger land spaniels. In 1892, however, the Cocker was recognized as a distinct breed in England. At one time, Cocker and Springer spaniels were taken from the same litter; they were distinguished only by size, the Cocker being the smaller of the 2. For many years, there was only one breed of Cocker Spaniel, but in 1935, the English Cocker Spaniel Club of America was formed to discourage interbreeding between the English and American varieties. It took an extensive pedigree search to sort out the purities of the 2 types.
Finally, in 1946, the American Kennel Club recognized the English Cocker Spaniel as a separate breed. Slightly larger than its American cousin, the English Cocker appears somewhat leggier and has a larger muzzle. And, unlike the Cocker Spaniel, the English Cocker Spaniel is not shown in different color varieties.

Recommendation
This alert and merry breed is known for its loyal and affectionate manner and its intelligence. It is an ideal family dog that loves to play. Such a good-natured pet deserves to be exercised sufficiently, especially when living in the city. The English Cocker Spaniel does not suffer from the same health problems as its American cousin, the Cocker Spaniel.

Plate 45

English Springer Spaniel

Characteristics
Broad head
Long, hanging ears
Compact body
Feathering
Docked tail

Personality
A great tail-wagger and an appealing family pet. First-rate field dog. Eager to please, intelligent, and loyal, the English Springer is extremely affectionate and exceptionally good with children. Although active and playful, it adapts well to city life.

Ideal Appearance
A balanced, symmetrical, and stylish breed. Males, ideally 20″ tall and 49 to 55 pounds; bitches, 19″ and proportionately lighter. Fairly broad head with long, wide, hanging ears. Compact body and docked tail. Flat or wavy coat, never curly. Feathering on ears, chest, belly, and legs. Permissible colors: liver or black, with white markings; liver or black and white, with tan markings; blue or liver roan; white with tan, black, or liver markings. Dark eyes.

Potential Health Problems
Basically healthy. Subject to hip dysplasia, allergic skin disease, ear diseases, retinal dysplasia, seborrhea, hypothyroidism, and rage syndrome.

Care and Exercise
Fine, glossy coat requires weekly grooming to keep it from matting. Professional trimming is also necessary several times a year. Although highly adaptable to urban life, this breed needs exercise as well as time and space to roam. It loves to romp and adores the water. Occasional trips to the country are a great treat for a deserving pet.

Puppies
Usually 7 puppies. Puppies should become accustomed to people and simple training at an early age.

Comment
When the English land spaniels were divided into toy breeds and working dogs, members of the latter group were assigned different responsibilities in the field. The smaller dogs were called Cockers, while the larger, taller dogs became known as Springers because their task was to work ahead of the gun, flushing or "springing" the game. Springers work rapidly and obediently, faster and farther ahead of the other spaniels. The breed standards for the English Springer Spaniel were developed to emphasize its natural sporting ability. In the show ring, the English Springer appears friendly and animated. As a family dog, it is completely delightful.

Recommendation
An all-around companion for either families or hunters, the English Springer Spaniel is gentle and easygoing. It is affectionate and playful, an ideal dog for children. Protective of its family, this alert watchdog is always ready to announce an intruder. The Springer will live happily in either the country or the city with equal ease, as long as it gets plenty of exercise and attention. Purchase a pet only from a fine specialty breeder. Some mass-produced strains have very poor dispositions, which is not at all characteristic of the breed.

Plate 79

Field Spaniel

Characteristics
Long, lean muzzle
Longer and lower
than other spaniels
Setter-like, silky coat
with feathering
Docked tail

Personality
Gentle, easy-going, and quick to learn. Very pleasant with other animals and children. This breed attaches itself to its family and, although friendly with everyone, makes an alert watchdog.

Ideal Appearance
Should appear well-balanced, noble, and active. Males, about 18″ tall and 35 to 50 pounds; bitches are usually smaller. Head has long, lean muzzle. Low-set hanging ears with setterlike feathering. Strong, muscular back and loins. Docked tail carried low, usually below level of back. Silky, glossy coat more setterlike than spaniel-like, with abundant feathering; should be flat or slightly wavy, never curly. Permissible colors: usually black; also liver, golden-liver, roan, mahogany-red, or any of these with tan markings. Dark hazel or brown eyes.

Potential Health Problems
Usually a healthy breed. Subject to hip dysplasia, retinal dysplasia, and ear trouble.

Care and Exercise
Silky coat requires only moderate care, which consists of about 5 minutes of brushing twice a week. Professional trimming is also necessary a few times a year. A very active breed, even indoors, the Field Spaniel needs frequent runs. It has a strong desire to roam and thus should be restricted to a leash or a fenced-in area.

Puppies
Usually a litter of 7 puppies. Bitch often has difficulty conceiving, but whelping is normal. Puppies need handling from a young age, as all dogs do.

Comment
One of America's rarest breeds, the Field Spaniel is one of the least-known spaniel breeds and possibly the youngest. Slower than the Cocker and lower to the ground than the Springer, the Field Spaniel was most likely developed from the Cocker, Springer, and Sussex spaniels for hunting in the underbrush. Its exact origins, however, remain somewhat ambiguous. At the end of the 19th century, emphasis on a fashionable look rather than a practical gundog resulted in an awkward-looking version of this breed whose long body, short legs, and heavy bones made it practically useless in the field. Subsequently the breed nearly vanished from England. In an attempt to correct the mistakes of the past, Cocker and Springer blood was bred into the Field Spaniel. Today the much-improved Field Spaniel is larger and stronger than its ancestors. This extremely agile dog has a good nose, is willing to work, and is well suited for hunting in open terrain.

Recommendation
This handsome but little-known animal is a tireless worker and a friendly companion. Docile and affectionate, intelligent, and eager to please, the breed is highly suited for family life. A city dweller should be prepared to spend a lot of time walking and running a Field Spaniel. Although still very rare, Field Spaniels may well be an up-and-coming sporting breed. It is a robust companion.

Plate 82

Irish Water Spaniel

Characteristics
Curly topknot
Ringlets overall,
except on face and tail
Large head and body
Rat tail

Personality
Highly intelligent and easily trained. Although generally fine in a family setting, the Irish Water Spaniel is a one-person dog that is naturally suspicious of strangers. May be stubborn and occasionally timid. Tends to be aggressive with other dogs. It is a fine, loyal pet when properly raised. Needs careful obedience training.

Ideal Appearance
Large and covered with thick ringlets. Males, 22″ to 24″ tall and 55 to 65 pounds; bitches, 21″ to 23″ and 45 to 58 pounds. Topknot of long, loose curls grows down into a well-defined peak between eyes, accentuating short, smooth hair on face. Rather large and cleanly chiseled head with square muzzle and long, low-set ears. Strong body with solid, athletic look. Ratlike tail, 2″ to 3″ of which is covered with short, smooth hair. Coat length is very important for show: on neck, back, and sides, should be dense with tight, crisp ringlets, but should not be woolly; curls or waves should be present on ears and legs. Underneath ribs, hair is longer; on lower throat, it is shorter. Permissible color: solid liver; no white allowed. Liver-colored nose and dark hazel eyes.

Potential Health Problems
Generally a healthy breed. Prone to hip dysplasia, ear infections, and skin disorders.

Care and Exercise
Special attention is required to keep this breed's coat in proper condition. Count on spending an hour a week in addition to significant professional trimming to retain the close curls. This active breed requires a great deal of exercise and is really unsuited to urban life. Loves water and should have the opportunity to swim whenever possible. Obedience training is required to control the dog's stubborn and sometimes aggressive tendencies.

Puppies
Litters of 4 to 12 puppies. Conception is sometimes difficult, but whelping is normal. Puppies need more than average socializing so that they get along well with people when grown.

Comment
A very ancient breed, the Irish Water Spaniel may date back to as much as 6000 years ago, when they inhabited Asia Minor. Carvings taken from old Roman ruins bear a striking resemblance to this dog. Its precise origin is unknown; however, this spaniel became known as a sporting breed in Ireland, where it was used to retrieve wildfowl from the icy waters. Judging from its curly coat, retrieving abilities, and coloring, the Irish Water Spaniel may have the Poodle, the old European Waterdog, and the Irish Setter among its ancestors, but this has not been proven. According to known records, a 19th-century dog named Boatswain was probably the first modern Irish Water Spaniel. It sired many of the outstanding gundogs and show dogs that followed. Recognized in England in 1859, the breed appeared in the first Westminster Kennel Club show in America in 1877. The Irish Water Spaniel is considerably larger than any of the other spaniels. A skilled and extremely hardy water dog, it is a better watchdog than most sporting breeds are.

Recommendation
Despite a somewhat stubborn nature, this highly intelligent breed can be an excellent performer or companion if trained early. The Irish Water Spaniel is reserved and occasionally tricky with strangers. A special kind of dog, this ancient, skilled, and independent breed is not for the casual owner, but is for a person who takes the role of master seriously. This is a fine but assertive dog.

Plate 129

Sussex Spaniel

Characteristics
Broad head
Heavy brow
Drooping lips
Low, muscular body
Short legs
Moderate feathering
Docked tail

Personality
Quite different from other spaniels.
Easygoing but stubborn. Gentle and
cheerful with everyone, including
children. An alert watchdog. May be
unpredictable with other dogs. Learns
somewhat slowly, yet is determined and
trainable. Overall, this breed's
personality falls somewhere in between
that of the phlegmatic Clumber and the
demonstrative, peppy Cocker or
Springer. Generally noisier than other
sporting breeds.

Ideal Appearance
Massive, long, low, muscular body.
Males and bitches, 35 to 45 pounds.
Although standard does not specify
height, males usually measure about 16";
bitches, approximately 15". Moderately
long, wide head with full stop, fairly
heavy brows, and large eyes. Long,
square muzzle about 3" long; lips droop
somewhat. Fairly large ears sit close to
head. Deep, wide, and round chest and
long, very muscular back. Short, strong
legs. Low-set tail docked between 5" and
7". Abundant, flat, slightly waxy coat
with moderate feathering on ears, legs,
stern, and tail. Permissible color: rich
golden-liver. Hazel eyes.

Potential Health Problems
Overall, a hardy breed. Ears need to be
checked routinely, as do all drop ears.

Care and Exercise
Only moderate coat care needed: about
10 minutes of brushing twice a week.
Like all sporting breeds, the Sussex
Spaniel loves the outdoors and needs a
fair amount of exercise.

Puppies
Average litter of 5 to 6 puppies. Born
brown, puppies develop gold tipping as
they age. Young puppies are very fragile,
especially females, and have a high
mortality rate. They are generally strong
by 6 months. Puppies do best if handled
from an early age.

Comment
An old English breed, the Sussex Spaniel
is named after the location of the first
and foremost kennel where the rich
golden-liver color that is so characteristic
of this breed was developed. In its early
days in England, when game was
abundant and men still hunted on foot,
this dog proved a fine sporting
companion. Conscientious and
persevering, it has a good nose, but lacks
the speed of the Springer or the Cocker.
With proper training, it can be an
excellent retriever. It is the only spaniel
that "gives tongue" (hunters' jargon,
meaning "bays") on the trail. The Sussex
Spaniel is still one of the rarest breeds in
the United States.

Recommendation
Not well suited to modern hunting
needs, the Sussex Spaniel is a soft and
affectionate house pet that will adapt
well to a family. It is loyal, easy to train,
and does not require any unusual care or
exercise. This quality breed deserves
more popularity as a companion animal,
though its rarity makes puppies quite
hard to find. The serious dog owner may
want to consider an import from England
to add to the American line.

Plate 81

Welsh Springer Spaniel

Characteristics
Shorter body than
English Springer
Square muzzle
Small, hanging ears
Feathering
Docked tail

Personality
Sensible and steady. May be less exhuberant than the English Springer Spaniel. A bold and alert watchdog. The Welsh Springer Spaniel is an intelligent one-family dog that is fine with children and pleasant to other animals. A tireless hunting companion and a devoted pet, it is adaptable to most environments.

Ideal Appearance
Symmetrical, compact build; shorter than English Springer. Although standard does not specify size, males are usually about 17″ tall and approximately 45 pounds; bitches, around 16½″ and some 38 pounds. Moderately long, slightly domed head has clearly defined stop and fairly square muzzle. Comparatively small ears hang close to cheeks. Strong body proportionate to length of leg. Tail docked to two thirds of the original length. Flat, straight coat is thick and silky, not wiry or wavy. Feathering on ears, chest, belly, and legs. Permissible color: only dark, rich red and white. Hazel or dark eyes.

Potential Health Problems
Generally healthy. Subject to epilepsy and progressive retinal atrophy. Ears should be kept clean to prevent infection.

Care and Exercise
Elegant coat requires brushing a couple of times each week and minor professional trimming. This active dog needs a great deal of exercise outdoors, where it can race around to its heart's content. No weather is too harsh for this hardy breed.

Puppies
Average litter of 6 to 10 puppies. Puppies will approach full size by 9 months. They do best if around people from an early age. Should be given obedience training and retrieving lessons at about 6 months of age. They do not do well in a kennel.

Comment
Although similar in appearance, the Welsh and English springer spaniels are different in many ways. The Welsh Springer is smaller, has shorter ears, and its only color is red and white. This breed was developed in Wales over 400 years ago; a very similar dog, always with the characteristic red and white, appears in ancient Welsh prints and writings.
The breed is exceptionally versatile, and able to withstand extreme heat or cold. As a result, Welsh Springer Spaniels—called Starters in Wales—have been exported to a variety of different climates throughout the world, from the States to India and Thailand. An excellent game dog, the breed has a fine nose and is an admirable retriever on land or in water. Its pleasant temperament makes it a good family pet.

Recommendation
This dependable breed is not as well known in the United States as its English cousin but is an equally fine game dog and pet. Playful yet even-tempered, easygoing but bold, it will adapt to city life if provided with regular long walks and frequent romps in an open park. Regardless of weather, the Welsh Springer expects exercise. If this breed is given what it needs, it will be a devoted, responsive, fit, and happy pet.

Plate 80

Vizsla

Characteristics
Pointer-like build
Lean, muscular head
Broad, deep chest
Short, silky coat
Docked tail

Personality
Livley, gentle, and intelligent.
Demonstratively affectionate and
easygoing. An alert watchdog. May be
very slow to warm up to strangers. This
steady-tempered breed does very well in
the family setting. Clean, fast, and
smart.

Ideal Appearance
Robust pointer build. Males, 22″ to 24″
tall, bitches 21″ to 23″. Although
standard does not specify weight, Vizslas
usually weigh 55 to 60 pounds. Lean yet
muscular head with moderately wide
skull between ears. Slight stop and
square, tapering muzzle. Thin, low-set
silky ears with rounded ends hang close
to cheeks. Strong, well-proportioned
body with broad, deep chest and short
back. Docked tail. Short, smooth, close-
lying coat. Permissible colors: different
shades of golden rust—from rusty gold
to dark sandy yellow. Eyes harmonize
with coat; brown nose.

Potential Health Problems
Overall a healthy breed, but some
subject to skin problems, bleeding
disorders, and epilepsy.

Care and Exercise
Short, dense coat requires little care; a
few minutes of brushing a few times a
week is sufficient. A sporting dog by
nature, the Vizsla needs an enormous
amount of exercise. Boundless energy
may turn into destructive behavior if
confined indoors. Long walks are a must,
and good long runs every day will keep a
Vizsla from becoming hyperactive. May
be hard to housebreak in some cases.
Dogs can be extremely headstrong and
should have significant amount of
obedience training at an early age.

Puppies
Average litter, 6 to 8 puppies. Colors do
not usually change. Puppies should be
taught basic obedience commands
beginning at 8 weeks; formal training
should begin at 6 months. To avoid
hyperactivity or timidity, puppies should
be exposed to many people and
experiences.

Comment
Tenth-century stone etchings of a dog
resembling the Vizsla suggest that this
breed's ancestors were the companions of
the Magyars, who settled in the area now
known as Hungary. In this agriculturally
rich terrain where game was plentiful,
the Vizsla, or Hungarian Pointer,
flourished for centuries as a hunting dog.
Its robust body, keen nose, and speed
made it ideal for tracking partridges and
rabbits through tall grasses.
The Vizsla's numbers diminished
dramatically between World Wars I and
II. During the Russian occupation of
Hungary in 1945, families fleeing to
Austria, Italy, and Germany took their
dogs with them, thereby extending the
breed's boundaries. The Vizsla was
admitted to the American Kennel Club
in 1960.

Recommendation
A superior gundog, the Vizsla works
equally well hunting rabbit or
waterfowl. It makes an even-tempered,
affectionate household pet under the
proper conditions. But like so many of
its sporting relatives, this breed is filled
with energy. To deprive it of exercise
may be the ruin of an otherwise
delightful dog. Hyperactivity and
destructiveness are often the results of an
improper environment. The Vizsla is not
suited to city living and frequently not
even to suburban life. This is a country
dog for owners who make their authority
clear from the beginning.

Plate 120

Weimaraner

Characteristics
Gray, with light eyes
Powerful build
Deep chest
Straight back
Docked tail

Personality
Intelligent, assertive, bold, and stubborn. A one-family dog that is reserved with strangers and a bit too impetuous for young children. Can make a good watchdog. When well trained, this breed has great character and is loyal and attentive. If untrained, however, it may be pushy and difficult to manage.

Ideal Appearance
Aristocratic, intelligent look. Males, 25" to 27" tall; bitches, 23" to 25". Although standard does not specify weight, males usually weigh 85 pounds; bitches, about 70 pounds. Overall appearance of grace, speed, stamina, alertness, and balance. Clean-cut, moderately long head. Long, high-set hanging ears. Deep, well-developed chest; strong, straight back; and strong forelegs. Tail docked to about 6". Short, smooth, sleek coat. Permissible colors: shades of gray from mouse to silver; blue or black coat not allowed. Light amber, gray, or blue-gray eyes. Gray nose.

Potential Health Problems
Generally hardy, although may be subject to bloat, hip dysplasia, mast cell tumors, gait abnormality, and bleeding disorders.

Care and Exercise
Short, sleek coat requires practically no care. Occasional brushing with natural-bristle brush will keep ordinary shedding under control. Highly active, this breed is really unsuited to city life. It needs frequent and rigorous exercise and is more manageable if given the space and opportunity to express its energetic, outgoing personality. May be hard to housebreak, and destructive if untrained and confined alone. Count the cost of a first-rate obedience school as part of the price for this breed.

Puppies
Average litter, 5 to 7 puppies. Starting at 5 weeks or even earlier, puppies should get used to handling by different people. They do not do well in a kennel. Obedience training at 5½ to 8 months.

Comment
The Weimaraner is a German breed dating to at least the early 19th century. It probably developed from ancient Bloodhound stock that was bred with the German Shorthaired Pointer, although some people believe that the dog originated much earlier. A similar light-colored dog appears in a 17th century Van Dyck painting.

By the 19th century, these dogs were, without a doubt, the favorite gundogs of the sporting nobles at the Court of Weimar, and they became known throughout Germany as the Weimar Pointers. They were jealously guarded, and it was all but impossible to obtain one outside the court. Used to hunt big game, as well as smaller animals, the Weimaraner was valued for its nose, intelligence, courage, and speed.

As its popularity grew in Germany, severe rules governed breeding; only German Weimaraner Club members were allowed to purchase dogs, and only puppies whose lineage met the scrutiny of a breed survey could be entered in the stud book. In 1929 Howard Knight, an American, joined the club, brought 2 dogs to the United States, and helped found a club here. The Weimaraner became an AKC breed in 1943.

Recommendation
The Weimaraner should not be an owner's first dog. It requires an intelligent, experienced person or family that is capable of being in command and is familiar with obedience training. Purchase a dog from only the most reputable breeders to avoid puppy-mill dogs. Exercise must be frequent.

Plate 119

Wirehaired Pointing Griffon

Characteristics
Pointer-like build
Stiff, wiry outer coat
Bushy eyebrows,
mustache, and beard
Short back
Tail usually docked

Personality
A pleasant companion and a skillful, multipurpose hunting dog. Loyal and obedient. Somewhat nervous or cautious with strangers, but gentle by nature. The Wirehaired Pointing Griffon is an alert watchdog and is exceptionally good with children.

Ideal Appearance
Powerful build. Males, 21½" to 23½" tall; bitches, 19½" to 21½". Although standard does not specify weight, males usually weigh about 60 pounds; bitches, approximately 55 pounds. Most striking characteristic is harsh, stiff outer coat forming eyebrows, mustache, and beard. Soft undercoat. Long, narrow skull with square muzzle. High-set, medium-length ears. Short back. Tail usually docked to a third of its length. Permissible colors: steel-gray, gray-white, or dirty white (all 3 with chestnut splashes), or solid chestnut; never black. Yellowish or light brown eyes. Brown nose.

Potential Health Problems
A robust breed overall. Subject to hip dysplasia, like most large dogs.

Care and Exercise
Wiry coat needs only minimal care—about 15 minutes grooming once a week. It does require some trimming and stripping every couple of months; this can be done at home. This dog naturally looks shaggy and should not be trimmed close like the German Wirehaired Pointer. Highly active both indoors and out, this breed must have plenty of exercise if it is to be calm and well-adjusted. May be hard to housebreak. If not trained and taught to get along with people, may be timid and high-strung.

Puppies
Average litter, 8 puppies. Newborns are white or white with liver spots; dogs later change to silver-gray or gray, both with liver spots, or solid liver. These hearty puppies do well if trained early. Should get used to people.

Comment
This shaggy sporting dog comes from a long line of hunting breeds, including setter, spaniel, Pointer, Otter Hound, and the medieval Griffon Hound. It is a fine example of 19th-century experiments in breeding. During the 1870s, a young Dutch banker's son, E. K. Korthals, set out to develop a new breed of sporting dog, starting with some Griffon-like dogs he purchased in Amsterdam. A family quarrel forced Korthals to continue his breeding in Germany and later in France, where he eventually produced the Wirehaired Pointing Griffon, still called the Korthals Griffon in France.
By the beginning of this century, the breed type was well established as an admirable hunting dog combining the skills of both pointer and retriever. Its harsh coat is perfectly suited to rough terrain and miserable weather. A strong swimmer, the Wirehaired Pointing Griffon is an excellent water retriever. It is a slow but deliberate worker.

Recommendation
This intelligent, good-tempered breed is a fine companion at home or in the field. Although generally calm, the Wirehaired Pointing Griffon may be very high-strung if confined to a strictly city life. It requires enormous amounts of exercise and thrives under the harshest working conditions. Truly a dog of the country.

Plate 90

Hounds

An Ancient Heritage

Hounds may be the oldest purebred dogs. The Saluki dates back seven or eight thousand years to Sumeria, and the Greyhound, the Ibizan Hound, and the Pharaoh Hound were all favored hunting dogs in ancient Egypt. The Ibizan Hound and the Pharaoh Hound closely resemble Anubis, an Egyptian god with the head of a jackal. The Afghan Hound is nearly as old. And the Bloodhound—probably the forerunner of all modern scent hounds—can be traced to Rome in the period before Christ; this ancestor was most likely quite similar to the dogs we now know.

Today the hound group consists of twenty-one breeds recognized by the American Kennel Club as well as five others recognized by the United Kennel Club (see page 253).

Types of Hounds

Hounds can be divided into three main AKC categories. Dogs that hunt using only their eyesight are, appropriately enough, called sight or gaze hounds; there are nine breeds in this category: the Afghan Hound, Borzoi, Greyhound, Ibizan Hound, Irish Wolfhound, Pharaoh Hound, Saluki, Scottish Deerhound, and Whippet. There are seven scent hounds, which hunt by scent without depending on eyesight: Basset Hound, Beagle, Black and Tan Coonhound, Bloodhound, American Foxhound, English Foxhound, and Harrier. Five breeds use a combination of sight and scent: Basenji, Dachshund, Norwegian Elkhound, Otter Hound, and Rhodesian Ridgeback.

Perhaps the Basenji, the Norwegian Elkhound, and the Rhodesian Ridgeback do not belong in the hound group at all. Although no one knows where in Africa the Basenji originated, the dog was brought to the Egyptian court thousands of years ago and today is rarely used for hunting. The Norwegian Elkhound and the Northern Spitz are the same breed; both are related to the sled dogs in the working group and the Keeshond in the non-sporting group. There is almost certainly some hound in the Rhodesian Ridgeback, but other strains exist as well. Many people also question the Dachshund's inclusion, because its size has been greatly reduced since it was used as a hunting breed in Germany; the breed is really a companion dog today. The five additional UKC hounds include the Bluetick Coonhound, the English Coonhound, the Plott Hound, the Redbone Coonhound, and the Treeing Walker Coonhound. This club also registers the greatest number of Black and Tan Coonhounds.

Diverse Uses of Hounds

Originally the hounds were hunting dogs, although they are clearly distinct from these breeds in today's sporting group. A number of the scent hounds—the Beagle, the American and English foxhounds, and the Black and Tan Coonhound—are still field dogs. The Greyhound and the Whippet are racing animals, and a limited number of people use the Borzoi and the Irish Wolfhound to course coyotes. Although the Bloodhound is still very prevalent in police work, most dogs of this breed are kept purely for companionship.

Miniature to Giant Companions

Hounds typically have gentle personalities. Unless raised as kennel dogs or in packs for field use, most of them make fine pets. The tallest dogs in the world—Irish Wolfhound, Scottish Deerhound, and Borzoi—belong to this group, and their homes must be quite large. These giants are balanced by the smaller of the two Beagle varieties, as well as by the miniature versions of the Dachshund. There is, in short, a hound for almost every taste and lifestyle.

Afghan Hound

Characteristics
High-fashion look
Long, wedge-shaped head
High-set hips
Natural tail
Long, silky hair
Superbly graceful

Personality
Somewhat aloof. Friendly but not fawning. Not aggressive with strangers, taking its own time to adjust to them. Remarkably good watchdog. Very pleasing companion of great style and beauty, although not terribly intelligent.

Ideal Appearance
A tall, slim dog of the Greyhound or coursing type. Males, approximately 27" tall and about 60 pounds; bitches, approximately 25" and about 50 pounds. Hips set high, enabling the dog to race over rough terrain when coursing. Long, wedge-shaped head bears topknot of silky hair. Level bite preferred; scissors type acceptable. Long, silky hair on ribs, flanks, legs, tail, and feet; short hair on top of neck, saddle, and back. Permissible colors: from champagne to black, either solid or with exotic patterns. White markings, particularly on head, are not desirable because they detract from dog's overall appearance. Dark eyes.

Potential Health Problems
As a rule, healthy. Tends to be sensitive to drugs, particularly topical types—such as flea powders, tickicides, and drugs on flea collars—which may cause allergic reactions. Prone to hip dysplasia and cataracts. Occasionally contracts a progressive paralysis, a fatal disease unknown in other breeds. Afghans have a low tolerance for pain.

Care and Exercise
No special grooming required except for regular combing and an occasional bath with mild soap. Dogs do best on a diet of the better grades of prepared dry or kibbled dog foods.
Runs in open fields should be a routine part of the dog's life; once or twice a day is most desirable. Also plan to take it on long walks on a leash.

Puppies
Litters average 6 to 8 puppies, although up to 14 have been recorded. Puppies may have jaw malformations at birth, but these often correct themselves by the age of 9 months.

Comment
The Afghan Hound originated almost 6000 years ago in an area along the Afghan border known as Seistan. A ruthless hunter, this breed was used to run down leopards and gazelles in the borderland mountains. Until the early 20th century, people simply lumped the Afghan with other coursing breeds and called them all Eastern Greyhounds, or sometimes Persian Greyhounds. However in 1907 a so-called Persian Greyhound named Zardin, upon being shown in England, became the model type for a distinct breed known as the Afghan Hound. The original savage nature had been eliminated, and the aristocratic, docile character of this dog became the norm for the breed. Although no longer really a hunting dog, the Afghan is becoming increasingly popular in the sport of lure coursing. But most Afghans are kept as pets today.

Recommendation
The Afghan is a special breed with classic, aristocratic looks. For experienced, dog-oriented owners only, as it is, in short, "a lot of dog." It can be kept in a roomy apartment as long as there is one athletic member of the household ready to provide regular exercise.
If you intend to buy an Afghan, it is best to get an 8- to 12-week-old puppy; at that age, it can adjust to your home more easily than an older dog can. Give it a bed of its own. Be sure to introduce your puppy as often as possible to children and strangers to help it overcome its innate shyness.

Plate 133

Basenji

Characteristics
Does not bark
Prick ears
Wrinkled forehead
Square build
Flat back
Ring tail
Virtually odorless

Personality

Docile and anxious to please. Playful, but may resent strangers. Carries itself with considerable majesty. Quiet. Breed does not bark; chortles or yodels instead. Extremely clean, attractive, and graceful.

Ideal Appearance

Males, 17″ tall and about 24 pounds; bitches, 16″ and 22 pounds. Body length is about the same as height. Dogs should look proud and lively. Prick ears and wrinkled forehead create a contemplative expression. Head tapers to medium-length muzzle; neck should be arched, back level, and tail tightly curved and carried to either side or directly over the spine. Short, silky coat. Very fast, beautiful, high-stepping trot. Permissible colors: chestnut-red, pure black, or black and tan, with white on legs, feet, chest, or collar; cream and other off-colors not allowed. Dark hazel eyes.

Potential Health Problems

Overall, a sturdy breed. Dogs sometimes have persistent pupillary membrane. Occasionally incidences of inguinal and umbilical hernias. These conditions can be treated or corrected by a veterinarian. Basenjis may have allergic skin disease. Anemia and diarrhea are common.

Care and Exercise

No special care required. Bathe in the mild soap. Give dog a draft-proof bed. Dog blankets are recommended for cold weather.

Exercise regularly on a leash. Curiosity may cause this breed to wander if allowed off leash or left alone in an unfenced area. Competes well in lure-coursing events.

Puppies

Dams come into heat only once a year, for 30 days. Whelping seldom difficult. Average litter contains 6 puppies, but as many as 12 have been recorded. Allow puppies to become accustomed to people and handling at an early age; this will help avoid difficult dispositions in mature dogs.

Comment

When the Basenji first came out of Africa, it was called the Congo Barkless Dog and, sometimes, Dog of the Forest. The present name, Basenji, is a Swahili word meaning "savage," and was inspired by the fierce personality of the wild predecessors of this breed. Swift and silent hunters, the early Basenjis were unequaled at tracking game through the jungle. During ancient Egyptian times, these curious dogs were given as presents to the pharaohs by traveling dignitaries. Their origin, however, remains a mystery.

The Basenji was first brought to America in the mid-1930s, and was recognized by the American Kennel Club in 1943. The Basenji retains characteristics of the primitive dog: It does not bark, and bitches come into heat only once a year, instead of following the usual biannual cycle. Dogs of a roughly similar type are still found in many places in Central Africa, but it is doubtful that purebred Basenjis still exist there. Despite their equatorial origin, Basenjis do well in northern Canada and Alaska.

Recommendation

An excellent house pet, the Basenji is quiet, clean, and does not shed much. This breed loves to play and is always a curious and insistent participant.

Plate 65

Basset Hound

Characteristics
Large head with
loose, elastic skin
Long, low body
Short legs
Long, low-set ears
Deep-set eyes
Natural tail

Personality
A gentle, slow-moving dog with a droll appearance. Adjusts quickly to home life. Easily spoiled, and can be stubborn. The Basset enjoys and needs human companionship. Very responsive to its family. It has a superbly deep, rolling bark that can be quite amusing.

Ideal Appearance
Has been described as having a Bloodhound's head and a fat Dachshund's body. Males, up to 14″ tall (over 15″ disqualifies from show ring). Although standard does not specify weight, males usually weigh about 60 pounds. Bitches are characteristically smaller and more feminine-looking. The head of this breed indeed resembles that of the Bloodhound: Loose skin forms forehead wrinkles when head is lowered, and, because eyes are deep set, lower eyelid also falls forward, exposing the third eyelid, or haw. Low-set ears are so long that they can fold over the nose. This massive breed has huge, long, low body, large feet, and the heaviest leg bones of any dog. Permissible colors: typical colors are combinations of black, tan, and white, but all hound colors and markings are acceptable. Brown eyes.

Potential Health Problems
Generally a healthy breed. Susceptible to shoulder and foreleg lameness caused by somewhat deformed leg bones. Glaucoma and bloat sometimes occur. Look between toes for signs of infection, which can be treated by your veterinarian. Possible disc disorders, ear disease, epilepsy, and bleeding disorders.

Care and Exercise
Easy to keep. Ears should be monitored since they are the hanging type. For a shiny and healthy coat, massage dog's skin occasionally with your fingers, then rub its coat with your palms to remove dead hair. Dog may get too fat if its diet is not watched carefully.

Daily exercise is a must and helps prevent bloat. Bassets often remain active up to the age of 12.

Puppies
Often delivered by cesarean section, litters average 8 to 10 puppies, and sometimes contain as many as 14. Puppies grow rapidly. Very large litters may require supplemental feeding and need calcium to prevent bone problems. Basset puppies are ungainly and endearing—constantly stepping on their own ears or tugging at each other.

Comment
An ancient breed, the Basset apparently came from Bloodhound stock, as is evidenced by its long ears, wrinkled brow, and excellent sense of smell. It also has the same stamina on the trail, although it is somewhat slower. The extraordinarily long ears allow the Basset to swirl scent particles up into its nose, an especially valuable ability on cold, damp days. The breed name may derive from the French word *bas,* meaning "low," or from a term once used in hare hunting that meant "the set of the hare." American show Bassets and most pets of this breed are lower to the ground and heavier than those used for actual hunting and field trials. Hunting dogs have lighter bones and shallower bodies that ride higher on the leg. These characteristics make them much more agile in the field. The American Kennel Club recognized this breed in 1885.

Recommendation
A lovely and amusing household pet for people with a good sense of humor. Good-natured, and is easily taught manners. The Basset is a short-legged version of the Bloodhound and has retained this giant dog's benign disposition. This breed requires and expects attention and care.

Plate 53

Beagle

Characteristics
Drooping, low-set ears
Sloping shoulders
Clean, neat look
Short coat
Natural tail

Personality
Gentle and lovable. Very responsive, naturally curious, and affectionate. Good watchdog. Sweet hunting voice, but pets tend to howl loudly if left alone. They can be trained not to howl, however. Beagles used in hunting and in field trials are apt to be much more high-strung than show dogs and pets.

Ideal Appearance
2 AKC varieties, based solely on size: those 13″ tall and under, and those over 13″ but not over 15″. Although standard does not specify weight, the smaller variety usually weighs about 18 pounds; the larger, approximately 20 pounds. Breed standard is written for the show dog, and field dogs only slightly conform to it; size varieties are the same. Overall build appears square, solid, and muscular. Beagles should look healthy, alert, and frisky. Bright, shiny, shorthaired coat; drooping, high-set ears; and sloping shoulders. Tail is carried gaily, with a slight curve, but not over the back. Permissible colors: usually a mixture of black, tan, and white, but any hound color is acceptable. Brown or hazel eyes.

Potential Health Problems
Generally Beagles are healthy, active dogs. Possible congenital heart disease, disc problems, bleeding problems, glaucoma, and epilepsy.

Care and Exercise
Remarkably little special care is required. To groom, massage the skin with the fingers, then stroke the dog from head to tail with the palms of the hands. Bathe using a mild shampoo. The Beagle is inclined to roam and so should be exercised on leash or in enclosed areas, such as Beagle club training grounds.

Puppies
Litters average 5 to 7 puppies, although up to 14 puppies have been recorded. Puppies grow rapidly without problems. Do not mate a 13″ bitch with a 15″ male or vice versa. The 2 varieties are distinct and should be maintained. Not all breeders agree, but whelping problems can arise when sizes are mixed.

Comment
During the Middle Ages and the Renaissance, hunting on foot using dogs known as "begles" or "begels" became a popular sport, particularly in England, Wales, and France. Although these early dogs came in all sizes, the name "beagle" became associated with the small hound now recognized as the supreme rabbit-hunting breed. Today hunters usually own a few Beagles and take them out individually to trail rabbits and hares. However, some Beagles are still used in packs.

Over the breed's long history, the Beagle has been so popular that it has been and remains one of the most familiar dogs in the world. No longer considered strictly a hunter, the Beagle makes a first-class household pet.

Recommendation
Since Beagles love to roam and often get lost, a pet should always wear a collar with a license and a visible name tag. A tattoo on the ear can also help prove identity. The Beagle is extremely friendly and, unfortunately, is thus easy to steal. It is best to keep your dog where it can be supervised. Excellent with children, other dogs, and cats, a Beagle will accept as much attention as you offer, then demand more.

Plates 43, 44

Black and Tan Coonhound

Characteristics
Long, soft ears
Muscular hound build
No skull wrinkles
Natural tail
Strong, healthy look

Personality
Fairly quiet and even-tempered, an excellent companion. Essentially a working hound. While trailing a raccoon it is basically silent, but will bark occasionally to indicate game is being trailed. When the animal has been or is about to be treed, the bark changes to a more bawling bark. Seldom noisy when not working, although it has a fine hound voice.

Ideal Appearance
Very close in appearance to Bloodhound, but not as heavily built and with much shorter ears. Males, 25″ to 27″ tall; bitches, about 2″ less. Although the AKC standard does not specify weight, males generally weigh about 85 pounds, bitches approximately 80 pounds. Dog lacks Bloodhound's loose skin, skull wrinkles, and furrows. Skull and muzzle are in roughly parallel planes. Dewclaws on hind legs are considered a serious fault; they are easily removed by a veterinarian, which prevents their being torn in the field. Coat should be shiny and smooth. Permissible colors: black and tan, preferably with no white. Dogs typically have a tan spot the size of a pumpkin seed over each eye. A white spot on chest 1½″ or smaller in diameter is allowed; if larger, dog is disqualified. Hazel to dark brown eyes.
UKC differences:
Dogs may be up to 2″ shorter. They also weigh less: males, 50 to 75 pounds; females, 40 to 65 pounds. Slightly underweight hunting dogs are not penalized.

Potential Health Problems
Generally strong and healthy with great heart and stamina. Hip dysplasia, progressive retinal atrophy, and hemophilia B (factor IX deficiency) occur occasionally.

Care and Exercise
This breed requires no special care, merely grooming 2 or 3 times a week. Ask your veterinarian to show you how to clean the long ears.
If a Black and Tan Coonhound is to be used for hunting, it needs steady exercise of an hour or more daily. For pets, walks on a leash or gallops in an open field are sufficient, but they should all be part of a regular routine.

Puppies
Black and Tans whelp easily. Average litter is 7 or 8 puppies, but up to 13 have been recorded. Usually solid black at birth, but tan markings soon appear on legs and muzzle. Dogs usually reach maximum height at 10 months.

Comment
Descended from the long-extinct Talbot Hound of the 11th century, the Black and Tan Coonhound's ancestors also include the Bloodhound, the American Foxhound, and the English Foxhound. Not only has this breed inherited the Bloodhound's coloring, but the Black and Tan has similarly large bones, long ears, and a famous cold nose. This breed is a superior track animal, used today to hunt raccoon, bear, and wild cats.
The Black and Tan Coonhound was first recognized by the United Kennel Club in 1900 as the American Black and Tan Coonhound, and was admitted to the American Kennel Club in 1945. Many owners cross-register their dogs, with a majority competing in UKC field events rather than in AKC shows because the United Kennel Club places greater emphasis on hound events.

Recommendation
Black and Tans make excellent house or farm dogs as long as they have ample room for their active lifestyle. Because of their large size, care should be taken in adjusting them to small children and vice versa.

Plate 118

Bloodhound

Characteristics
Very large
Loose skin, especially
on head and neck
Long, low-set ears
Powerful build
Otter tail

Personality
Gregarious. Gentle with people, especially children. Generally compatible with other animals, although a stud male can be aggressive and domineering with other male dogs. Can be stubborn, but anxious to please. Demands attention. Extremely clean except for drooling.

Ideal Appearance
A true giant. Males, 25″ to 27″ tall and 90 to 110 pounds, and even up to 140 pounds; bitches, 23″ to 25″ and 80 to 100 pounds or more. Handsome, solid, and powerful physique. Dogs should look massive yet refined. The wrinkles and long, low-set ears give the dog a distinctive, noble, and amusing look. Fine, straight topline and heavy, cylindrical otter tail essential. Permissible colors: Black, tan, reddish brown, or any combination of these colors; small amounts of white allowed on chest. Eye color corresponds to coat, from deep hazel or brown to yellow.

Potential Health Problems
A strong, sturdy breed, Like many large dogs, susceptible to hip dysplasia. Prone to bloat or gastric torsion, which is potentially fatal. Possible eyelid defects. Should be bred only after hips are X-rayed and certified normal at age of 2.

Care and Exercise
Short, dense coat needs occasional stroking with rough cloth. Bathe as needed. For show, whiskers may be trimmed. Pendulous ears should be cleaned weekly to prevent infection. Unusual odor is a signal to see veterinarian. Nails should be kept trimmed; long nails will cause a dog to splay its toes and break down in the pasterns.
A Bloodhound should be walked several miles daily. Long leash should be strong, since this dog pulls—even with obedience training—when it picks up an interesting scent. This breed should spend as much time as possible outdoors, but it must also be with people. With enough outdoor time, dog will housebreak itself. Bloodhounds have no road sense and thus should not be allowed to wander near traffic. A fenced yard or a very large run is ideal.

Puppies
Litters generally range from 6 to 12 puppies. All are born black, or at least very dark; some lighten as they mature. They do not have wrinkles at birth. Bloodhounds mature very slowly: 3 years for males, 2 for females.

Comment
The breed probably originated in ancient Greece or Rome well before the Christian Era. The name was coined in England during the Middle Ages, when there were 2 grades of hound: a coarse version owned by common people, and a refined, scent-trailing hound that belonged to the nobility, or "people of the blood"— hence the name "blooded hound" or "bloodhound."
As a scent hound on the trail, the Bloodhound is considered king. Police agencies use these dogs mostly for "mercy runs": the pursuit of lost children, elderly people, and campers who have gone astray. The Bloodhound is never used for attack, no matter what its quarry. Whether on the trail of criminal or child, the Bloodhound is more likely to lick than bite the person it has been trailing. Bloodhounds are never trailed off-leash. The record for a single run on a trail was 138 miles.

Recommendation
This specialized breed is recommended for experienced dog people—not as a first dog or for people unwilling to devote time to its care and especially to its exercise. It is an unsuitable breed for confined living quarters or the city.

Plate 157

Borzoi

Characteristics
Tall
Streamlined build
Long, silky coat
Long tail
Graceful and
aristocratic

Personality
A gentle but boisterous pet. Loves to coax other dogs into races, to clown in front of people, and to gambol with children. Gets along with other dogs. Somewhat slow to train for obedience, yet once trained is dependable. A large, pleasant dog.

Ideal Appearance
An exotic giant. Males, 28″ to 34″ tall at withers and even higher at top of arched back, 75–105 pounds; bitches, at least 26″, and 15 to 20 pounds less. Sleek lines of a racing dog, streamlined from its muzzle to unusually long tail. Narrow but deep rib cage. Heavily muscled hindquarters, considerably angulated at stifles and hock joints. A strongly arched back usually indicates a sprinter; a flatter back, a distance runner. Long, silky coat; feathering on hindquarters and tail, some on chest. Any color permissible, though most Borzois are white; dark eyes.

Potential Health Problems
Overall, a healthy breed. Extremely sensitive to barbiturates and other drugs, such as those in insecticides, particularly on flea collars. Sometimes prone to bloat and progressive retinal atrophy.

Care and Exercise
No special care is required, although brushing should be a daily routine if the breed's splendor is to be maintained. Self feeders, which allow dog to snack at any time, are recommended and may aid in preventing bloat. Avoid heavy meals. Exercise frequently on leash or, better yet, in open fields at least twice a week.

Puppies
Borzois average 6 to 7 puppies per litter, and occasionally have up to 13. Puppies grow rapidly, but may remain very loose and floppy until near maturity. Do not overwork young puppies, but gradually increase running as puppy approaches 1 year of age. Males should not be used as studs until 2 years old, and bitches should not be mated until the third heat.

Comment
The Borzoi (pronounced Bor-zoy) was developed sometime during the late Middle Ages to course wolves and hare on the great plains of Russia. Known as the Russian Wolfhound until 1936, this breed is believed to be a cross between the long-extinct Steppe Greyhound and the Collie. Its exotic good looks and size soon made this breed the darling of the Russian aristocracy, and it is still photographed throughout the world with high-society ladies in long, flowing gowns.

Like the Greyhound, the Borzoi hunts by sight, and its extreme speed allows it to run down any game. In South Africa, Borzois have been used to course jackals; in the United States and Canada, they have aided hunters in pursuit of coyotes. The sport of lure coursing is becoming popular across North America, and the Borzoi is a prominent competitor.

Recommendation
A dog of extremely high style, the Borzoi is a very expensive breed to buy and one that needs a great deal of exercise. Not a typical first dog nor a breed for a casual dog owner, the Borzoi is for the truly committed. This dog is stubborn and needs an assertive owner to train it. A pet should be monitored around cats and other creatures that move suddenly.

Plate 147

Dachshund

Characteristics
Long body
Short legs
Deep chest
Long, rounded ears
3 coat types
Natural tail

Personality
Fun-loving, often comical, little dog. Good spirits and winning ways have enabled the breed to live down the unflattering nickname "sausage hound." Enjoys play and responds well to obedience training. Loyal friend and companion.

Ideal Appearance
A short-legged, long-bodied dog. Deep chest and compact, muscular body. Long ears set near top of head. 2 sizes: standard size, 10 to 20 pounds and, although AKC standard does not specify height, usually about 9" (for both males and bitches; dogs over 20 pounds are not disqualified); miniature size, under 10 pounds at one year or older and about 5". More coat types and colors than any other breed. Coats can be smooth (shorthaired), longhaired, or wirehaired. Permissible colors: solid red, which covers various shades of tan to yellow; black, chocolate, gray, or white, each with tan markings; or dappled gray or brown with darker patches. Eyes are reddish-brown to brownish-black.

Potential Health Problems
Most are healthy. Prone to crippling invertebral disc disease or diabetes. Possible pattern baldness, adrenal gland problems, urinary stones, and acanthosis nigricans.

Care and Exercise
Grooming should be done on a table. For the smooth variety, an occasional rubdown with a damp cloth is sufficient. The longhaired dog requires daily combing and brushing to remain stylish. To maintain the wirehaired coat in top condition, consult a professional; some trimming and stripping are required. Avoid chills. The Dachshund should have a draft-proof bed at floor level. When coming in out of the rain, mud, or snow, dry the dog's belly and feet. If kept as a pet, a Dachshund requires no particular exercise. To avoid injury to the long back, do not allow your dog to jump off beds and chairs.

Puppies
Most litters average 3 to 4 pups; as many as 12 have been recorded. Puppies normally progress well.

Comment
Developed in Germany several hundred years ago, the Dachshund and the Basset Hound probably had common ancestors. The smaller dogs were called Dachshunds, *hund* meaning "dog" and *dach* for the badger they were originally bred to hunt. Low to the ground, strong, and incredibly courageous for their size, these small dogs could effectively tackle game far larger than themselves. Larger dogs—those that weighed 35 pounds or more—were used to trail deer and foxes, while smaller dogs were employed in the pursuit of stoats and ferrets. In the early 20th century, miniatures were introduced to hunt rabbits.

In North America, where Dachshunds are kept mostly as pets and for show, their deep chests generally reach nearly to the ground. But in Germany, France, Belgium, and other European countries where the breed is still used for hunting, shallower-chested dogs are the norm. In America, however, the shallower-chested dogs now also compete in field trials.

Recommendation
An excellent, happy pet for any home—apartment or house, city or country. The smooth variety is especially easy to care for. Odorless, full of energy, and alert to announce visitors, this variety is one of the most popular dogs. To get the weight and coat style you prefer, consult an established breeder. The Dachshund is so popular, it is often poorly bred by mass producers.

Plates 1, 21, 22, 23

American Foxhound

Characteristics
Back gently arched
Sloping shoulders
Hindquarters
moderately angulated
Short coat
Natural tail
Clean look

Personality
This outstanding scent hound has a keen nose, a sweet disposition, and 2 remarkable talents: an instinct to bark on the fox's trail only when taking the lead or challenging the leader; and an incredible homing sense, which brings the dog back to the place where it started the chase. Good voice.

Ideal Appearance
Males, 22" to 25" tall; bitches, 21" to 24". Although standard does not specify weight, males usually weigh approximately 70 pounds; females, about 65 pounds. Back arched from withers to tail, and shoulders slightly sloping. Moderate angulation of hindquarters. Deep, strongly arched feet. Tail is carried up, but not over back. Typical, hard hound coat. Permissible colors: any hound colors and markings, typically black, tan, and/or white; sometimes white with piebald or hare color. Brown or hazel eyes have a pleading expression.

Potential Health Problems
In the main, healthy and relatively free of genetic problems. A blood disease that is limited to this breed occurs rarely. Possible deafness, hip dysplasia, and vertebral osteochondrosis.

Care and Exercise
Short coat requires only routine groomings such as a rub down with a cloth or hound glove. Must get plenty of hard exercise if dog is to hunt well. This active, outdoor dog should not be allowed to become obese. Some are more dependent on human interaction than others.

Puppies
Litters usually contain 5 to 7 puppies. Whelping problems seldom occur. Dam usually has plenty of milk and is a good mother.

Comment
Robert Brooke, an English colonist, brought the first pack of English Foxhounds with him to Maryland in 1650, and over the next 2 centuries, others arrived from England, Ireland, and France. These hearty dogs eventually evolved into the American Foxhound and a strain still recognized today as the Virginia Hound.

Favored for its speed and endurance, the American Foxhound is a unique hunting dog because, unlike the English Foxhound, it hunts as an individual rather than in packs, and does not bark until it is in the lead. American Foxhounds are believed to have greater stamina and stronger hearts than any other dogs. They are exceptionally athletic and very willing to work.

Recommendation
Some lines of American Foxhounds make excellent home companions. Loyal and protective, this breed takes time to adjust to strangers. In the city, a pet will go stir crazy without frequent, long runs in a field, park, or an open area. Not a typically sedentary pet, this dog simply has to move. Breed only after dog has been proven in the field and is certified free of genetic problems.

Plate 76

English Foxhound

Characteristics
Heavier than
American Foxhound
Level back
Hindquarters quite
angulated
Short coat
Natural tail

Personality
An excellent field dog with a nonquarrelsome, steady disposition. Adjusts well to living in packs; in fact hunts in packs. Moves more slowly than the American Foxhound. Neat and clean.

Ideal Appearance
A well-balanced dog, with heavier bones and body than American Foxhound. Although standard does not specify size, males are usually about 25″ tall and weigh around 70 pounds; bitches, 24″ and 62 pounds. Hindquarters slightly more angulated than those of American Foxhound; level back. Legs very straight. For show, ears are usually rounded off; 1″ to 1½″ may be cut away. Hard, short, dense, glossy coat. Permissible colors: any hound colors and markings, usually black, white, and tan, sometimes combined with yellow. Symmetry of markings is important. Dark eyes.

Potential Health Problems
Like its American cousin, the English Foxhound has no serious genetic faults.

Care and Exercise
Coat requires minimal care—only an occasional hard stroking with a rough cloth. English Foxhounds need frequent, hard exercise. They are usually kept in pack kennels of about 20 to 30 dogs under the supervision of a trained huntsman. Do not allow them to get fat.

Puppies
Litters of 5 to 7 puppies; occasionally more. Whelping usually without problems, and puppies develop normally. Only the finest are used for breeding.

Comment
English Foxhounds were used originally to rid the English countryside of foxes, which had become pests during the late Middle Ages. Landowners soon began to appreciate the fun of the chase, and "riding to hounds" became a sport. Fox hunting gradually became embroidered with colorful ceremony, involving buglers, mounted horsemen, and packs of baying hounds.

Recommendation
Though not a typical pet breed, selected strains of the English Foxhound do well in the home as long as they are properly exercised. This breed is best suited for people who really know and care about dogs. The English Foxhound must be taken seriously as a family member; although it tends to wander, it is generally loyal to its owners.

Plate 75

Greyhound

Characteristics
Streamlined body
Chiseled appearance
Ears folded against
neck when racing
Long tail
Firm, short coat

Personality
Bodily perfection in the racing hound, and a passionate, competitive spirit. In the home, a quiet, clean breed. Usually calm around other dogs, but the safety of neighborhood cats cannot be guaranteed.

Ideal Appearance
A superb combination of bone, muscle, and competitive instinct in a streamlined body. Show males weigh 65 to 70 pounds; bitches, 60 to 65. Racing dogs weigh between 40 and 80 pounds. Although standard does not specify height, both males and bitches usually measure 27″ to 30″ tall. Streamlining begins at tip of nose, continues to ears (which fold against neck when racing), along arched neck, narrow body, powerfully muscled hindquarters, ending in fairly heavy, long tail (which acts as a rudder to steady the speeding dog). Dark eyes are prominent and lustrous. Permissible colors: any colors or markings, usually white, gray, or fawn.

Potential Health Problems
Fairly healthy, although susceptible to hemophilia (factor VIII). Occasional esophageal disorders. Subject to bloat and a serious eye disease. Coursing and racing Greyhounds may suffer from a variety of muscle and limb injuries.

Care and Exercise
Little grooming is required. Nails should be cut regularly, and ears checked for cleanliness. In the home a Greyhound can get lazy and fat. Control diet rigidly and exercise dog on leash as often as possible.
Track and coursing Greyhounds need professional care and training.

Puppies
Large litters of 10 to 15 puppies are not uncommon. Male pups may weigh as much as 1½ pounds; their unusually long tails are easily broken. Part way through whelping, dams may rest before continuing. Occasionally they have trouble expelling puppies and need help. Like all puppies, Greyhounds need to be handled by people at an early age.

Comment
Dogs of the chase that hunted by sight were known in ancient times in Greece, Egypt, Persia, and Rome. The ancients called them gaze hounds and made carvings of Greyhound-like dogs on their tombs. Similar dogs were known as early as the 9th century in the British Isles. Among the fastest dogs in the world, Greyhounds were at first hunters, especially of game; only later were they used for racing.

The origin of the breed name has inspired many guesses. Some say that only men of degree were allowed to own these dogs, whence the name "degree hounds." This was eventually shortened to "gree hounds," or Greyhounds.

Others connect the name with the old English word "grech" for dog, and still others associate it with Greece (*Graicus*). While the true derivation is unknown, it is certain that Greyhounds arrived on this side of the Atlantic in the 1500s, brought over by the Spanish conquistadors.

Recommendation
The Greyhound makes an excellent pet for people who want a fairly large dog, but one that is both streamlined and clean in its habits. Be prepared to give it plenty of exercise. This breed is not for the average or inexperienced owner.

Plate 135

Harrier

Characteristics
Resembles undersized
English Foxhound
Level back
Straight legs knuckle
over slightly
Short coat
Natural tail

Personality
A charming, gentle dog. Basically a hunting dog, but can be a loving pet. Responsive and obedient. Friendly to people, but must be taught to respect other animals, especially cats.

Ideal Appearance
Resembles an undersized English Foxhound or an oversized Beagle. Males, 19″ to 21″ tall; bitches slightly smaller. Although standard does not specify weight, males usually weigh around 50 pounds; bitches, about 45 pounds. AKC standard stresses similarity to Foxhound, but Harrier generally more closely resembles a Beagle. Strong, active, well-balanced dog. Deep chest; level, muscular back without arching; and straight legs that knuckle over slightly. Hard, short, dense, glossy coat. Permissible colors: any hound colors and markings; also a blue, mottled color found only in Harrier. Dark eyes.

Potential Health Problems
One of the most healthy dog breeds. Knuckling over occurs occasionally, when dog has a faulty wrist that doubles forward under the animal's weight. Sometimes suffers from dental malocclusion, usually associated with abnormal development of jaws.

Care and Exercise
Coat requires only minimal care, including routine rubdowns with harsh cloth and massaging to release dead hair. Keep ears clean and nails trimmed. An extremely active outdoor animal, and must be treated as such. Inclined to wander if allowed free, so should be exercised on a leash except while training in hunting areas, where dog can be controlled. Do not allow dog to become lazy and obese. Should be given obedience training.

Puppies
Litters average 7 to 8 puppies. Normal whelping. Puppies benefit from contact with people at an early age.

Comment
In about 400 B.C., the Greek historian Xenophon described hare hunting using hounds resembling the Harrier, but the breed as we know it probably dates from the Middle Ages. English hunting records mention Harrier packs as early as the 13th century. Yet since hounds were common in Europe before then, Harriers may have traveled to the British Isles with the Normans. The name Harrier may in fact come from the Norman word *harier,* meaning hound. Many people believe the Harrier is merely a smaller version of the Foxhound.

By the 17th and 18th centuries, hunting hare on foot using packs of Harriers had become the poor man's alternative, in England, to the mounted fox hunt of the upper classes. In the United States, the Harrier has been used since Colonial days. Today packs of Harriers are occasionally used for hunting in both countries.

Recommendation
This excellent rabbit dog is quite rare in America. Its popularity has been hurt by the fact that it is intermediate in size between the Beagle and the English Foxhound. Yet this lack of popularity has in fact proved a safeguard: Only the best dogs are mated, so buyers are assured of getting good, unusually healthy puppies. You do not have to be a hunter to own this breed, but you must be able to provide ample opportunity for outdoor activity. With proper exercise, the Harrier makes a fine family pet, especially for people living in the country.

Plate 73

Ibizan Hound

Characteristics
Streamlined body
Long, narrow head
Prominent prick ears
2 coat types, smooth
and wirehaired
Natural tail

Personality
Friendly; used to living intimately with families. Gets along with other dogs but does not adjust well to kennel life. Alert and farsighted, as is common in coursing dogs. Ancient breed with a charm all its own.

Ideal Appearance
Streamlined body typical of Greyhound family. Males, 23½" to 27½" tall and about 50 pounds; bitches, 22½" to 26" and 42 to 49 pounds. Long, narrow head has very prominent prick ears set about level with eyes, which are small for sight hounds. Belly is slightly tucked up. 2 coat types, smooth and wirehaired. Permissible colors: red and white, lion and white, solid white, and solid red; solids rare but very desirable. Amber to caramel-colored eyes; pinkish nose.

Potential Health Problems
Healthy overall. Sensitive to insecticides, flea collars, sprays, and dips. May be dangerously sensitive to anesthetics. Severe false pregnancies are common. Dogs used for breeding should be X-rayed for hip dysplasia and checked by a veterinarian for eye problems.

Care and Exercise
To groom, massage skin with your fingers, then rub it down with the palms of your hands. Brush and give a final rubdown with a damp cloth. Check ears and keep nails trimmed. Should have a draft-proof bed. The Ibizan does well on a standard prepared dog food, but the cheaper varieties should be avoided. Frequent long walks on a leash are required as minimum exercise.

Puppies
Excellent mothers, Ibizan bitches whelp easily. Litters range from 6 to 12 puppies, each weighing about 1 pound. Very large litters need supplementary feeding beginning at 3 weeks. All puppies require a balanced diet. Puppies should become accustomed to handling.

Comment
Dogs very similar to the Ibizan Hound are pictured in drawings and carvings found in Egyptian tombs dating back as far as the First Dynasty (3100 to 2700 B.C.). Phoenician or Libyan sailing vessels probably brought the breed to the Balearic Islands off the coast of Spain and to Ibiza, the island that inspired the breed's English name. The islanders culled litters so rigidly—keeping only the purest dogs—that the breed has emerged reasonably free of genetic problems. Extremely resilient and strong, Ibizan Hounds were at first used to course and capture hare. This breed arrived in the United States in 1956 and was recognized by the American Kennel Club in 1979.

Recommendation
The Ibizan Hound is a splendidly graceful, athletic sight hound that easily adapts to family life. A true hound, it needs to learn to respect small animals such as cats. This breed is fairly large, but this is not a heavy dog, and it has a pleasing manner.
Since genetic defects usually appear by the time a dog is 2 years old, do not breed Ibizans at a younger age.

Plate 136

Irish Wolfhound

Characteristics
Huge size
Wiry eyebrows and
beard
Deep chest
Wide hips
Long tail

Personality
This gentle giant possesses an almost placid disposition and is completely trusting. Can be timid—a difficult personality problem to work out—but its great size and strength are all the protection it needs in its contacts with man and beast. Few creatures will challenge this dog.

Ideal Appearance
Largest of the Greyhound family. Males, 32″ to 34″ tall and at least 120 pounds; bitches, a minimum of 30″ and 105 pounds. Body should be longer than tall, arched over loins, with belly drawn up. Narrow but deep rib cage. Muscular thighs, well let-down hocks, and great breadth across hips. Long tail. Rough, hard hair covering body is particularly long and wiry over eyes and under jaw. Permissible colors: gray, brindle, red, black, fawn, or pure white. Dark eyes.

Potential Health Problems
Free of most genetic faults. Hip dysplasia, elbow hygroms (a type of benign tumor), and bloat may cause problems. Particularly sensitive to anesthetics. Possible congenital eye defects, bone tumors. Lifespan of males is only slightly over 5 years; bitches live about 1 year longer.

Care and Exercise
Pets require only routine brushing of coat, but show dogs need stripping of dead hairs. Coat should look natural. Ears should be checked and nails kept short. Bathe as needed. This dog is a huge eater while growing, but adults require proportionately less food than do smaller breeds. Should not be confined to a city apartment.

Puppies
Normal litter contains 3 or 4 puppies, but up to 13 have been recorded. At 6 months, a puppy may weigh 100 pounds; dogs reach full maturity at about 20 to 24 months.

Comment
In 391 A.D. the Roman Consul Quintus Aurelius received a present of 7 Irish Wolfhounds, and all of Rome was amazed at their size. Even in the 16th century, the peaceful disposition of these enormous dogs created comment. Yet they proved powerful and fierce hunters during the late 18th century, when they helped rid Ireland of wolves. Once the wolves were gone, the breed nearly became extinct. In 1862 Captain George Graham, a Scot in the British Army, started a great rescue effort, which resulted in the establishment of the first breed standard in 1885. The AKC standard was passed in 1950.

Recommendation
Only people living on country estates or at least in suburban areas with large fenced yards should own an Irish Wolfhound. These dogs do not make good watchdogs, although their great size will scare any intruder. Because of their enormity, care should be taken in accustoming children to them. This breed has enjoyed the backing of a small group of dedicated—and usually wealthy —fanciers. Expensive to obtain and not very easy to keep, the Irish Wolfhound is not a casual pet for an inexperienced owner.

Plate 146

Norwegian Elkhound

Characteristics
Northern sled-dog
Wedge-shaped head
High-set, erect ears
Flat double coat
Compact, square build
Full, curled tail

Personality
Extremely versatile: Hunts a variety of game, and a great family pet and home guardian. Takes its job seriously. Very loyal and can be exceptionally protective. Piercing bark. Good watchdog.

Ideal Appearance
Northern sled-dog type. Males, 20½" tall and about 55 pounds; bitches, 19½" and about 48 pounds. Wedge-shaped head with skull and muzzle in parallel planes. Lips tightly closed; scissors bite. High-set, erect ears. Compact body forms a square; hindquarters only moderately angulated. Small feet. Tail tightly curled over center of back. Flat double coat. Permissible colors: any shade of gray, with black-tipped outer hairs; other overall colors disqualify. Dark brown eyes.

Potential Health Problems
Usually very healthy dogs. Susceptible to subcutaneous cysts and tumors which do no particular harm. Hot spots may develop in the summertime. Some dogs get progressive retinal atrophy, lens luxation, glaucoma, and congenital kidney disease.

Care and Exercise
Regular combing and brushing are a must, particularly during shedding periods. Hot spots can be controlled with diet supplement of unsaturated fatty acids, available at pet stores. Diet must be carefully monitored or dog will become obese.
Does well in either a kennel or a home. Needs an average amount of exercise; thoroughly enjoys daily walks on leash. Easy to train if started early.

Puppies
Bitches whelp easily. Litters average 7 puppies, and, on rare occasions, may contain up to 14. Newborns are black, but turn gray in about a week as their fur develops. Weaning usually occurs between the 5th and 6th weeks.

Comment
A hardy Nordic breed, the Norwegian Elkhound goes back to the days of the Vikings, some 6000 years ago, when its ancestors guarded village herds against wolves and bears, hunted great elk, and even pulled sleds. Despite its relatively small size, this breed's enormous stamina and keen senses of smell and hearing made it ideally suited to ruthless weather and rugged northern terrain.
When these dogs were brought to the United States in the early 20th century, the name "Elkhound" was mistranslated from the Scandinavian word *hund,* which means "dog," not "hound."
Nevertheless, since the dog is a highly competent hunter, "Elkhound" has stuck. Because the dog does not resemble other breeds in the hound group, there is currently some discussion about regrouping it with other Nordic dogs.

Recommendation
When purchasing Elkhound puppies, avoid those with so many black-tipped outer hairs that the coat appears black rather than gray. As soon as possible, and by 12 weeks certainly, the Elkhound puppy should start obedience training. Elkhounds are classic hardheads and must understand who leads the pack. This breed has a high-pitched, piercing bark; thus too much vocalizing should be discouraged. Its natural protectiveness makes the Elkhound a superb watchdog.

Plate 101

Otter Hound

Characteristics
Coarse outer coat
Woolly undercoat
Large head
Long, hanging ears
Powerful body
Natural tail

Personality
One of the most amiable, but little-known, breeds. Gets along well with other dogs and is remarkably gentle with children and puppies. Very vocal; one of the great pleasures in owning an Otter Hound is to hear its grumbling, either in pleasure or annoyance.

Ideal Appearance
Large dog; roughly as tall as it is long. Males, 24″ to 27″ tall and 75 to 115 pounds; bitches, 22″ to 26″ and 65 to 100 pounds. Only hound with double coat: coarse, crisp outer coat and a soft, woolly, oily undercoat that repels water. Huge head: on a 26″ dog, about 12″ long from tip of nose to back of skull. Deep chest; heavily muscled hindquarters; moderately angulated at stifle and hock joints. Heavy bones in legs and webbed feet. Well-feathered tail carried sickle-style. Despite its size, long pendulous ears and sheepdoglike mop of hair over its eyes give this breed a friendly appearance. Permissible colors: any; combination of blue and white preferred. Dark eyes.

Potential Health Problems
Extremely healthy breed. Nearly free of genetic problems. Few get hip dysplasia. Possible bleeding disorders. Still should be X-rayed for hip dysplasia, and puppies should be given blood tests.

Care and Exercise
Thick double coat requires moderate brushing and combing. No special diet is needed, unless prescribed by a veterinarian.
This hound's love of swimming—it is the most powerful swimmer of all dogs—makes this the ideal exercise. But it should also get plenty of runs as well as extensive rough play. Treated well, Otter Hounds generally live 10 to 12 years.

Puppies
Bitches whelp easily and usually have 7 to 10 puppies; rarely litters of 13. Puppies weigh about 1 pound at birth. Dams are attentive and normally raise a full litter of strong, healthy puppies.

Comment
No one quite agrees about the origin of the Otter Hound—whether its bloodline traces back to the Harrier, the Bloodhound, the Water Spaniel, or the Bulldog; or whether it comes from England or France. The dog probably existed in England by the reign of Edward II (1307–1327), when packs of hounds were used to hunt otters, which were depleting the rivers and streams of fish. French origin is also possible, since the build and double coat of the Otter Hound are almost the same as those of the old French Vendee Hound. During the late 19th century, otter hunting with packs of these hounds was a popular sport. Since otter hunting has long since been banished, the breed is now kept primarily as a companion and for show.

Recommendation
Definitely a country dog, the Otter Hound makes a friendly, energetic, albeit sometimes headstrong, pet. It loves hunting, is an expert swimmer (an ability that is facilitated by its webbed feet and waterproof coat), and is easily trained to be a watchdog. The dog's irrepressible hunting instinct does not discriminate between chipmunks, rabbits, and cats. Although large, this hound is not expensive to raise and keep. Its loud, baying voice and shaggy appearance make the Otter Hound deserving of the title "the Bloodhound in sheep's clothing." A fine pet for an assertive owner.

Plate 110

Pharaoh Hound

Characteristics
Long, narrow head
Large, erect ears
Streamlined body
Short coat
Natural tail
White star on chest
Extremely elegant

Personality
An intelligent and affectionate dog to those it knows, but somewhat aloof with strangers. Playful; likes children and enjoys a fast romp. Graceful.

Ideal Appearance
Resembles small Ibizan Hound. Males, 23″ to 25″ tall; bitches, 21″ to 24″. Although standard does not specify weight, both males and bitches usually weigh 40 to 60 pounds. Flat, triangular head. Muzzle longer than skull, which is lightly chiseled under eyes. Large, erect, high-set ears. Body is Greyhound-like, lithe, and lean, with belly slightly drawn up; back is level. Ribs reach nearly to elbows and are moderately sprung. Strong, arched cat feet. Tail reaches to hocks and, when dog is excited, is carried high with a curve, but not curled over the spine. Short, shiny coat. Permissible colors: rich tan; white on tail tip, toes, star on chest, and sometimes a slender blaze on centerline of skull. Amber eyes; pinkish nose.

Potential Health Problems
Relatively free of genetic problems. Sensitive to anesthetics, flea collars, and certain other drugs. Puppies should nonetheless be X-rayed for hip dysplasia. Possible bleeding disorder and congenital heart disease.

Care and Exercise
Pharaoh Hounds are light eaters; for centuries they have lived on what would for other dogs be a subsistence diet. On modern diets, they tend to grow fat very quickly; thus they must be fed lightly. Requires little grooming other than routine brushing or rubdown with a hound glove. Should get plenty of exercise. Walks on a leash and occasional romps in open fields are essential.

Puppies
Bitches whelp easily. Litters generally range from 3 to 7 puppies, although larger litters have been recorded. Puppies grow rapidly. Watch to be sure they do not damage their long tails.

Comment
The Pharaoh Hound unquestionably originated in ancient Egypt. It has an extraordinary resemblance to dogs pictured by the Egyptians 4000 years ago. Pharaoh Hounds were probably taken to the Islands of Gozo and Malta by Phoenician traders, and eventually a few reached Sicily. For generations, the people of Gozo called them "rabbit dogs," or *kelb-tal-fewek*.

Surprisingly, despite its longevity, this breed has only recently been recognized in the United States. It was not until 1968 that 8 dogs were taken from Gozo to England, where they quickly gained English stud-book recognition under the name Pharaoh Hound. Others were brought to the United States. The American Kennel Club recognized the breed in 1983.

Recommendation
Fun-loving, good-natured, and gentle with children, the Pharaoh Hound is especially suitable for young families living in the suburbs, where the dog can get plenty of exercise. Remember that this breed is still a passionate hunter and loves to chase any four-legged game—from rabbits to neighborhood cats. An apartment is too confining for this active breed.

Plate 67

Rhodesian Ridgeback

Characteristics
Ridge of stiff hair
along spine
Large head
Broad chest
Strong back
Natural tail
Clean, powerful lines

Personality
Highly intelligent, but stubborn. Requires an understanding owner who will be stern. Without training, this breed may become either overly aggressive or silly and shy.

Ideal Appearance
Strong, muscular dog. Male, 25" to 27" tall and 75 pounds; bitches, 24" to 26" and 65 pounds. Unique symmetrical ridge of stiff hair growing along spine is widest at start just behind shoulder blades; ends at hips, and has identical crowns on either side near beginning. Large, wide head with deep, powerful muzzle and high-set, pendulous ears that taper to rounded ends. Level bite. Broad chest with moderately sprung ribs; strong back; muscled, heavy, slightly arched loins. Heavily boned forelegs, with elbows close to the body; well-arched toes with hair between them. Tail carried with slight curve upward, but never curled. Short, hard, glossy coat. Permissible colors: wheaten or red-wheaten. Dark amber eyes.

Potential Health Problems
Generally strong and healthy. Major problem is development of cysts, called dermoid sinuses, which occur near the ridge and require surgery to remove. Many veterinarians recommend that puppies with dermoid cysts be put to sleep. Some subject to hip dysplasia, eyelid abnormalities, and cervical deformity.

Care and Exercise
Except for plenty of exercise, the Rhodesian Ridgeback requires no special care. This breed thrives on American dog foods of the dry or kibbled varieties.

Puppies
Bitches have little problem whelping. Litters of 7 or 8 puppies are common; very rarely, as many as 15 have been reported. Pups thrive on dam's rich milk supply, and mature at about 18 months.

Comment
A native of southern Africa, the Rhodesian Ridgeback traces its lineage back to the Boer period, during which it hunted game on the African veld. This breed was especially suited to withstand rugged bush and dramatic changes in temperature—scorching days and freezing nights. No other breed has the Ridgeback's curious raised tuft of hair. At one time, the origin of this ridge was attributed to the Phu Quoc of Thailand. Today it is believed that a half-wild, prick-eared breed that lived among the Hottentot people had the same bizarre hairs down its back, and interbred with a variety of settlers' dogs in Cape Province, producing the breed stock for today's Ridgeback. In 1876, these dogs were taken to Rhodesia, where settlers adopted them for big game hunting, calling them the African Lion Hound. The Ridgeback was imported to the United States in 1950, and adopted by the American Kennel Club in 1955.

Recommendation
A good house pet for assertive owners who have had some experience with dogs. The Ridgeback's deep voice is sufficient to keep intruders away. This breed seldom quarrels with other dogs, and is easy to keep.

Plate 121

Saluki

Characteristics
Streamlined body
Wedge-shaped head
Hanging, silky ears
Longhairs have
feathering
Smooths lack
feathering

Personality
An aloof, cautious dog. Strongly committed to its family. Seems to depend upon human ties more than most other dogs. Regal, fast, and extremely elegant. Very strong coursing instinct.

Ideal Appearance
Greyhound-like build with streamlined body and perfect, wedge-shaped head. Males, 23″ to 28″ tall; bitches, considerably smaller. Although standard does not specify weight, males and bitches weigh up to 55 or 60 pounds. Body appears emaciated, but extremely fine, bony look is natural and healthy. Skull and muzzle are in nearly same plane. Large, lustrous, dark to hazel eyes; wide-angled vision. Large, silky ears hang close to skull. Chest reaches to elbows. Narrow but deep ribcage; abdomen is moderately tucked up. Hind legs somewhat angulated at stifle and hock joints. Long, narrow toes. 2 coats: longhaired, marked by feathering on legs, ears, and tail; and smoothhaired, with no feathering. Permissible colors: white to red; black and tan, with or without white.

Potential Health Problems
Remarkably free of most common genetic faults; hip dysplasia is almost unknown, and progressive retinal atrophy is rare. Leg bones are sometimes broken when racing at great speeds. Sensitive to many drugs, particularly barbiturates; great care must be taken when anesthetics are given. Because of intense empathy with people, Salukis sold when nearly adult may suffer from psychosomatic illnesses, such as hives.

Care and Exercise
Keep diet consistent and feed only a minimum amount of junk food. In the house, provide a soft bed to prevent leg sores. Coat requires only routine brushing to remove dead hair. Needs a lot of exercise to keep from getting fat.

(In areas where lure coursing is available, Salukis should take part.)

Puppies
Litters of 5 to 7 hardy puppies. To minimize shyness, expose puppies to people at an early age.

Comment
Possibly the oldest existing breed; dogs resembling the Saluki appear on Sumerian carvings made almost 9000 years ago. The ancient Egyptians were so impressed with the regal appearance of these dogs that they often mummified and buried them along with pharaohs and people of noble birth. Centuries later, Arabs treasured the Salukis, considering them sacred dogs sent by Allah. They are just about the only breed that escapes traditional Moslem prejudice against dogs, which is the result of a belief that they are unclean.
Extraordinarily swift, the Saluki once ran down gazelles, antelope, and other quick game. Even today the breed is used to course hare in England, and in the United States, it competes with other breeds in lure coursing using mechanical rabbits.
The Saluki was officially recognized by the American Kennel Club in 1927.

Recommendation
The Saluki definitely belongs in the home, but because it needs plenty of exercise, it is not especially suited to city life. Be prepared to take your Saluki for long walks on a leash, and never allow your dog to run free in areas near roads. Remember that the Saluki is a hunter and the mortal enemy of chickens and cats, unless strictly taught not to chase them. Plan to include your Saluki in as many family activities as possible. This breed is a strong-willed, splendid animal for committed dog people.

Plate 134

Scottish Deerhound

Characteristics
Silky hair on head
Wiry hair on body
Greyhound-like body
Long tail

Personality
Calm and gentle with both children and adults, but may be boisterous as a puppy. Gets along with other dogs and is not a fighter by nature.

Ideal Appearance
A giant in the Greyhound family. Males, 30″ to 32″ tall (sometimes taller) and 85 to 110 pounds; bitches, at least 28″ and 75 to 95 pounds. Long, narrow head with pointed muzzle and small button ears. Silky mustache, beard, and ears. Harsh, wiry coat on body and long, arched neck. Typical Greyhound body: Chest reaches to elbows; stomach is tucked up; and back falls away slightly from hips to long tail. Hindquarters moderately angulated at stifle and hock joints. Permissible colors: a solid color with lighter marking; blue-gray preferred, but darker or lighter grays and brindle acceptable. Ears always blackish; toes, sometimes white; and a white star may be present on brisket. Eyes dark, usually brown or hazel.

Potential Health Problems
Robust overall. Prone to gastric torsion or bloat. Unlike many other large dogs, not susceptible to hip dysplasia. In dogs older than 10 years, heart trouble may cause death. Occasionally gets a broken tail at birth, but this does not affect its health.

Care and Exercise
Natural, wiry coat requires minimal care. Brush out dead hair using a pinbrush. Keep nails clipped short and check teeth routinely for tartar build-up. This huge breed requires plenty of exercise, either on a leash, in open fields away from roads, or in fenced areas of 30 to 100 square feet. If lure coursing using mechanical rabbits is available, dogs should be trained to take part. Do not exercise or give water after a heavy meal, since either may stimulate bloat (stress may also contribute to this ailment). To prevent torsion and bloat, provide a self-feeder, which permits the dog to snack at any time and thus to avoid heavy meals. Pets should be trained to respect, not hunt, smaller animals.

Puppies
Pregnant bitches should be given light exercise during gestation. They usually whelp easily, sometimes bearing 2 pups in quick succession and then relaxing for a short period. Litters average 8 to 9 puppies, each weighing about a pound. Males mature at 3 years; bitches, at about 2½ years.

Comment
The familiar staghound of chivalrous romances, the Scottish Deerhound was the pride of kings and lords. Sir Walter Scott immortalized the breed, calling it "the most perfect creature of the Heaven." Ironically, despite this legendary nobility, the historical origin of the breed remains a puzzle. Some relate it to the Irish Wolfhound, while others consider it a descendant of the now-extinct Picts Hound. When the Irish Wolfhound standard seemed to be slipping, it was bred with the Scottish Deerhound to return it to its present size and form.
Scottish Deerhounds do not do well in kennels, although they are not quarrelsome and live amicably with other dogs. Excellent as house dogs, but not as guard dogs. They want—and deserve—to be in the home.

Recommendation
This dog is extremely loyal and even-tempered; its love of family and children is remarkable. Despite its great size, the Scottish Deerhound will fit into almost any home as long as it gets frequent exercise. Never allow this breed to run free in the city or near country roads; the automobile is its deadly enemy.

Plate 148

Whippet

Characteristics
Streamlined body
Ears folded against
neck when racing
Tail carried under
body
Extreme grace and
speed

Personality
Charming personality and highly
intelligent. Extremely responsive and
affectionate. Makes an outstanding house
or apartment dog. Loves to race, with or
without another dog. Epitome of grace
and elegance; incapable of assuming an
awkward pose. A dog for all people,
although often called the "poor man's
Greyhound."

Ideal Appearance
A half-size Greyhound. Males, 19" to
22" tall; bitches, 18" to 21". Although
standard does not specify weight, males
usually weigh about 28 pounds; bitches,
approximately 20 pounds. Streamlined
from narrow muzzle to tip of tail.
Scissors bite. Prominent ears fold over
and back against neck when racing.
Chest should be deep rather than wide;
stomach, tucked up; hindquarters,
heavily muscled and well angulated at
stifle and hock joints. Tail normally
carried under body. Permissible colors:
any; usually gray, tan, brindle, or white.
Dark eyes.

Potential Health Problems
Much stronger and healthier than
appearance may indicate. Tends to have
weak stomach and may get attacks of
diarrhea. Sensitive to flea collars, other
insecticides, and to anesthetics. Old dogs
may get skin cysts, but most are benign.

Care and Exercise
A Whippet is remarkably clean and
seldom needs more than a rubdown with
a damp cloth. If bathed, pin towels
around dog until dry. Watch diet
carefully to prevent obesity.
Take for long walks on a leash at least
twice a day, and allow to run in the open
whenever possible. Exercise is very
important. Do not exercise off leash
except in large, open areas, and then
only if your dog has been trained to obey
when called. Needs to be taught not to
pursue the neighbor's cat or any other

small animals it may see. Track
Whippets need professional care and
training.

Puppies
Litters average 5 to 8 puppies, but
unusual instances of as many as 11 have
been reported. Puppies grow rapidly.

Comment
Whippets were developed about 150
years ago, apparently by crossing small
Greyhounds with one or more terrier
varieties, and perhaps adding some
Italian Greyhound blood. From the first,
the breed was used to course hare and
rabbits, as well as for competition in rat-
killing contests. Traditionally raced on
200-yard courses, these dogs were said to
be raced "to the rag," because helpers,
called "slippers," held and started the
dogs, while owners urged them to the
finish by yelling and waving white rags
at the end of the course. Today starting
boxes are used, and, at some events,
Whippets do lure coursing in fields.
The Whippet is one of the fastest dogs
for its weight and is capable of speeds of
up to 35 miles an hour. The breed is
sometimes referred to as the "wheel-
backed hound" because, when racing, it
doubles up its body so that the hind legs
pass the front ones.

Recommendation
English Whippets are slightly smaller
than American-bred dogs and, some
think, slightly more graceful and
elegant. Prospective owners desiring a
Whippet for show purposes should search
for one under 20" at the shoulder. A
Whippet minds the cold unless a blanket
is available to curl up in; thus owners
should expect their beds to be unmade.
Affectionate to a fault, the Whippet is
characteristically spoiled rotten, but that
is the fun of owning this breed.

Plate 68

Working Dogs

Exceptional Guard Dogs

The nineteen breeds included in AKC's working-dog group are all hardworking animals. Most are also exceptionally large. Their enormous bulk has made them especially suitable as guard dogs and watchdogs.

Of the thirteen guard dogs in this group, twelve breeds were originally bred to assume this role: Akita, Bernese Mountain Dog, Boxer, Bullmastiff, Doberman Pinscher, Giant Schnauzer, Great Dane, Great Pyrenees, Komondor, Kuvasz, Mastiff, and Rottweiler. Unlike herding dogs, which round up or drive flocks, guard dogs protect the flocks from such predators as wolves, bears, and mountain lions. The ancestors of both the Bernese Mountain Dog and the Rottweiler accompanied the Roman army throughout Europe, since it was the Roman custom to bring cattle with them as a source of food for their troops. The Mastiff dates back to ancient Egypt and China, while for hundreds of years, the Akita stood watch in the imperial palaces of Japan. And in medieval Europe, the Kuvasz served as a prized protector of kings and nobles, at a time when all royalty had to be forever on the alert for assassins. Although one breed, the Standard Schnauzer, was originally developed to hunt weasels, foxes, and other vermin, it eventually also became known as a guard dog. Today many of these breeds work with the police or are watchdogs in homes.

Northern Sled Dogs

Three arctic breeds—the Alaskan Malamute, the Samoyed, and the Siberian Husky (which the UKC calls the Arctic Husky)—probably descended from the same Asian ancestor. These hardy dogs were raised to pull sleds or herd reindeer. Their thick double coats enabled them to withstand subzero temperatures and incredible winds. While the Alaskan Malamute and the Samoyed were developed for great endurance, the Siberian Husky was bred for speed. Today these breeds still play a vital role in arctic expeditions and dog-sledding competitions. More often, they are prized as superb family dogs.

Rescue Dogs

The remaining three breeds in the working-dog group are best known for their rescue work. The Newfoundland and the Portuguese Water Dog work alongside fishermen, hauling nets and, when necessary, plunging into the water to save drowning people or shipwreck victims. The Saint Bernard's heroic exploits in alpine mountains are legendary. Although these three breeds still accomplish their original duties in their homeland areas, they are now usually kept as pets in America.

Energetic Breeds

All of the working dogs need a great deal of exercise to keep them in top condition. Because most are also very large, they require especially spacious homes with large yards for runs or active play. Although some breeds, notably the Saint Bernard and the Great Dane, have become increasingly popular with city dwellers preoccupied with rising crime rates, these giant dogs are really best suited to country life, and it is not fair to confine them to an urban setting. Of course, any breed can adapt, given the exercise and care it needs.

Because of their great size and strong wills—qualities that enhance their ability to perform—the working breeds generally need intensive obedience training. It is important that a working dog have an assertive owner who can establish his or her role as boss from the beginning. Given the training, exercise, and love it needs, a working dog can make a wonderful pet and a responsible family member.

Akita

Characteristics
Resembles sled dog
Thick double coat
Triangular head
Powerful, heavy-
boned build
Full, high-set tail

Personality
Extremely faithful. Marvelous as both a
watchdog and a companion. May be
reserved with strangers. Can adapt to
many different situations. Tends to
be aggressive toward other dogs,
particularly males. Obedience training
is very important to keep this breed in
check.

Ideal Appearance
Powerful build. Males, 26″ to 28″ tall;
bitches, 24″ to 26″. Although standard
does not specify weight, males usually
weigh 85 to 100 pounds; bitches, 75 to
85 pounds. Body is slightly longer than
tall. Heavily boned and muscular.
Broad, triangular head; small, dark
brown, deep-set, triangular eyes; and
erect, triangular ears. Thick, large, full
tail set high and carried over back or
against flank. Thick double coat of short
to medium-length hair; no ruff or
feathering. Permissible colors: various
solids and parti-colors, including white,
brindle, and pinto.

Potential Health Problems
Basically quite hardy. Tendency toward
hip dysplasia. Breeding stock should be
X-rayed at 2 years, and only dogs
certified normal should be used for
breeding. Subject to hypothyroidism and
allergic skin disease, both of which are
easily treatable. Possible congenital eye
defects.

Care and Exercise
Profuse coat with dense undercoat needs
weekly grooming. Unlike many other
double-coated breeds, the Akita is not a
big shedder.
It needs plenty of unconstrained exercise,
especially while growing, and after the
age of 18 months, a regular routine of
roadwork. Keeping the dog in a large,
fenced yard is ideal. With its thick coat,
the Akita does well living outdoors, even
in cold weather. Must be obedience-
trained.

Puppies
From 4 to 10 puppies in a litter. Follow
the immunization schedule set up by
your veterinarian. Puppies need
thorough socialization—handling by
people and exposure to new situations—
at a young age.

Comment
Bred for many hundreds of years in Japan
as the guardian of home and hearth, the
Akita is a superb watchdog and
companion. It is named for its homeland
—Akita, a town on northern Honshu
Island in Japan. These dogs have been
used successfully to hunt deer, bear, and
wild boar, as well as to retrieve
waterfowl. During World War II, Akitas
served as military guard dogs, and many
are still trained as guard dogs today.
After the war, returning American
soldiers brought these dogs home with
them. Since then the breed has been
increasingly popular here in the United
States.

Recommendation
The Akita is a large, impressive, and
strong working dog. Its heritage must be
taken into consideration by a prospective
dog owner. This breed cannot be fed and
forgotten—it must be given a chance to
be a member of the family. It needs
room, love, training, and exercise. More
dog than a first-time dog owner may
want to try, the Akita is for assertive,
dog-oriented people.

Plate 151

Alaskan Malamute

Characteristics
Northern sled dog
Broad head
Wolflike expression
Facial cap or mask
Powerful build
Coarse double coat
Plumed tail

Personality
People-oriented and friendly, a devoted companion. Loves children, and is an eternal puppy. Basically an outdoor dog, the Alaskan Malamute is happiest drawing a sled or a wheeled cart.

Ideal Appearance
A northern sled dog with a substantial, powerful build. Males, 25″ tall and 85 pounds; bitches, 23″ and 75 pounds. Good, strong bones. Compact, deep-chested build; muscular back. Broad head with keen, wolflike expression and erect, wedge-shaped ears. Large, plumed tail carried over back. Proud carriage. Thick double coat: harsh outer coat, 1″ to 2″ long; and woolly undercoat. Permissible colors: various hues, usually light gray to black with white under body and white markings on legs, feet, and face; or all white. Facial markings form either a cap or a mask. Brown eyes; blue eyes are a show fault.

Potential Health Problems
A hardy breed. Possible hip dysplasia. Before breeding, dog should be X-rayed. Subject to anemia and zinc-deficiency-induced skin disease; both are usually manageable. Possible day blindness and dwarfism.

Care and Exercise
Full coat needs to be kept clean, well brushed, and free of parasites. Tends to shed heavily in spring and early summer, when it needs daily brushing to remove excess hair. Keep toenails clipped or filed so that long nails do not break down feet; this routine is best started when dog is a puppy. Wipe ears using baby oil on a cotton swab, and check teeth for tartar regularly.
This breed needs a lot of exercise and intensive obedience training. Permit it to fulfill its sled-dog instincts by allowing it to pull a sled in winter or let it drag a wheeled cart anytime. Keeping dog in a large, fenced yard is ideal. Do not allow it to run loose or to get fat. Dog is happiest in cool weather; does not do well in extreme heat and humidity.

Puppies
Litter of 4 to 10 cute, roly-poly puppies. They benefit from exposure to people, especially children, soon after birth. Good sanitation and proper immunization are important.

Comment
One of the oldest northern sled dogs, the Alaskan Malamute comes from the northwestern region of Alaska. It is related to other arctic dogs, such as the Samoyed and the Siberian Husky of the Soviet Union, and the Eskimo dogs of Greenland and Labrador, but its exact origins are unknown. Russian explorers, upon first traveling to western Alaska, reported seeing dogs pulling huge sledges across the ice. Other adventurers described teams of dogs used by an Innuit tribe called the Malamutes, whence the breed's name. Unlike other sled dogs, which are bred for speed, the Malamute became known for its unbounding endurance, loyalty, and ability to haul heavy loads.

Recommendation
This large breed is suited for the country, not the city. It needs a family that will spend time with it—training, exercising, and loving it. If allowed to become bored, the Alaskan Malamute can be troublesome and make a nuisance of itself by barking and by chewing up its owner's things. This is a highly specialized dog, bred for a particular purpose. It should have plenty of outdoor space. Unless trained early and well, the Alaskan Malamute can be a problem around livestock—or neighborhood cats.

Plate 139

Bernese Mountain Dog

Characteristics
Robust, compact build
Slightly wavy coat
Thick tail
Tri-color

Personality
Steady and loyal. Not inclined to fawn or be overly friendly with strangers. Its reserved nature is a sign of caution, not pettiness. Must be dominated by its owner; otherwise the Bernese will try to be boss.

Ideal Appearance
Males, 24½" to 27½" tall; bitches, 22½" to 25½". Although standard does not specify weight, males usually weigh 80 to 105 pounds; bitches, 75 to 90 pounds. Rather compact build with level back, deep chest, and good bones. Strong muzzle with defined step. V-shaped, hanging ears come forward slightly and are raised at base when dog is alert. Natural tail, fairly thick and well covered with hair, is not carried over back. Slightly wavy, moderately long coat. Color is very important. Permissible colors: jet-black, with deep tan or rust markings on all 4 legs, a spot just above forelegs, a spot on each side of white chest markings, and spots over eyes. White tail tip, white feet, white blaze, and white star markings on chest. Dark hazel to brown eyes.

Potential Health Problems
Generally quite healthy. Prone to hip dysplasia and bloat. All breeding stock should be X-rayed and certified normal. Possible eyelid abnormalities, which can be repaired by surgery; and serious metabolic bone disease.

Care and Exercise
Thick coat should be brushed regularly. Bathe as necessary. Wipe ears clean with a little baby oil on a cotton swab. Keep toenails filed, and be sure teeth are free of tartar.
This breed needs a great deal of exercise, as befits its working-dog heritage. Because of its thick coat and sturdy build, it can be kept in unheated quarters. Although it does best in the country, the Bernese Mountain Dog may be kept in a city as long as its needs for strenuous exercise are met.

Puppies
From 4 to 10 puppies in a litter. Dams have a good maternal instinct. Puppies need to become used to people and handling.

Comment
The Bernese Mountain Dog can trace its lineage to the dogs of ancient Rome. Invading Roman soldiers brought their guard dogs with them to Switzerland over 2000 years ago, and from these canines the Swiss developed 4 breeds of large working dogs. While the other Swiss mountain dogs were used for herding, the Bernese Mountain Dog was bred by the basket weavers of Berne, Switzerland, for the sole purpose of drawing their carts to market. In Europe, the breed is still a superb draft animal. It has been popular in the United States as a farm dog, protector, and family friend.

Recommendation
A large, handsome animal, the Bernese Mountain Dog makes a marvelous pet for a family with a large home and space for outdoor exercise. To be sure of getting a dog with a good temperament, choose a puppy that appears bold and robust. Be sure to give it obedience training early.

Plate 144

Boxer

Personality
A fun-loving, energetic dog whose
energy seems to have no bounds—ready
for anything. Alert. Good watchdog.
Very intelligent. Male may challenge
other males, and can become a
neighborhood bully. Requires careful
obedience training. Should never be
permitted to wander free.

Ideal Appearance
Medium-size breed. Males, 22½" to 25"
tall; bitches, 21" to 23½". Although
standard does not specify weight, males
usually weigh about 70 pounds; bitches,
about 60 pounds. Head shows Mastiff
heritage in undershot jaw and fairly well-
broken, upward-tipped muzzle. Dark,
alert-looking eyes. Ears cropped and
erect, or folded just above top of skull
with tips falling forward toward corners
of eyes. Deep chest, and level topline.
Well-bent rear legs. Docked tail carried
high. Permissible colors: brindle or
fawn, generally with white markings and
a darker face or mask.

Potential Health Problems
Rather healthy. Early death at about 10
years sometimes caused by faulty heart.
Skin tumors, digestive complaints,
hypothyroidism, and cornea ulcers are
common but treatable problems. Some
dogs subject to hip dysplasia, colitis, and
bleeding.

Care and Exercise
Smooth, shiny coat is easily cared for.
Nails should be kept clipped. Feed a
balanced diet and do not allow pet to
become fat.
This very eager, bouncy breed needs to
express its exuberance and get plenty of
exercise. A large, well-fenced yard is
ideal, and walks on a leash are beneficial.

Puppies
Litter of from 5 to 10 puppies. Dams are
generally attentive. An occasional boxer
puppy will be born all white or mostly
white with a few brindle or fawn
markings. These cannot be shown,
because these colors are disqualifications.
If ears are to be cropped, this should be
done at 8 to 12 weeks, after good
immunization program against
distemper, hepatitis, and parvovirus.
Healing, setting, and taping of ears
must be carefully supervised to ensure
correct ear set and carriage; follow
veterinarian's recommendations to the
letter.

Comment
The Boxer gets its name from the way it
positions its front legs in play—just as a
human boxer does when sparring in the
ring. This fighting pose is hardly
coincidental, for the Boxer descends from
a long line of Bulldog types that were
common in medieval Europe. It is
related to the English Bulldog and the
Great Dane, as well as the Mastiff of
Tibet, whose history goes back thousands
of years.
Like the Bulldog, the Boxer was
originally bred to participate in the
blood sports of dogfights and
bullbaiting. The ferocious temperament
has been removed, and the Boxer is
today an excellent, even-tempered family
dog. Highly intelligent, it has also been
used as a guide dog for the blind, and
some Boxers have been trained for police
work.

Recommendation
This breed has many admirers. It does
well in homes in both rural areas and
urban settings. Although the Boxer's
short coat is easily cared for, it cannot
withstand inclement weather for long
periods. A Boxer is not content to sit in
the sun and snooze; this is a breed for
active people.

Plate 138

Bullmastiff

Characteristics
Large, wrinkled head
Broad, deep chest
Compact build
Strong limbs
Natural tail
Imposing appearance

Personality
Awesome. Excellent watchdog. Fearless; will not back down from a fight with either beast or man. Must be obedience-trained early and well. Most are very mild-mannered; when cranky or tricky, a Bullmastiff is an intolerable menace, given its size.

Ideal Appearance
Large, powerful dog—totally imposing animal. Males, 25″ to 27″ tall and 110 to 130 pounds; bitches, 24″ to 26″ and 100 to 120 pounds. Undershot jaw; wrinkled muzzle is one third of skull. Hanging ears. Strong limbs and broad, deep chest. Natural tail. Smooth, short coat. Permissible colors: red, brindle, or fawn, with black face or mask; very small white spot on chest. Dark eyes.

Potential Health Problems
Usually healthy. Subject to hip dysplasia and bloat. Hips should be X-rayed, and only dogs that are over 2 years of age and free of hip dysplasia should be used for breeding. Possible hypothyroidism, a manageable condition; occasional eyelid abnormalities, which can be corrected with surgery; and some bone ailments.

Care and Exercise
Short, smooth coat can be kept clean and bright quite easily; requires only routine brushing or rubdowns with a cloth. Trim toenails on a regular basis. Nutrition is very important for the Bullmastiff, as for all large dogs.
Dogs need daily walks at least, but do much better with a lot of exercise. Large, well-fenced yard with a lot of running space is ideal. Obedience training is mandatory.

Puppies
Normally about 5 to 8 puppies in a litter. Early socialization is important: Puppies need to get used to people and handling. This big breed needs to learn its lessons well from the beginning to be a proper part of the family.

Comment
Bred to help the gamekeeper keep poachers from private English estates, the Bullmastiff combines the power and courage of the Mastiff with the speed and ferociousness of the Bulldog. It is deliberately big and imposing.

Recommendation
This breed requires time, and common sense in its rearing and training, as well as a lot of good food and exercise. It is not a breed for everyone. However, those with the time and know-how to raise a Bullmastiff correctly will have a staunch friend and protector. The Bullmastiff is so impressive that some people are overwhelmed with a desire to own one. It should be remembered that this is not a large dog, but a huge one. It is not a dog to buy on a whim. The Bullmastiff is a major commitment.

Plate 153

Doberman Pinscher

Characteristics
Long, wedge-shaped head
Erect and cropped ears or folded ears
Smooth coat
Square build
Docked tail

Personality
Energetic, watchful, and determined. Alert and fearless—a good watchdog or guard dog. Can be very aggressive. Loyal and obedient, but obedience training is absolutely essential. Breed has mellowed over last 3 or 4 decades as a result of careful breeding.

Ideal Appearance
Males, 26" to 28" tall, ideally 27½"; bitches, 24" to 26", ideally 25½" Although standard does not specify weight, males usually weigh 70 to 75 pounds; bitches, 60 to 65 pounds. Long head resembles blunt wedge. Ears cropped and erect, or natural, folded just above top of skull with tips falling forward toward corners of eyes. Dark eyes. Clean-cut, sinewy, and muscular body. Short, docked tail. Short, fine, close-lying coat gives the impression of smoothness and class. Permissible colors: gleaming black, deep red, blue, or fawn; all colors with sharply defined rust markings above each eye, on muzzle, throat, forechest, legs, and feet, and below tail.

Potential Health Problems
Generally a healthy breed. Some dogs are subject to hip dysplasia, bleeding disease, and congenital eye defects. May also be susceptible to bloat, skin diseases, and hypothyroidism, all of which are manageable. Possible bone and liver diseases. Have puppy checked by veterinarian before purchase, and do not select puppy with bluish coat, as this may indicate a skin condition.

Care and Exercise
Short coat requires little care, usually just a brisk rubdown with a rough cloth. Bathe as needed. Whiskers are normally cut for show purposes. Nails usually keep themselves worn down, but sometimes may require further filing. Help keep teeth clean by feeding dog a hard biscuit daily; if doing this is not sufficient, teeth may need scraping by a veterinarian.

This athletic breed must be exercised regularly and carefully to maintain its look, condition, and agility. Roadwork —following a car, bicycle, or jogger—is essential, as is free play such as chasing a ball, although only in a safe fenced area. Dobermans become tense when deprived of sufficient exercise. Should be obedience-trained well and early. Best kept on leash unless it has had advanced obedience work.

Puppies
Litters normally from 3 to 8 puppies. Ears may be cropped at 8 to 12 weeks, after immunizations against distemper, hepatitis, and parvovirus. Follow your veterinarian's instructions carefully to aid the ears' healing process; freshly cropped ears must be taped so that they stand correctly. Puppies must become accustomed to people and different situations at an early age.

Comment
A German breed, the Doberman Pinscher traces its heritage to some of the old, basic German dogs such as the Rottweiler and the German Pinscher, as well as to the Black and Tan Terrier of England. It is named after Louis Dobermann of Apolda in Thueringen, Germany, who developed the breed in the 1890s, primarily as a guard dog and a watchdog. The Doberman blossomed into a superb police and army dog, and is still used as a guard dog throughout the world.

Recommendation
This breed is recommended only for an experienced dog person or family. It needs good and proper exercise, and makes a superior dog if raised well and trained carefully. It should never be trained to attack.

Plate 137

Giant Schnauzer

Characteristics
Huge
Angular profile
Wiry outer coat
Eyebrows, mustache, and beard
Short, docked tail

Personality
Usually a friendly, gregarious giant. Good with the entire family, including children, although this may depend on early social training. Agile and active. Good watchdog with keen awareness of its surroundings. Generally will want to check out all strangers. Will challenge other dogs.

Ideal Appearance
A true giant. Males, 25½" to 27½" tall; bitches, 23½" to 25½"; medium sizes preferred. Although standard does not specify weight, males usually weigh 75 to 95 pounds; bitches, slightly less. Square build. Powerful, rugged, and robust. Short, docked tail. Sharp, cropped ears, or neatly folded natural ones. Dense double coat: wiry, bristly outer coat, and short undercoat. Arched eyebrows, good mustache and beard, and thicker furnishings on legs and under body. Permissible colors: black or pepper-and-salt. Dark brown eyes.

Potential Health Problems
Generally quite healthy. Subject to hip dysplasia. Breeding stock should be X-rayed. Skin should be kept from drying out. Possible demodectic mange or epilepsy.

Care and Exercise
Coat needs good, vigorous brushing; beard and legs should be combed daily. Remove long, dead hairs from body by plucking. Legs, eyebrows, and beard must be shaped using scissors. Keep toenails short.
This breed needs good brisk exercise, including long walks on a leash and occasional free romps when it is safe. For such a big dog, correct nutrition, obedience training, and plenty of exercise are very important.

Puppies
From 5 to 8 puppies in a litter. Dams are attentive. Ears may be cropped at 8 to 12 weeks, after innoculations against distemper, hepatitis, and parvovirus. Have veterinarian show you how to tape ears so they heal correctly—this is a very important task in raising this breed and takes some extra time and interest on the part of the owner.

Comment
The Giant Schnauzer is the largest of the three Schnauzer breeds, the others being the Standard and the Miniature. Despite a strong resemblance to each other, the 3 breeds are distinctly different animals. The Giant Schnauzer is a German dog, originally bred to drive cattle. Because of its keen intelligence, it was later trained for police work.

Recommendation
This lovable giant is a marvelous dog for a country family with time and interest in a large working dog. Its coat needs attention, and it must have proper obedience training. The Giant Schnauzer does not do well on its own, and it deserves the care and attention it needs. It is not a dog for a casual owner.

Plate 114

Great Dane

Characteristics
Tall
Large head
Erect, cropped ears or
natural, folded ears
Broad, deep chest
Muscular build
Natural tail

Personality
Friendly, spirited, and gentle for its size.
Dependable. Interacts well with people;
very good with children. Male may be
domineering with other male dogs. This
good watchdog can be very intimidating.
Requires obedience training.

Ideal Appearance
Large, impressive, and elegant. Males,
no less than 30″ tall, preferably over 32″;
bitches, no less than 28″, preferably 30″
or more. Although standard does not
specify weight, males usually weigh 135
to 150 pounds; bitches, 120 to 135
pounds. Males appear masculine, and
bitches, for all their size, feminine. Tall,
muscular, and coordinated; square build.
Long, narrow, finely chiseled head with
pronounced stop. Eaglelike look in dark,
expressive eyes. Long, cropped, erect
ears, or natural folded ears that droop
forward. Natural tail, never docked.
Permissible colors: brindle or fawn, with
dark face or mask; also blue, black, or
harlequin (ground of pure white, with
black patches over entire body).

Potential Health Problems
Not a long-lived breed; dogs survive 8 to
10 years or less. Nonetheless, most are
healthy. Some are prone to hip dysplasia,
so dogs should be X-rayed and certified
normal before breeding. Tends to get
bloat and hypothyroidism, which are
manageable. Some dogs are subject to
bleeding and bone diseases, demodectic
mange, urinary stones, epilepsy, or
wobbler's disease. Possibility of inherited
eyelid defects, which can be corrected.

Care and Exercise
Short coat needs minimal care. Bathe as
necessary. Whiskers are normally
trimmed for show. With proper exercise,
nails are worn down by themselves; if
necessary, shorten further with file.
Correct nutrition is very important with
the giant breeds: Provide a palatable,
well-balanced diet. To prevent bloat,
feed 3 small meals a day rather than 1
large meal. In addition, restrict exercise
and water consumption immediately
before and for 1 hour after feeding. Food
dish should be raised up off the floor so
that the Dane does not have to go down
on its knees to eat. This is more
comfortable for the dog and encourages
correct posture.
This large breed needs unconstrained
exercise, especially as a puppy. A large,
well-fenced yard is essential to protect
young dogs from road accidents or dog-
napping. After 12 months, give
moderate roadwork—at a speed of 10
m.p.h.—using a bicycle or a car. Or
provide long walks on a leash several
times a day. Should have obedience
training.

Puppies
Average litter is from 5 to 12 puppies. If
ears are to be cropped, this should be
done by a veterinarian at 8 to 12 weeks,
after immunizations.

Comment
Although known as the Great Dane, this
breed is not Danish, but of German
origin. It descended from an old game
dog at least 400 years ago. This giant
was originally bred as a wild-boar
hunter. It is extremely popular in many
countries in the world, as it is truly
handsome, and it is known as the Apollo
of the dogs. It is not exclusively a pet,
but is also used as a watchdog.

Recommendation
Not for everyone, the Great Dane
requires a family of dedicated people. Its
needs for space, nutrition, and obedience
training must be met. To own a Dane is
to accept a large responsibility. It does
far better in the country than in the city,
although in recent years, Great Danes
have appealed to loft-dwellers who want
to discourage robbers.

Plates 149, 150

Great Pyrenees

Characteristics
Long head
Deep body
Thick double coat
Large feet
Long tail

Personality
Rather quiet, ponderous, and introspective. Inclined to be a one-family dog. Wary of strangers; makes friends slowly. Should be watched when people it does not know enter its turf. Good watchdog. Will challenge other dogs.

Ideal Appearance
Very imposing. Males, 27" to 32" tall and 100 to 125 pounds; bitches, 25" to 29" and 90 to 115 pounds. Heavy bones and deep body. Large, wedge-shaped head with lovely, knowing, dark brown eyes and drop ears. Large, tight feet with double dewclaws on lower part of rear legs. Long, natural tail. Thick double coat. Permissible colors: all white with some gray, tan, or badger markings.

Potential Health Problems
Very healthy. Subject to hip dysplasia; only dogs that are X-rayed and found normal at 2 years of age should be used for breeding. Watch for hot spot skin conditions, which are easily treatable. Possible eyelid defects and epilepsy.

Care and Exercise
Thick double coat must be kept clean, well-brushed, and free of fleas and ticks. Tends to shed, particularly in spring and early summer. Breed thrives on exercise —especially accompanying its master on hikes, and pulling a cart or a small sled. It requires a great deal of exercise and a large amount of space.

Puppies
A litter of 6 to 10 puppies. Dams are fair to good. Rear dewclaws or extra claws are a necessity in this breed, so should never be removed. Temperament must be a major concern; puppies must become used to people and different situations early and well to prevent shyness or sharpness.

Comment
The Great Pyrenees is one of the oldest natural breeds. Fossil remains of this type of dog that have been found in Europe date to the Bronze Age (1800 to 1000 B.C.), and even earlier ancestors are believed to have originated in the Middle East. The Babylonians depicted similar dogs in their art in around 3000 B.C. The dog as we know it today was developed in the Pyrenees Mountains of France for rugged mountain work: guarding flocks against wolves and bears, and drawing sleds. Its weather-resistant coat allowed it to withstand the intense cold of the mountains. In Europe it is still used with livestock, but in the United States, it is a pet, and not a very common breed.

Recommendation
This beautiful, hardy dog needs human companionship and attention. It is not for the apartment dweller or the haphazard dog owner. Future owners should be forewarned: This dog sheds a lot, since its coat was intended for outdoor living. The Great Pyrenees makes a marvelous addition to the family if its master is willing to spend the necessary time for its care and exercise.

Plate 160

Komondor

Characteristics
Long, corded coat
Muscular build
Long tail
White

Personality
Loyal and courageous. Wary of strangers. Must have a purpose in life; likes to work. Excellent watchdog. Extremely powerful and headstrong. Requires careful obedience training.

Ideal Appearance
Very large. Males, 25½" tall or more; bitches, 23½" or taller. Although standard does not specify weight, males usually weigh about 95 pounds; bitches, about 80 pounds. Robust and muscular. Unusual, white double coat covering body resembles long, white ribbons of felted or matted material, and consists of coarse outercoat and soft, woolly undercoat that intertwine to form tassel-like cords. It is parted in the middle and hangs down over head, body, and limbs. Dark eyes.

Potential Health Problems
Healthy overall. Prone to hip dysplasia. Dogs used for breeding should be X-rayed and certified to be normal at 2 years.

Care and Exercise
Unusual coat requires very special care. Ask a professional groomer to explain grooming technique, or trim the coat very short, which is not typical for the breed. A very large dog, the Komondor requires excellent nutrition and plenty of exercise, which should consist of both free running and long, controlled walks. Can live outdoors comfortably in a doghouse. Obedience training is essential to discourage assertive tendencies.

Puppies
From 3 to 10 puppies in a litter. Puppies are white and fluffy; the tendency to form cords becomes apparent by 3 to 4 months. They should become accustomed to people at an early age.

Comment
This very old breed was used primarily to protect flocks on the mountainsides of Hungary over a thousand years ago. Prior to that, it traces back to the long-legged dogs of the Russian steppes. Not a shepherd, but instead a working guard dog, the Komondor was responsible for driving wolves, foxes, and bears from the pasture, as well as prowlers from its master's estate.

Its great size, robustness, and thick coat enable it to withstand all kinds of harsh and inclement weather. Seen at work in the open mountains, the Komondor's long cords usually appear unkempt and matted. But in the show ring, the coat is carefully groomed into handsome, long, corded tassels. Pet owners can find a happy medium between the two extremes.

Recommendation
Because its coat requires much attention, the Komondor is not a good breed for a first dog. It should appeal to those who desire an unusual appearance and a grooming challenge. The Komondor is clearly a country dog that should not be taken lightly or casually.

Plate 145

Kuvasz

Characteristics
Long head
Almond-shaped eyes
Muscular build
White double coat
Long tail

Personality
Very active and robust. Loyal and protective. An exceptional watchdog, but requires intensive obedience training, and then life-long management. Likes to test people to see who is really in charge.

Ideal Appearance
Very large, white dog with no markings. Males, 28″ to 30″ tall and 100 to 115 pounds; bitches, 26″ to 28″ and 70 to 90 pounds. Long head with dark, almond-shaped eyes and drop ears that hang slightly forward. Sturdy, muscular build with well-developed hindquarters. Natural, long tail. Double coat is longer on neck, backs of legs, and tail; may be wavy or only slightly wavy. Short coat is usual in warm areas.

Potential Health Problems
Generally healthy. Subject to eyelid defects and hip dysplasia. Should be X-rayed at 2 years of age, and only normal dogs should be bred.

Care and Exercise
Coat must be kept brushed, clean, and free of parasites. Dog normally sheds a lot in hot weather. A large, fenced area is ideal for exercise, plus long walks or hikes as part of the daily routine. Needs obedience training. Because this breed is very large, nutrition is of great importance.

Puppies
Litter of about 8 puppies. Puppies should become used to people at an early age and be encouraged to be playful and responsive.

Comment
This handsome animal comes from Tibet, where it was bred as a guard dog for royalty. Dogs of this breed were kept as guardians of the home, both in rural areas and towns. By the Middle Ages, the Kuvasz was well known in the kingdoms of Europe, but it was in Hungary during the 15th century that the modern form developed at the court of King Mathias I. Huge dogs were used to guard the royal chambers, and packs of dogs were also trained to hunt. Gradually the breed became popular with the common people, who used it as a sheepdog and a cattle herder. Today the Kuvasz is still highly regarded as a working breed, primarily as a watchdog.

Recommendation
Space is important for this very large and active breed. It must have constant supervision to assure obedience, and a regular routine to channel its energy. In the right home, the Kuvasz can be a useful and intelligent member of the household. It is essential, however, that the owner be more assertive than the dog.

Plate 159

Mastiff

Characteristics
Huge head
Deep, broad build
Straight back
Stately appearance
Natural tail

Personality
Ponderous in its ways: slow-moving and a homebody. But can be quite active when aroused. Good watchdog. Beware of timid puppies, as they may bite out of fear when they grow up. Usually makes a fine pet.

Ideal Appearance
Massive. Males, 30″ or more; bitches, 27½″ or taller. Although standard does not specify weight, males usually weigh 180 pounds; bitches, 170 pounds. Deep, broad body with well-knit frame, strong limbs, and huge head. Deep foreface, shorter than back skull. Uncropped ears lie close to skull. Kindly, alert, dark brown eyes. Scissors bite preferred, but slightly undershot bite also permitted. Natural tail. Short, smooth double coat: coarse outer coat and dense undercoat. Permissible colors: brindle, fawn, or apricot, with dark face or mask.

Potential Health Problems
Healthy as a rule. Subject to hip dysplasia; breeding dogs must be X-rayed at 2 years old and certified normal. Possibility of hypothyroidism, a manageable condition, and eyelid defects, which can be corrected.

Care and Exercise
Short coat requires only routine care. Requires large quantities of correct food. Needs plenty of good exercise to keep from getting stiff. Regular roadwork, jogging, and games are recommended. Does best if given obedience training early in life.

Puppies
Very few puppies in litter. Adjusting puppies to people and different situations is of great importance in their development.

Comment
Giant dogs called Mastiffs have been known in Europe and Asia for thousands of years, but their exact origins are unclear. Dogs resembling the Mastiff are pictured on ancient Egyptian tombs, and are described in Chinese literature dating to about 1121 B.C. And when the Romans invaded Britain in 55 B.C., Mastiff-like dogs are said to have helped their British masters ward off the enemy. By the early 19th-century, the English Mastiff was a fighting dog that was well known in the pit, but eventually this sport was outlawed. Today the breed is prized as a guard dog, just as it was thousands of years ago.

Recommendation
Like so many of the giants, the Mastiff is not long-lived. An old and dignified breed, it deserves a good life and proper care. This dog is not for everyone; because of its size, it needs an exceptionally large home—ideally on an estate or farm—and lots of exercise, as well as human companionship.

Plate 154

Newfoundland

Characteristics
Massive head
Deep chest
Broad back
Heavy double coat
Long, bushy tail

Personality
Gentle with people; very kind to children of all ages. Despite its size, a sweet and intelligent giant. Males may try to dominate each other, particularly those that have been used as studs. Bitches are very anxious to please. Although a clean breed, tends to pant fairly constantly, and drooling accompanies the panting.

Ideal Appearance
Males, about 28″ tall and 130 to 150 pounds; bitches, about 26″ and 100 to 120 pounds. Massive head with foreface slightly shorter than back skull. Heavy bones. Deep chest with good ribs. Long, bushy tail. Broad back with level topline and muscular hindquarters. Heavy double coat. Permissible colors: all black, but perhaps with a touch of white on chest and/or chin, toes, and tail tips; black and white (called Landseer); or bronze (deep reddish-brown) and blue. Dark brown eyes.

Potential Health Problems
Short-lived but generally healthy. Prone to hip dysplasia, so all breeding stock should be X-rayed and found normal. Possible allergic skin disease or arthritis. Subject to congenital heart defects, eyelid defects, and epilepsy.

Care and Exercise
Coat needs regular brushing, preferably twice a week. Swimming, which is second nature to this breed, will keep coat clean, but should be confined to fresh water for the most part, because salt water is irritating to the skin. Keep ears clean, and check them after swimming. Odor or discharge is a sign of trouble and a reason for consulting a veterinarian. A flea collar is not recommended for this or any swimming breed, since such collars should not get wet.
Nutrition is also very important: Provide a well-balanced diet, and feed at least 2,

if not 3, small meals a day rather than 1 huge meal. Do not supplement the basic food too much.
A large, fenced-in yard is a must. The Newfoundland must have free (not forced) exercise as it grows. But starting at 12 to 18 months, take dog on long walks and begin a routine of serious roadwork, consisting of following a bicycle or a car at 10 m.p.h. Dog should have access to safe swimming on a regular basis.

Puppies
Litters of about 8 to 10 puppies. Immunize well with innoculations for distemper, hepatitis, and parvovirus, according to your veterinarian's recommendations. Puppies need to learn to adjust to people from an early age.

Comment
As its name implies, this breed originated in Newfoundland, Canada. It has long been valued for its ability to work in water: It can take lines out through heavy seas to shipwrecked vessels, save drowning people, or help haul heavy nets. Newfoundlands have also been used to pull carts and as pack animals for hunting. Most of the refined breeding of the Newfoundland was accomplished in England, after the breed was discovered in Canada.

Recommendation
The Newfoundland is a large dog for dog-oriented people who have the space to raise one properly and the time to train it. This breed needs room, understanding, and a chance to perform some of the tasks for which it was bred. It is better suited to cold climates than hot ones.

Plate 158

Portuguese Water Dog

Characteristics
Curly or wavy coat
Trimmed coat
Pompon at tip of
undocked tail

Personality
Intelligent and calm. A lovable clown. Alert and ready for anything. Very active and serious about exercise, particularly in the water.

Ideal Appearance
Males, 20″ to 23″ tall and 42 to 60 pounds; bitches, 17″ to 21″ and 35 to 50 pounds. Strong, nicely proportioned build. Wide head with tapering muzzle and well-defined stop. Medium-length natural tail arched over back when dog is at attention. Covered with thick, curly, or slightly wavy coat. Coat is groomed either into a lion clip (with shaved face and hindquarters) or into a working-retriever clip with hair shortened over body and slightly longer on legs and top of head; in both clips, tail is shaved, leaving a pompon on end. Permissible colors: solid black, brown, or grayish-white; or marked with varying degrees of white. Black or brown eyes.

Potential Health Problems
Healthy overall. Subject to hip dysplasia, so breeding stock should be X-rayed at 2 years of age and certified normal. Health history not well known yet in this country.

Care and Exercise
Coat must be kept brushed and groomed. Ears should be checked weekly, especially after swimming, when water is apt to remain in ears, possibly causing irritation and infection. Check teeth for tartar, and keep toenails filed. A fenced-in yard and access to safe, swimmable water are both ideal. This breed is active enough to take its own exercise, either playing or swimming, but dog loves to go on long walks with its owner.

Puppies
Litter of 4 to 8 puppies. Dams have strong maternal instincts. Follow your veterinarian's advice on a good immunization program.

Comment
At home in the sea as well as on water, the Portuguese Water Dog has strongly webbed feet, which serve it well in swimming. This breed comes from the Algarve province of Portugal, where, for centuries, fishermen trained these unusual dogs to haul nets and even to dive for escaping fish and catch them in their mouths. The breed is relatively new to the United States, and only gained AKC breed recognition in the working dogs group in 1983.

Recommendation
A marvelous dog for all family members, the Portuguese Water Dog will swim, retrieve, act the clown, and generally please everyone. It is a nonshedder and makes a good choice for people who are allergic to longhaired animals.

Plate 88

Rottweiler

Characteristics
Broad head
Hanging ears
Broad chest
Muscular body
Short, docked tail

Personality
Quite strong. Highly protective of its home and owners' property. Willing and very trainable. A good guard dog or watchdog. Must become accustomed to people and have obedience training at an early age if it is to adjust properly in a home. Males may be aggressive toward other males.

Ideal Appearance
Strong build. Males, 24″ to 27″ tall; bitches, 22″ to 25″. Although standard does not specify weight, males usually weigh 115 pounds; bitches, about 100 pounds. Slightly longer than tall. Broad, well-proportioned head with moderate length of muzzle and inquiring, dark brown eyes. Ears are folded at skull line. Thick body with deep chest and muscular legs. Short, docked tail. Short, flat, coarse coat; softer undercoat on neck and thighs. Permissible colors: black with tan markings on cheeks, muzzle, chest, and legs, and over both eyes.

Potential Health Problems
Basically quite healthy and hardy, although some dogs subject to bloat and hip dysplasia. Breeding dogs should be X-rayed at 2 years of age and certified normal. Possible eye problems and progressive spinal cord disorder.

Care and Exercise
Short coat needs relatively little care: A good rubdown with first a wet and then a dry towel will remove most surface dirt; bathe as needed. Keep nails short with a rasp or file. Feeding plays a very important part in correct development. Small meals 2 times daily, rather than 1 large meal, will help prevent bloat. This robust breed needs plenty of free exercise, especially as a puppy. After 12 or 18 months old, give it workouts on the road, allowing dog to follow your bicycle or car at about 10 m.p.h. In between workouts, a large, well-fenced yard is a necessity.

Puppies
From 4 to 10 puppies in a litter. Puppies need to become accustomed to people and handling, and to learn house manners early.

Comment
The ancestor of the Rottweiler was a Roman dog that was used to drive cattle over the Alps while the Roman army pushed into central Europe. (Because the army could not be sure of food provisions in the new lands, they brought this ready supply of beef with them.) When the Romans moved onward, some of their dogs remained behind in the vicinity of Rottweil in Württemberg, Germany. These were the foundation stock for the modern breed.
In recent times, the Rottweiler has been known for its outstanding police work. Strong, active, and alert, it is a natural watchdog.

Recommendation
This breed is for people who have had prior experience with large dogs. With the proper socialization and comprehensive training, it can be an outstanding family dog in a country setting. It is very possessive of its home and property.

Plate 152

Saint Bernard

Characteristics
Huge head
Short muzzle
Long or short coat
Broad back
Majestic and powerful
Natural tail

Personality
If correctly bred and raised, this is a gentle giant. Good disposition. Fine watchdog, but should never be encouraged to do more than bark. Obedience training is essential for control and management. Beware of mass-produced stock, which make poor pets.

Ideal Appearance
Very large. Males, 27½" tall; bitches, 25½" or more. Although standard does not specify weight, males usually weigh 165 pounds; bitches, 145 pounds. Immense bones. Massive skull with short muzzle and drop ears thrown forward. Deep chest and very broad back. Muscular legs. Long, broad, natural tail. 2 coat types: longhaired, with thick, heavy coat, ruff around neck and shoulders, and long hair on tail and backs of legs. Shorthaired or smooth coat is thick, rather short, and smooth over entire body. Permissible colors: red with white, or white with red; white markings, brindle patches, and dark muzzle and edges of ears. Dark brown eyes.

Potential Health Problems
Quite healthy. Subject to hip dysplasia, so all breeding stock should be X-rayed at 2 years of age. Possible hot-spot skin condition and bloat are treatable. Some dogs prone to arthritis, congenital heart defects, eyelid defects, and rage syndrome.

Care and Exercise
Both types of coats must be kept clean, brushed, and free of parasites. Clean ears regularly with baby oil, and clip or file toenails. This giant sheds a lot, especially in spring. It needs a large enclosed yard for exercise, as well as daily walks.

Puppies
About 6 to 8 puppies in a litter. To prevent shyness or aggressiveness, puppies should become accustomed to people and different situations at an early age.

Comment
To many people, the name Saint Bernard evokes images of romantic rescues from snowy slopes by a large dog with a brandy-filled barrel about its neck. In fact, the Saint Bernard lives up to legend: It has worked for centuries as a rescue dog in the Alps. During the 16th century, monks at a monastery near the Saint Bernard Pass in Switzerland used these dogs to patrol the area and warn of avalanches, and probably eventually to rescue the lost as well. The breed name, coined in the 19th century, refers to the Swiss pass, but the dog probably developed from earlier stock brought to Switzerland by the invading Roman army.

Recommendation
This large and powerful dog needs to be with people throughout its life. It can be messy, with its drooling and shedding, but it is a marvelous companion in the correct surroundings. Apartments should not be considered; this is truly a country dog. It needs reasonable exercise.

Plates 155, 156

Samoyed

Personality
Enjoys people. Smiles and chortles its way through life. Gentle, not aggressive, but a good watchdog. Lovely personality matches splendid appearance. Has style and a pronounced sense of humor. Good with children.

Ideal Appearance
Compact, agile, and alert northern sled dog type. Males, 21″ to 23½″ tall; bitches, 19″ to 21″. Although standard does not specify weight, males usually weigh 55 to 75 pounds; bitches, 40 to 55 pounds. Wedge-shaped head with triangular, erect ears and dark, almond-shaped eyes. Alert face should have sparkling expression with typical Samoyed smile: a true turning up of mouth in a grin. Muscular, deep-chested body with a straight neck and moderately long legs. Moderately long, bushy tail carried forward over back. Double coat: harsh, long outer coat; dense undercoat. Ruff around neck. Permissible colors: pure white, cream, or biscuit, or white-and-biscuit with a silver sheen.

Potential Health Problems
Usually quite healthy. Possible hip dysplasia; breeding dogs should be X-rayed. Subject to treatable skin diseases and some serious eye problems. Before purchasing a dog, have it examined by an ophthalmologist. Possible dwarfism.

Care and Exercise
Dog's coat must be groomed weekly, thoroughly brushed, and kept clean and free of parasites. Sheds heavily in spring and early summer. Keep toenails short. Clean teeth and ears when necessary. Must have vigorous exercise on a daily basis. A large, well-fenced yard is ideal, but free time in the yard should not replace long walks and hikes. Obedience training is strongly recommended.

Puppies
Litter of 5 to 9 puppies that look like little white teddy bears. They show their heritage early and are sturdy, adaptable, gentle, and kindly. Like all puppies, they should become accustomed to people at an early age.

Comment
A true northern breed, the Samoyed probably originated in Mongolia. These dogs roamed northern Asia for centuries as the companions of the nomadic Samoyed tribe. For generations they were used to herd reindeer, pull sleds, and as companions on the lonely trail. Today the Samoyed is still used as a sled dog in the Arctic.

Recommendation
The Samoyed is a beautiful breed to look at and live with. Breed thrives on human companionship, but must also have space and proper exercise. It is too much dog for the uncommitted or first-time owner. Keeping its white coat clean and brushed is a big responsibility.

Plate 104

Siberian Husky

Characteristics
Northern sled dog
Lithe build
Wedge-shaped head
Erect, triangular ears
Soft double coat
Longer than tall
Full, natural tail

Personality
Very natural, gentle, and friendly. Extremely trustworthy. Does well in a family, especially with children. A willing and hard worker. Its somewhat independent nature may keep it from becoming a good watchdog, and it can tend to wander.

Ideal Appearance
Medium-size northern sled-dog type. Males, 21″ to 23½″ tall and 45 to 60 pounds; bitches, 20″ to 22″ and 35 to 50 pounds. Body slightly longer than tall. Somewhat almond-shaped eyes, set at a slight slant, create a friendly and mischievous look. Wedge-shaped head widest at eyes. Erect, triangular ears, well-developed stop, and tapering muzzle. Deep chest, strong back, and well-muscled hindquarters. Bushy, foxlike tail carried arched over back. Furry, medium-length double coat: soft, dense undercoat and straight, smoothly-lying outer coat. Permissible colors: all hues from black to pure white, with many striking markings on head. Eyes may be brown or blue, or dog may have 1 of each color.
UKC differences:
Males, 21″ to 22″ tall and 40 to 60 pounds; bitches, 19½″ to 22″ and slightly lighter.

Potential Health Problems
Usually healthy. Tendency toward hip dysplasia; breeding stock should be X-rayed at 2 years of age. Subject to treatable skin problems. Possible laryngeal disease. May have serious eye problems, so before purchase, have your puppy examined by an ophthalmologist.

Care and Exercise
Soft, furry coat needs grooming weekly and must be kept free of dirt and parasites. Sheds heavily in spring, so requires more brushing and raking at that time, particularly if kept inside. Quite clean by nature, this breed is generally free of the doggy odor of many dense-coated breeds. Check teeth, ears, and toenails once a month.
The Siberian Husky was bred as a working dog and, even if kept as a pet, must get plenty of exercise to stay in top condition. If inactive and kept in a pen, a dog can become shy or even neurotic. Obedience training recommended.

Puppies
Normal litter of 6 to 8 puppies, resembling cuddly bears. Adjusting puppies to people and different situations is important for their development.

Comment
The Siberian Husky was developed by seminomadic people of northeastern Asia to be a sled dog capable of traveling great distances at moderate speed and of carrying light loads at low temperatures. Some authorities believe that the breed dates back to the time when a land bridge connected Siberia and Alaska. Russian explorers undoubtedly made many journeys charting the coastline of Siberia using packs of these dogs, hence the breed name.
Lighter in weight than many northern sled dogs, the Siberian Husky is consequently much faster. It often competes in Alaskan sled-dog races. The American Kennel Club recognized the breed in 1930, while the United Kennel Club began registering this breed under the name Arctic Husky in 1932.

Recommendation
This breed makes an excellent family dog. It is most happy in the country, but with attention to good exercise, adapts well to city life. It enjoys pulling sleds or wheeled vehicles, playing outdoors, and just being a companion.

Plate 108

Standard Schnauzer

Characteristics
Angular profile
Square build
Eyebrows, mustache,
and whiskers
Cropped or folded,
natural ears
Docked tail

Personality
Alert, active, vigorous, and inquiring.
Full of energy. Easy to train, and very
reliable. Males may be aggressive toward
other males. Headstrong, but has a good
sense of humor. Very loyal. Needs to
participate in family affairs. Not a breed
to own and ignore.

Ideal Appearance
Males, 18½" to 19½" tall; bitches,
17½" to 18½". Although standard does
not specify weight, males usually weigh
40 to 50 pounds; bitches, 30 to 40
pounds. Square build with angular
profile. Rectangular head with cropped,
erect ears or natural, folded ears. Bristly,
arched eyebrows, mustache, and
whiskers. Strong, well-boned, and
robust. Short, docked, erect tail. Dense,
harsh, wiry outer coat; soft undercoat.
Permissible colors: pepper-and-salt or
pure black. Dark brown eyes.

Potential Health Problems
Excellent health. Prone to hip dysplasia;
breeding stock should have normal hips.

Care and Exercise
Broken, harsh coat needs brisk brushing
with the lay of the hair. Legs,
underbody, eyebrows, and whiskers need
daily combing to be kept free of tangles.
Pluck out long dead hairs on body and
head using fingers or special stripping
comb. Eyebrows and beard may need
careful shaping with scissors to retain the
correct Schnauzer look; a professional
groomer can show you how. Breed
should not be clipped all over, because
hard outer coat is its protection, and
clipping may lead to skin problems. May
be washed with mild soap when
necessary; rinse well.
This breed loves walks and occasional
good runs off the leash—but make sure
this is in a safe place, since dog will dash
headlong after a ball, a cat, or another
animal, oblivious of traffic. Obedience
training recommended.

Puppies
Litters of 4 to 9 puppies. Dams are very
attentive and protective. If ears are to be
cropped, this is generally done at 8 to 12
weeks, after vaccinations. Taping and
healing of the ears must be learned by
the owner, as this is an important part of
cropping; follow your veterinarian's
instructions.

Comment
The Standard Schnauzer is a very old
breed that originated in Germany. It is
considered the original breed size (the
other 2 are the Miniature and the Giant,
which are now recognized as 2 distinct
breeds). The Schnauzer was originally
bred to hunt rats, weasels, and other
vermin, but proved itself a truly versatile
breed, serving as a guard dog, a water
retriever, and a house pet. It is an alert
and attentive companion.

Recommendation
This breed is recommended for active
people. However, its coat requires
grooming attention. The Standard
Schnauzer is not a dog to be left to its
own devices. It needs training and
thrives on attention.

Plate 91

Terriers

British Origins
These courageous, energetic dogs were originally bred to help control vermin and hunt small game. Distinguished by bravery far beyond their size, terriers were expected to face formidable opponents above and below ground—ranging from foxes to otters, weasels, and rats. The word "terrier" comes from the Latin *terra,* or earth, and designates how and where these dogs pursued their game. Even today terriers are diggers, and many dogs will "go to ground" without training or urging.

Almost all terriers have deep roots in Great Britain. Although this group is not as old as some others, sources dating to the 14th and 16th centuries specifically mention "earthe dogges" of various types, and these dogs probably existed even earlier. Terriers were originally the dogs of gamekeepers and ratcatchers. People of the lower social classes were more likely to keep terriers than were privileged aristocrats. The differences among the various breeds arose in response to local conditions and the type of game hunted.

Today the American Kennel Club recognizes twenty-four terrier breeds; one of these—the American Staffordshire Terrier—is also recognized by the United Kennel Club as the American Pit Bull Terrier.

A Varied Family
Early writings divide the terrier family into two groups: a long-legged, smooth-haired, English type, and a short-legged, rough-haired variety from Scotland. In time, breeds and varieties became more sharply defined, leading eventually to the terriers we now know.

The two main branches of the family are still the long-legged terriers—tall dogs with rectangular heads, button ears, and erectly carried, docked tails—and the short-legged terriers—which are low-slung dogs with a better-than-average sense of smell and incredible tenacity. Both of these types were originally developed as hunters. The Airedale and the Wire Fox Terrier are typical of the former group, while the Cairn Terrier is an example of a short-legged breed. The Bull Terrier, the American Staffordshire Terrier, and the Staffordshire Bull Terrier belong to a third group, which was originally bred more for fighting than for chasing vermin. Other terriers, such as the Bedlington, Manchester, and Border terriers, do not fall neatly into a category, although all were used either for sport or as ratters on farms.

Grooming Requirements
Except for the few smooth-haired breeds, terriers require a fair amount of trimming to appear presentable. Some call for considerable artistry, particularly for the show ring. Stripping and plucking involve pulling out and shaping the hair to enhance the color and texture of the new coat, and for a few breeds—such as the Bedlington, Kerry Blue, and Soft-Coated Wheaten terriers—skillful scissoring is necessary to put them in top form. Pet terriers are usually trimmed with clippers, which is easier and more economical for the owner, but the finished result is not as elegant.

Active Companions
Terriers are more closely related than members of other AKC groups and, as a result, generally have similar temperaments. Fun-loving and independent, they are ideal companions. Terriers characteristically throw themselves with vigor into everything they do and are always ready for adventure at a moment's notice. Their well-known love of life makes them perfectly suited to the rough play of older children, long hikes, or any vigorous activity that brings dog and owner together.

Airedale Terrier

Characteristics
Tallest terrier
Angular profile
Wiry double coat
Blanketed pattern
Button ears
Small, dark eyes
Erect, docked tail

Personality

An excellent family dog. Protective yet sensible. Particularly good with children: gentle with toddlers and rugged enough for older youngsters. Eager to please. Adaptable to both obedience-training and hunting. Keeping a male with other male dogs is not always wise.

Ideal Appearance

Classic, long-legged, rugged look; the tallest terrier. Males, about 23″ tall; bitches, slightly shorter. Although standard does not specify weight, both males and bitches usually weigh 45 to 60 pounds. Angular profile and muscular build. Button ears; small, dark eyes. Moderately long, erect, docked tail. Covered with harsh double coat that is sometimes straight and sometimes wavy. Permissible colors: tan, with black or dark grizzle saddle extending from upper side of neck down back and sides and up front of tail, fading as it blends into legs. Sometimes red mixed in with black, or small white spot may be present on chest.

Potential Health Problems

Usually hardy. May get hip dysplasia. Possible skin allergies because of harsh coat.

Care and Exercise

Wiry coat needs to be trimmed at regular intervals for both pets and show dogs. For show, additional plucking and stripping are required. Although pets may be trimmed with clippers, this adversely affects coat color and texture. Dogs should be brushed and combed at least 3 times a week. With regular grooming, bathing will be needed only about once a month. Keep nails short, and clean teeth and ears at regular intervals.

Airedales need vigorous workouts. Dogs should be exercised on a leash, in a fenced yard, or in safe areas far from traffic. A passing cat or wandering canine intruder could divert even the best-trained Airedale and spell trouble. Obedience training advisable.

Puppies

Litter size ranges from 5 to 12 puppies. Newborns are almost solid black; pups become two-toned as they grow. Most breeders paste ears to skull several times before onset of maturity to ensure that they will be positioned correctly on the adult dog. Maturity is indicated by eruption of permanent teeth. Growing puppies need firm, gentle handling.

Comment

There is a great deal to admire about the king of terriers. The largest of the terrier group was developed in Yorkshire during the 19th century in order to help Otter Hounds clear the local waterways of otters and other animals that were then considered vermin. The Airedale boasts a wide repertoire of talents: It has been successfully used in many countries around the world as a bird and big-game hunter, and as a war and police dog. It combines the courage, agility, and spirited personality that are typical of the terriers with the swimming and tracking abilities of its Otter Hound ancestors. The Airedale came to the attention of dog lovers at large by way of the show ring. Today this giant terrier is universally loved as a family dog.

Recommendation

The Airedale makes a wonderful companion. For both physical and mental development, it needs and loves human contact. However, this breed should be trained early to know its place in the family framework. It adapts well to training and, because of its size and strength, must be kept under firm control. Many Airedales live happily in confined urban spaces, but the breed benefits from a lot of physical activity.

Plate 95

American Staffordshire Terrier

Characteristics
Powerful build
Broad head
Deep stop
Usually cropped ears
Smooth, sleek coat
Undocked tail

Personality
Completely at home in a family. Very responsive to its owners. A breed with extremely well-developed protective instincts. Responds well to obedience training. Will fight other dogs unless properly supervised. Never allow this breed to roam free.

Ideal Appearance
Active, muscular build. Males 18″ to 19″ tall; bitches, 17″ to 18″. Although AKC standard does not specify weight, males usually weigh about 50 pounds; bitches, approximately 45 pounds. Broad, powerful, wedge-shaped head with deep stop. Round, widely spaced, dark eyes set low on skull. Ears either cropped or short and uncropped; held in prick or half-rose position. Muscular neck, deep chest, and strong, short back. Big-boned legs. Undocked, fairly short tail tapers to fine point. Smooth, glossy coat. Permissible colors: any color but white; however coats that are liver, black and tan, or over 80 percent white are not desirable.
UKC Differences:
Weight is not important. Males, preferably 35 to 90 pounds; bitches, 30 to 50 pounds. Any color of markings permitted.

Potential Health Problems
Generally robust. Juvenile cataracts have been reported. Hip dysplasia and mast cell tumors possible.

Care and Exercise
Smooth coat requires little maintenance, only minor trimming for show. Regular brushing with a bristle brush and a rubdown with a chamois will keep coat healthy and shiny. Baths need be given only about once a month if the dog is brushed routinely.
Be sure breed gets vigorous exercise. Long walks on a leash and trotting alongside a bicycle are good and will help tone the body. When not on a leash, an AmStaff should be confined to a secure, fenced yard: The exercise area should be strong enough to keep the terrier in and wandering animals out.

Puppies
Litters usually contain 5 to 10 puppies, which develop early. It may be necessary at times to separate some or all of a litter if puppy bickering gets too serious. AmStaff puppies need firm handling in order to develop properly. If cropped ears are desired, this should be done by a veterinarian at about 12 weeks.

Comment
No doubt about it: The American Staffordshire Terrier was developed and bred to fight! The breed stems from the same roots as the Staffordshire Bull Terrier and the Bull Terrier, and, like them, possesses phenomenal courage and amazing strength for its size. This breed was recognized first by the United Kennel Club in 1898 under the name American Pit Bull Terrier (plate 62), and then by the American Kennel Club in 1936 under the name Staffordshire Terrier. In 1972 the AKC name was changed to American Staffordshire Terrier, also known as AmStaff, to distinguish it from the lighter-weight Staffordshire Bull Terrier of England. Today this breed is still claimed by both of the American dog clubs.

Recommendation
The American Staffordshire Terrier is not an ideal choice for a first dog, but can be a satisfying pet for experienced dog lovers. Ownership involves a substantial commitment to supervision, as well as a rigorous schedule for exercise. These dogs must be trained in obedience and exercised on a leash or in a secure area.

Plate 60

Australian Terrier

Characteristics
Small
Harsh double coat
Longer than tall
Topknot on head
Ruff around neck
Erect ears
Docked tail

Personality
Alert and active. Very responsive to people, and wants to please. A natural watchdog with tremendous courage. Quick to notice unusual happenings or strangers. Adaptable to training, and very good with children. Sensible and not hyperactive.

Ideal Appearance
One of the smallest working terriers. Males and bitches, about 10″ tall and 12 to 14 pounds. Overall look of balance and sturdiness, despite small size. Erect, high-set ears enhance breed's energetic appearance. Eyes dark and small, but never prominent. Body slightly longer than it is high. Level topline. Docked tail. Harsh double coat forming topknot on head and ruff about throat. Permissible colors: blue-black or silver-black, with tan markings; or solid red or sandy color.

Potential Health Problems
No special problems reported. Watch for possible hot-spot skin condition if fleas go unchecked.

Care and Exercise
Very easy to maintain coat without professional attention. Ears should be plucked to remove all long hair, and feet plucked or stripped for neatness. Brush and comb at least twice a week to keep coat tidy; pluck the longest hairs to maintain it in good shape for extended periods. With regular brushing, frequent bathing is unnecessary. Check ears, nails, and teeth routinely.
Exercise in a fenced yard or on a leash. Even on spacious, secluded property, this lightning-fast dog can dart away and become lost or be killed in traffic.

Puppies
Litters usually contain 3 to 4 puppies. Although newborns are usually almost completely black, they may be any hue, and they change to adult color as they mature. Ears become erect in 6 to 8 weeks, but may rise and fall several times until adult teeth fully appear.

Comment
The Australian Terrier was developed down under during the 19th century by Australian pioneers who needed a small terrier for specialized working conditions typical of a tropical, generally rather uncivilized environment. They blended the traits of the Cairn, Dandie Dinmont, Irish, Scottish, probably Yorkshire, and perhaps several other terriers to create this breed. The result was a small dog that was equal to the demanding climate and rugged hunting conditions prevalent in Australia at the time. Adept at hunting all vermin, including snakes, Australian Terriers were also much prized as watchdogs for property and livestock in those rough-and-ready times.
The Aussie made its initial appearance in England in 1906, but did not catch on immediately; in fact it was not until 1933 that the breed was recognized by the Kennel Club in England. After a most vigorous campaign by the Australian Terrier's Supporters, the American Kennel Club recognized the breed in 1960. Today the Australian Terrier offers the dog lover all of the most desirable features of a small terrier.

Recommendation
The Australian Terrier is a fine breed for anyone who likes terriers but does not want to devote a lot of time to grooming and exercise. Although the Aussie is typically active, it is easy to live with. It thrives in any environment—urban, suburban, or rural—and gets along well with other pets and children.

Plate 31

Bedlington Terrier

Characteristics
Lamblike appearance
Hanging ears
Arched back
Curved, smoothly
trimmed tail
Linty, mixed coat

Personality
Courageous, loyal family companion.
Tends to be jealous of other animals in
the household. Ordinarily not as hard-
charging as some other terriers, but once
aroused is a fierce fighter. Very clean
house dog with nonshedding coat.
Generally adaptable to training, but can
be stubborn. Likes to run.

Ideal Appearance
Distinctive, lamblike appearance,
achieved in part by skillful trimming.
Males 16″ to 17½″ tall, ideally 16½″,
and from 17 to 23 pounds; bitches, 15″
to 16½″, ideally 15½″, with
proportionate weight. Build combines
aspects of terrier and Whippet-like
frames. Head trimmed to a Roman-nosed
profile. Low-set, hanging ears clipped
clean, with tassel at tip. Topline of back
curves in graceful arch, and tail is
continuation of spine. Long legs. Curly,
linty double coat consisting of both hard
and soft hairs. Permissible colors: blue,
liver, or sandy, often combined with tan.
Light hazel to dark eyes.

Potential Health Problems
Generally healthy and hardy. May be
affected by hereditary liver disorder
known as copper toxicosis. Some have
tear duct abnormalities. Recessive retinal
dysplasia, renal disease, and distichiasis
have also been reported.

Care and Exercise
To maintain lamblike appearance,
expert, regular trimming with clippers
and scissors is required. Groom
regularly, using slicker and comb. Bathe
as needed, paying usual attention to ears,
teeth, and nails.
Because of its speed, the Bedlington
Terrier should never be exercised off
leash unless in a secure enclosure. The
dog's hound background asserts itself in
its swiftness and need to run, so give it
the chance to do so under safe
conditions. A scampering cat or a stray

dog might tempt an alert Bedlington,
causing it to give chase and get lost.

Puppies
Litters usually number from 3 to 6
puppies. Coats of black newborns turn
blue as puppies mature; dark brown
coats change to liver. Coat lightens and
usually assumes mature color by dog's
first birthday. Because of trimming
requirements, it is best to accustom
Bedlington puppies to grooming
routines when they are very young.

Comment
The Bedlington was developed in the
district of Northumberland in northern
England during the early 19th century.
Miners and other workers in the district
wanted a terrier that would take game
such as ferrets and foxes with great speed
and courage. Because it had these
qualities, this breed was much
appreciated by poachers; ironically it also
prospered in the hands of the very gentry
it was used to poach from!
Although its ancestry remains somewhat
ambiguous, the Bedlington Terrier is
closely related to the Dandie Dinmont
Terrier. It combines the terrier's good
hearing and eyesight with the legs of a
small coursing hound, possibly—but not
positively—the Whippet.
The breed has always had its band of
faithful supporters. Considering the
breed's origins as a workingman's
sporting animal, the Bedlington's
current status as a top-notch show dog is
a bit ironic.

Recommendation
The Bedlington combines the best
characteristics of a small hound and a
terrier. It is the ideal companion for the
dog lover who appreciates this mix and
the Bedlington's singular appearance.
Grooming is a must, but the breed is
adaptable to any environment.

Plate 89

Border Terrier

Characteristics
Distinctive, otterlike head
Drop ears
Thick, loose-fitting hide
Wiry double coat
Undocked tail

Personality
A strong-willed, determined character, but one that can relate to all family members and that responds well to obedience training. Proverbially courageous, but not as argumentative as some other terriers. Gets along well with children and family pets.

Ideal Appearance
A "no-frills" working breed; some people say it looks like a mongrel. Males, 13 to 15½ pounds; bitches, 11½ to 14 pounds. Although standard does not specify height, males usually measure about 13″ tall; bitches, approximately 12″. Body slightly taller than it is long. Very distinctive head, similar to an otter's. Small, V-shaped drop ears. Thick, loose-fitting hide. Harsh, wiry double coat. Undocked, relatively short tail. Permissible colors: red, grizzle and tan, blue and tan, or wheaten. Dark hazel eyes.

Potential Health Problems
Healthy and strong overall. Watch for skin conditions during tick and flea season, and in dry environments such as an overheated house or apartment. Congenital heart conditions possible.

Care and Exercise
A good coat needs very little trimming in order to appear neat. Head, feet, neck, and tip of tail should be tidied, and long hairs on the body need to be plucked. Otherwise the coat needs only regular brushing and maintenance.
Even though this is a small breed, the Border Terrier needs sufficient exercise in order to keep fit and happy. Long walks on a leash are best, whether the dog's home is in the city or the country. Excursions can be interspersed with yard time, but take care that time spent in the yard or paddock is not passed in total boredom. The Border has an active, working heritage and likes to have something to do.

Puppies
Litters usually number between 3 and 6 puppies. Newborns can be any color. No unusual developments during growth.

Comment
The Border Terrier traces back to a large group of terriers that existed for centuries in the Cheviot Hills, which separate Scotland from England—hence its name. This terrier was much valued by farmers of the region for its remarkable ability to destroy foxes and other vermin that posed serious threats to crops and livestock. The Border Terrier's combination of courage and good sense has always been an asset.
Today the Border Terrier is a great dog to have in a home. The breed has never become faddish or stylish and retains the same unspoiled character it exhibited hundreds of years ago. Interestingly, breeders of Jack Russell Terriers— strictly a working type that is not recognized by the American Kennel Club —often cross their dogs with Border Terriers to enhance the hunting ability of their own breed.

Recommendation
Anyone who likes terriers should enjoy a Border Terrier. Its pleasant personality, ease of care, and impish appearance make it very appealing. This dog is very willing to hunt. Its rarity is an added attraction; if you own a Border Terrier, you have a splendid canine companion without looking like everyone else in the neighborhood. This is a dog lover's dog.

Plate 41

Bull Terrier

Characteristics
Egg-shaped head
Erect ears
Eyes close together
Smooth coat
Big-boned legs
Powerful build
Natural tail

Personality
A delightful pet and a real people-lover. Companion to every member of the household, and accepting of visitors. May not tolerate other pets and may fight, often with disastrous results. Amenable to training, and very clean in its habits. Must be supervised when off leash: A Bull Terrier on its own will not back down from challenge and can be a lethal opponent.

Ideal Appearance
Muscular build with big-boned legs that are rather short. Although standard does not specify size, males are usually about 22″ tall and 50 to 60 pounds; bitches, approximately 21″ and about 50 pounds. Small, neat, erect ears on distinctive, egg-shaped head. Small dark eyes set close together high upon head, with intelligent, determined expression. Smooth, close-lying coat. Moderately short, undocked tail carried just above level of back. Permissible colors: all white, or white with red or brindle markings on head only; colored variety brindle or red, often with white blaze and white on chest, legs, feet, or tail tip. Black nose.

Potential Health Problems
An extremely robust breed. In the white variety, there is a tendency toward congenital deafness, so a puppy should be checked.

Care and Exercise
Smooth, dense coat needs little trimming. Bathe only when needed (a white variety will need more bathing than a colored one, particularly in a city). Use a rubber- or natural-bristle brush or hound glove. Keep nails short, and ears and teeth clean. Two grooming sessions a week should keep any Bull Terrier presentable.
Exercise should always be scrupulously supervised in order to prevent fights with other dogs. The owner who lacks a securely fenced yard should take the dog on at least 1 long walk every day—and 2 or 3 would better suit the dog's needs.

Puppies
Litters of 4 to 8 puppies. Ears stand up at 3 to 4 months, but may fall and rise again before permanent teeth are in place. The noses of newborns are usually pink, but darken with time.

Comment
Bull Terriers were developed in England just before the middle of the 19th century for only one purpose—dog fighting. The Bull Terrier was created by crossing the now-extinct White English Terrier with the Bulldog of that time. The result was a resolutely courageous animal that would stand up to anything; it was unfortunately used to satisfy a sadistic side of Victorian society. Blood sports were eventually abolished by an act of Parliament, and fanciers of the breed discovered its other virtues.
The white variety came into being after the colored—somewhere around 1860. At first looked down upon as inferior, the white dogs were soon enthusiastically taken up by fashionable sportsmen of the day. Some still consider the "white cavalier" to be less desirable, but most people accept both color varieties of this wonderful breed, which is as loving as it is lion-hearted. The 2 varieties often appear in the same litter.

Recommendation
For the right owner—and the right owner only—the Bull Terrier is an ideal choice. These dogs give of themselves fully, are loyal, and do all they can to please. However, unless you are assertive enough to provide firm training and safe handling, the breed should be admired from a distance. It is by no means a good choice for someone who has never owned a dog.

Plates 63, 64

Cairn Terrier

Characteristics
Small
Longer than tall
Shaggy double coat
Broad head
Erect ears
Short legs
Undocked tail

Personality
Everything one could want in a small terrier. A good family dog: not argumentative under ordinary circumstances and good with children. Intelligent and sensitive, amenable to training, and eager to please. Males of the breed may fight with each other, as is generally true of all terriers.

Ideal Appearance
Males, 10″ tall and 14 pounds; bitches, 9½″ and 13 pounds. Body length, 14¼″ to 15″. Short, broad head with dark, intelligent eyes and small, erect ears. Undocked tail carried erect. Shaggy double coat is naturally water-resistant. Permissible colors: any other than white; typically red, black, brindle, or silver.

Potential Health Problems
Generally a very healthy breed. Watch for hot-spot skin conditions if skin and coat are too dry. Older dogs may get allergic skin diseases. Bleeding tendency (factor IX deficiency) and progressive neurologic disorder reported.

Care and Exercise
Since a shaggy coat is the natural look of this breed, little grooming is required. Ears, head, neck, feet, and tail must be tidied. Check under tail periodically for accumulations in hair. Keep nails short, and teeth and ears clean. Check eyes regularly and remove any accumulated matter. A wig brush will stimulate the coat and prevent mats from forming. Brush and comb (with a strong steel comb) at least 3 times a week.
The Cairn Terrier does not require an excessive amount of exercise, but will benefit from long walks on a leash. At other times, a securely fenced yard will allow sufficient opportunity to be active. Make sure your dog does not try to dig under the fence or take other steps to escape.

Puppies
Litters of 3 to 5 puppies of any color.

Cairns go through many color changes as they approach maturity, and some grown dogs change color as well. Ears usually become erect by 8 to 12 weeks, but may fall, only to come up again after second teeth have fully erupted.

Comment
Developed in northwestern Scotland over the course of several centuries, the Cairn Terrier takes its name from the cairns, or heaps of stones that are characteristic of its homeland. Cairns are natural hiding places for all manner of small game, and a little terrier that could squeeze into them and exterminate rats and other vermin pleased the Highlanders. These dogs were well known in the 1840s, but were not recognized as a breed until after the start of the 20th century.
The Cairn is closely related to the West Highland White Terrier, and there was considerable crossing between the 2 breeds until the American Kennel Club moved to discourage the practice in 1916. Today the 2 breeds are separate, although they share many favorable traits. The modern Cairn Terrier is a good pet and an enjoyable show dog.

Recommendation
Anyone who has seen *The Wizard of Oz* knows that a Cairn is a faithful and courageous friend that will stand up to witches, flying monkeys, and just about anything else. Happily, there are many real-life Totos. Cairns thrive in any environment and are easy to keep contented. Very young children should be supervised around puppies.

Plate 32

Dandie Dinmont Terrier

Characteristics
Small
Large head
Soft topknot
Long, curved body
Short legs
Curved tail
Crisp coat

Personality
Good family dog, but likely to reserve deepest devotion for one person. Can be stubborn, yet learns well with a patient trainer. Clean in the home, and a good watchdog. Not overly vocal. Inadvisable to keep males together.

Ideal Appearance
A small dog. Both males and bitches, 8" to 11" tall and 18 to 24 pounds. Large, distinctive head marked by deep, melting eyes with wise expression, topknot of soft hair, and hanging, tasseled ears. Short, powerful legs. Fairly short, curved tail. Permissible colors: pepper, from silver to blue-black; or mustard, from pale fawn to dark red. Head may be cream-white. Hazel eyes.

Potential Health Problems
Healthy overall. Some dogs—particularly those past middle age—may develop intervertebral disc disease.

Care and Exercise
Let an expert show you how to handle the Dandie's coat; with a little practice, it is easy to look after. Keep nails short, teeth and ears clean, and watch for any accumulated matter in eye corners. Use terrier palm brush or pin brush at least 3 times a week, and follow with a light combing. Bathe only when necessary. Very little shedding, so coat must be kept in order or it will mat.
The Dandie benefits greatly from long walks on a leash: The regular rhythm of the exercise tones its body and fosters closeness to its owner, which is important in developing the unique personality that is so prized in the breed. Remember, though, that the Dandie is very stubborn, so take no chances by letting it off the leash—it may streak off and not return. A yard that cannot be dug out of also offers a good exercise alternative.

Puppies
Litters of 3 to 6 puppies. Coats that are black and tan at birth turn a peppery hue as puppies mature; sable newborns with black masks become mustard-colored dogs. These color changes generally occur in 6 to 8 months. Most puppies have white marking on chest that disappears with age. Dandies are slow to mature, with 3 years being the average age of complete maturity.

Comment
The Dandie Dinmont comes from the border between England and Scotland, and is the only dog breed to take its name from a character in literature. Dandie Dinmont appeared in the 1814 novel *Guy Mannering,* which was written by one of the world's greatest dog lovers, Sir Walter Scott. Over the years, this breed, a first cousin to the Bedlington Terrier, has held on to a faithful—if limited—following in both Great Britain and the United States. Originally developed for hunting small game, Dandies were said to be particularly good for tracking otter, and were favored by poachers and gypsies. Like the Bedlington, when the Dandie became stylish, it became the darling of the gentry, on whose lands it had earlier helped poachers. Today the Dandie Dinmont is kept mainly as a pet and a show dog.

Recommendation
Quite different from most other terriers, this enigmatic fellow, with its curved body and waggish attitude about life, requires a special type of owner. To be successful with a Dandie, you must be patient. Although dogs of this breed are very loving, they are also stubborn and frequently assertive. However, the Dandie is a delightful pet for the right person or family. It adapts to a house or apartment and gets along well with children. Stairs can pose a problem for it, especially for an older dog.

Plate 24

Irish Terrier

Characteristics
Angular profile
Wiry double coat
Rectangular head
Button ears
Small, dark eyes
Erect, docked tail

Personality
An excellent family dog. Big enough to withstand the rough handling of younger children, but small enough to fit into most households. Extremely courageous, an excellent watchdog. Responds well to training, but may require firm handling. Males do not get along with each other.

Ideal Appearance
Built like a Fox Terrier, but longer-bodied and of lighter weight than expected for a dog of this height. Males, about 18″ tall and 27 pounds; bitches, same height and 25 pounds. Rectangular head; button ears; and small, dark eyes with a keen expression. Erect, docked tail. Dense, wiry double coat; curly or kinky coat undesirable. Permissible colors: solid colors ranging from bright red to wheaten. Small white patch on chest permissible, but not desirable.

Potential Health Problems
Strong and healthy, despite a tendency to develop kidney or bladder stones. Corns on the feet used to be a concern, but this is less of a problem today, since breeders have worked to eradicate the complaint.

Care and Exercise
The more an Irish Terrier's coat is groomed, the more beautiful it becomes. Regular brushing and combing is easy, and frequent plucking improves the color and texture of the coat. Bathing should only be done when dog cannot be cleaned by other means, but pay regular attention to ears, teeth, and nails. Be sure to check foot pads for corns.
This active dog requires exercise to keep fit. Games that combine both vigorous activity and human contact will do wonders for the dog's mind and body. As with other terriers, long walks on a leash and outdoor exercise in a fenced yard round out a sensible routine.

Puppies
Litters of 4 to 8 puppies. Occasionally puppies will have some black hairs at birth, but these usually disappear before the dog reaches adulthood.

Comment
Known in Ireland for centuries, the Irish Terrier is currently experiencing a much-deserved renaissance. In Ireland, terriers were the dogs of the commoner—the farmer and the laborer. As a result, these dogs had to be able to do everything. It was not unusual for an Irish Terrier to guard a homestead, watch over the animals, accompany the children on their various rounds, provide sport for the master, and ward off human or animal prowlers at night. It took a determined dog to thrive under these heavy demands; the result is the modern Irish Terrier—self-reliant, brave, and all that can be asked for in a companion.

Recommendation
A top-notch working terrier and a splendid sporting companion, the Irish Terrier adapts well to any environment and is staunchly loyal to every member of its family. It is an excellent watchdog: alert, protective, and ready to defend its loved ones against any peril. These dogs make wonderful companions for anyone who enjoys terriers.

Plate 96

Kerry Blue Terrier

Characteristics
Angular profile
Button ears
Small, dark eyes
Erect, docked tail
Soft, silky, grayish-
blue coat

Personality
Very outgoing and friendly with people.
A fine family dog, and a courageous
protector of life and property. Training
must combine patience and firmness.
Will not back down from a fight, so
keeping males together is usually
inadvisable.

Ideal Appearance
Fox Terrier build. Males, 18″ to 19½″
tall and 33 to 40 pounds; bitches, 17½″
to 19″ and proportionately lighter. A
solid, well-proportioned body with
forward-angled, docked tail typical of
terriers. Small, dark eyes, and button
ears. Angular profile. Unusual single
coat is silky-soft but very dense and
wavy. Permissible colors: any shade of
blue from light silver-gray to midnight
or slate blue, often with darker points
about head, feet, and tail.

Potential Health Problems
Breed is generally healthy and active.
Hair-follicle tumors, entropion,
keratoconjunctivitis, tear deficiency, and
gait ataxia have been noted. Corns on
feet used to be a concern, but this is not
a problem today.

Care and Exercise
Brush and comb at least every other day
with a steel comb and a slicker brush.
Bathe dog monthly. Check eyes, ears,
teeth, and nails regularly. Breed is
properly trimmed with scissors and
clippers, and many owners become very
adept at trimming their own dogs.
A Kerry needs vigorous daily exercise.
Long walks on a leash and robust games
build body and spirit. Exercise should
always be supervised, especially when the
dog is allowed to run at large. Dogs also
need to be close to people. Obedience
training essential; sharpness must be
discouraged.

Puppies
Litters of 4 to 8 puppies. Born black;
attain typical color at around 18 months.

Coat goes through several color phases,
including casts of red, brown, gray, and,
finally, Kerry blue.

Comment
A native of southwestern Ireland, the
breed takes its name from County Kerry,
where it was widely used and admired as
a farm, guard, and hunting dog. The
Kerry was known in the 19th century,
but came to general notice only after
fanciers promoted it, trimmed it up,
calmed it down, and stabilized its
volatile nature, showing the world what
a fine fellow this dog can be. To many,
Kerries have a reputation for fighting,
and indeed they can be aggressive.
However, this temperament should be
directed only at other dogs and can be
controlled by an assertive owner.
Kerries are wonderful around people and
act like eternal puppies, retaining their
bounce far into old age. The coat neither
sheds nor has the typical doggy odor of
most breeds, which makes this terrier
even more attractive. As a show dog, the
Kerry has made quite a name for itself.

Recommendation
If you can be assertive, can train
patiently, firmly, and fairly, and would
enjoy a dog with an enthusiastic outlook
on life, the Kerry Blue Terrier could be
your breed. But if a strong-willed dog
could pose problems for you, do not
consider the Kerry Blue.

Plate 93

Lakeland Terrier

Characteristics
Angular profile
Wiry double coat
Button ears
Small, dark eyes
Erect, docked tail

Personality
A game, frolicsome pet that enjoys activities with adults as well as with children. Generally likes everyone, but can distinguish friends from strangers. An alert watchdog. Can be vocal. Males can be quarrelsome together.

Ideal Appearance
Small, resembling the Wire Fox Terrier. Males, 14″ to 15″ tall, ideally 14½″, and about 17 pounds; bitches, up to 14″ and proportionately lighter. Angular profile. Rectangular head with small, dark eyes and button ears. Erect, docked tail. Double coat: soft underneath, dense and wiry on the outside, often in tight waves. Permissible colors: blue, black, liver, black and tan, blue and tan, red, red grizzle, grizzle and tan, or wheaten.

Potential Health Problems
Generally a healthy breed. Skin should not be allowed to dry out in an overheated environment. Lens luxation reported.

Care and Exercise
Pluck or strip the harsh double coat to maintain strongest color and proper texture. This is absolutely essential in show dogs, but pets may also be clipped if the owner wishes. A properly textured coat will shed dirt and, if brushed at least twice weekly, can be well maintained between trimming sessions. Pay regular attention to ears, teeth, and nails. Check eyes routinely, since the breed is trimmed so that the eyes are partly covered; stray hairs touching the eye surface can cause irritation.
A Lakeland needs vigorous exercise to keep trim. Walk it on a leash and also let it have free exercise, either in a fenced area or indoors. Like most terriers, Lakelands have a strong territorial sense and will fight.

Puppies
Litters of 3 to 5 puppies. Newborns often have soft, curly coats until they have been plucked once or twice. Dark colors fade out or clear, especially around the saddle. This process is usually complete by the time the dog becomes an adult.

Comment
The Lakeland Terrier was developed in the Lake District in the north of England and is related to the Border, the Bedlington, and the Dandie Dinmont. Unlike many other terriers which were bred to be diggers, the Lakeland was used to hunt foxes and other wildlife that preyed on livestock. Its courage earned it fame as a dauntless exterminator of predators. Soon after the turn of the century, a club was formed in England for the advancement of the breed. The Lakeland was recognized in England in 1921, and recognized in the United States in 1934. Since then the Lakie has accomplished much as a show dog, which is remarkable in view of its modest numbers.

Recommendation
Anyone who wants an energetic and enthusiastic breed will like the Lakeland. It enjoys whatever its owner does, although it would rather be active than sedentary. It is not common anywhere in the United States; thus most people do not recognize the breed when they see it. The Lakeland Terrier is a flawless companion. Short-tempered or impatient people will do better with a less demanding—and possibly less intelligent—breed. This is a dog lover's dog.

Plate 39

Manchester Terrier

Characteristics
Long, narrow head
with almost no stop
Ears usually cropped
Slightly arched back
Whiplike tail
Smooth coat
Graceful

Personality
Pleasant and well-mannered. Notably clean in its habits. A lively dog, but very easy to live with. A good companion for adults and children; may not tolerate other pets.

Ideal Appearance
2 sizes: standard and toy. Standard size is 12 to 22 pounds. Although standard does not specify height, males usually measure about 16″ tall; bitches, approximately 15″. In the show ring, dogs are often divided by weight into a 12-to-16 pound group and a 16-to-22 pound group. Toy size, 11″ and under (see Toy Manchester Terrier, page 214). Long, narrow head with practically no stop. Dark eyes. Ears of standard size may be button, cropped, or natural. Back slightly arched over loins (roach back). Long, whiplike tail. Sleek, smooth coat should be thick and dense, never soft. Color and markings are important: jet-black and mahogany-tan, with division between colors well-defined; white is undesirable, and more than ½″ of it is not allowed for show.

Potential Health Problems
Hardy overall. Lens luxation and secondary glaucoma have been reported.

Care and Exercise
Smooth coat requires little care. Regular brushing with a natural-bristle brush will leave the coat clean and shiny and the skin healthy. Check nails, teeth, and ears routinely. Bathe as needed. Pets do not require trimming. For the show ring, coarse feelers are removed from the muzzle, from above the eyes, and from the sides of the head; long hairs behind the legs and thighs, under the tail, and on the sides of the neck are also cut. Dogs benefit from long walks on a leash as well as off-leash exercise in an enclosed area. The more the dog is exercised, the closer the bond it will have with its owner, and the happier both will be.

Puppies
Litters usually contain 2 to 4 puppies, which are born the same colors as their parents. If ears are cropped, this operation is usually performed when puppies are 8 weeks old.

Comment
One of the oldest terrier breeds, the Manchester Terrier has ancestors that date back to before the 16th century. In the 19th century, another precursor was probably produced by crossing sporting terriers with Whippets or Greyhounds. The goal was offspring that would excel both at hunting rats and other vermin and at racing rabbits. Manchester, England, became the breeding center, and the dogs were named for the city. When Parliament first banned blood sports and, later, ear-cropping, the Manchester suffered some setbacks, but devoted fanciers perpetuated the breed, which has been appreciated in America since the early part of the century. There are 2 varieties: the standard, which is included in the terrier group, and the toy, which is now classified with other toy breeds.

Recommendation
The Manchester Terrier combines good temperament with a handsome appearance. It is easy to care for, clean, alert, and pleasant. This breed adapts well to any environment: it is a good family dog, makes a challenging yet sensible pet, and is a good watchdog. It is also an excellent companion. The Manchester Terrier gives the distinct impression that it cares, as it is very sensitive to people's moods.

Plate 66

Miniature Schnauzer

Characteristics
Small and stocky
Angular profile
Wiry double coat
Cropped ears
Small, dark eyes
Erect, short, docked
tail

Personality
A friendly and companionable family dog. Good with children and tolerant of other family pets. Not inclined to fight. Content to stay close to home. An alert, vocal watchdog.

Ideal Appearance
A stocky terrier. Both males and bitches 12″ to 14″ tall, ideally 13½″. Although standard does not specify weight, males usually weigh about 15 pounds; bitches approximately 14 pounds. Rectangular head with appealing face: cropped ears and bushy eyebrows and whiskers give dog an elfin expression. Strong, compact build with muscular hindquarters and angular profile. Small, dark brown eyes. Double coat: harsh and wiry outer coat; close undercoat with abundant hair on legs and feet. Short, docked tail. Permissible colors: solid black, black and silver, salt-and-pepper; tan shading is allowed.

Potential Health Problems
Normally, a healthy, robust little dog. Liver diseases, diabetes, bilateral cataracts, progressive retinal atrophy, bladder and kidney stones, and von Willebrand's disease reported. Some dogs have skin acne and tear deficiency.

Care and Exercise
Distinctive salt-and-pepper color can only be maintained by plucking or stripping. A clipped coat will soon lose this handsome effect, even on a black animal, but clipping is easier for the pet than orthodox grooming procedures are. In any case, to look its best, a Miniature Schnauzer must be trimmed; the method depends on the needs and wishes of the owner. Ears, eyes, teeth, and nails require routine care. Bathe the dog only when needed.
Breed does well with whatever exercise it gets, but the more the better. A long walk on a leash once a day along with a few shorter excursions will keep the dog fit. Supervised off-leash exercise is excellent when conditions permit.

Puppies
Litters average 3 to 6 puppies. Salt-and-pepper animals are considerably darker when born than at maturity; they clear to the adult shade.

Comment
The most popular of the terriers, the Miniature Schnauzer is the only one that cannot be traced to the British Isles. It is generally conceded that the breed was developed in Germany. A smaller replica of the Standard Schnauzer, the Miniature Schnauzer is a distinct breed. It was used on farms and around stables as a ratter and still lives up to the name it made for itself in this respect. Today this dog may look more glamorous than its ancestors did, but it has just as much courage. Its handsome appearance and flashy showmanship win it friends and honors in the show ring.

Recommendation
This intelligent little companion dog has all the assets we admire in a terrier and much less built-in aggression. Highly recommended for either city or country living, it is an ideal pet in any setting. It even travels exceptionally well. This breed is splendid with both elderly people and small children. It loves to be spoiled, but that is easy to control. The Miniature Schnauzer is a great little character in the world of dogs.

Plate 37

Norfolk Terrier

Characteristics
Small
Drop ears
Wiry double coat
Compact, short body
Short legs
Short, docked tail

Personality
A thoroughly likable, active little dog.
Self-sufficient, but happy to be with
people. Does well with children and is
tolerant of other pets. A natural digger,
so any outdoor enclosure should be made
escape-proof.

Ideal Appearance
Both males and bitches, 10″ tall and 10
to 12 pounds. Compact, short, stocky
body with short legs. Slight whiskers
and eyebrows, with suggestion of mane
around neck and on chest. Ears are very
important: They are the most obvious
difference between this breed and the
Norwich Terrier. The Norfolk has small
drop ears with rounded tips; they break
just above the skull, are carried close to
the cheeks, and do not fall below the
outside corner of the eye. Tail docked
fairly close to body. Harsh, wiry double
coat. Permissible colors: any shade of
red, wheaten, black and tan, or grizzle;
white marks or patches are not desirable.
Dark eyes with black rims.

Potential Health Problems
Quite healthy overall; may suffer from
allergic skin disease.

Care and Exercise
Wiry coat requires only regular brushing
and combing, including judicious
tidying of ears, feet, and tail. Extensive
grooming is strongly frowned upon; this
breed should look natural. Check eyes,
ears, teeth, and nails regularly. With
sufficient brushing, baths are seldom
necessary. This robust breed needs a fair
amount of activity despite its small size.
The Norfolk Terrier is a ground hunter
and, if not watched, could dig its way
out of a yard. Provide regular walks on a
leash.

Puppies
Litters are usually small, averaging 3
puppies. Like all puppies, they should
become accustomed to being with people
at an early age.

Comment
The Norfolk was developed as a hunting
terrier about the turn of the century in
the urban communities of Cambridge,
Market Harborough, and Norwich in
England. Often termed the Jones
Terrier, after the breed's best-known
early proponent, Frank Jones, the
Norfolk was a great favorite in sporting
circles in America and England. The
breed is still a familiar sight around
foxhound packs, often riding in a
saddlebag or a special pouch, and being
slipped down to the ground when the fox
takes refuge underground.
Originally recognized in England in
1932, the Norfolk and Norwich terriers
were considered one breed in Britain
until 1964, when the Kennel Club ruled
that drop ears would henceforth denote
the Norfolk and prick ears, the Norwich.
The same distinction was made in the
United States in 1979.
The modern Norfolk retains its working
character and no-frills appearance. What
it lacks in glamour, it more than makes
up for in character.

Recommendation
If you want a small, personable dog to
accompany you on long country rambles
or to sit by you in moments of quiet
communication by a fire, you should
consider sharing your life with this
breed. It does very well in city
apartments, suburban homes, or on the
farm. It will pose on a satin cushion or
hunt rats and mice in the barn. You pick
the lifestyle, and the Norfolk will jump
right in and love it, as long as you are
nearby.

Plate 29

Norwich Terrier

Characteristics
Small
Erect ears
Wiry double coat
Compact, short body
Short legs
Short, docked tail

Personality
Like the Norfolk Terrier, the Norwich is friendly with adults and children, and lives in harmony with other household pets. Vigilance is necessary in discouraging both digging and wandering in quest of adventure.

Ideal Appearance
Both males and bitches, 10″ tall and 11 to 12 pounds. Low build: compact, short body on short legs. Head has slight whiskers and eyebrows, with suggestion of mane around neck and on chest. Sharply pointed, erect ears, which distinguish it from the Norfolk. Tail docked fairly close to body. Harsh, wiry, relatively short double coat; longer on head. Permissible colors: red, wheaten, black and tan, or grizzle; white markings on chest not desirable. Dark eyes with black rims.

Potential Health Problems
Generally robust. Does not tolerate very dry conditions. Possible allergic skin disease.

Care and Exercise
Needs same care as the Norfolk Terrier. Trimming is confined to tidying up coat and clearing long hair from ears, feet, and around tail. Brush and comb at least 2 or 3 times a week to keep coat and skin healthy and to eliminate the need for frequent bathing. Keep ears and teeth clean and nails trimmed.
Long walks on a leash are best and safest. When walks are not practical, the dog should have the run of a secure yard out of which it cannot dig. Easy to care for and pleasant to live with.

Puppies
Small litters, averaging 3 puppies. Ears usually come up by 6 to 8 weeks.

Comment
The history of the Norwich and Norfolk terriers is a shared one: they were developed in the same place, at the same time, and for the same purpose. By recognizing 2 distinct breeds, the English Kennel Club—in 1964—and the American Kennel Club—in 1979— enhanced the development potential of both types.
In recent years, the Norwich has taken an increasing number of top awards in the show ring, both in this country and in Great Britain. Despite its growing popularity, the Norwich retains the natural, unspoiled character of its ancestors. It can still bolt foxes and cause rats to flee, and its value as a companion has not been lessened.

Recommendation
The Norwich is among the most personable dogs. Many who have experience with other dogs take up this breed enthusiastically because of its tremendous combination of positive features. Farm living and an apartment lifestyle are equally acceptable, for the Norwich adapts to any environment or person. This is a delightful dog to have close by.

Plate 30

Scottish Terrier

Characteristics
Small
Wiry double coat
Shaggy eyebrows and
whiskers
Moderately long head
Erect ears
Undocked tail

Personality
A very independent, one-person dog.
Can be stubborn in a clash of canine and
human wills. A dog of tremendous
character: Thinks of itself as a giant and
has considerable self-esteem. Very
sensitive to the moods of those around it.
Better suited to slightly older children.
Can be aggressive with other pets.

Ideal Appearance
Sturdy, compact body on short, powerful
legs. Males, about 10″ tall and 19 to 22
pounds; bitches, same height and 18 to
21 pounds. Moderately long head with
dark brown to almost black eyes. Keen,
penetrating expression helped by thick
eyebrows, whiskers, and erect ears.
Undocked, erect tail. Hard, wiry double
coat. Permissible colors: brindle, black,
steel- or iron-gray, grizzle, sandy, or
wheaten; small markings permitted on
chest.

Potential Health Problems
Generally healthy. Tends to get bladder
and kidney stones and allergic skin
disease. Von Willebrand's disease,
craniomandibular osteopathy,
demodectic mange, and Scottie cramp
reported.

Care and Exercise
To look its best, coat must be plucked or
stripped. Show preparation requires
considerable skill, but a pet can be
clipped if the owner wishes. A stiff,
natural-bristle brush, a pin brush, and a
strong steel comb are the chief grooming
tools needed. Comb at least 3 times a
week. Pay regular attention to eyes, ears,
teeth, and nails, and routinely check to
make sure hair around the anus is
short.
Exercise either on leash or in a securely
fenced yard that the Scottie cannot dig
out of. If off leash and unsupervised, a
Scottie can get into trouble easily.
Obedience training is recommended, and
any sharpness should be discouraged.

Puppies
Average litter consists of 3 to 5 puppies.
Brindle coats often go through color
changes. Ears are usually up within 8
weeks, but may fall before permanent
teeth erupt; ears will usually come up by
themselves, but sometimes need to be
braced. Puppies need to be handled from
an early age so they get used to people.

Comment
The Scottish Terrier has been around for
centuries. Although there is some debate
about its exact ancestors, this breed's
background is linked to that of all the
other Highland terriers—Dandie
Dinmont, Skye, Cairn, and West
Highland White—since much
interbreeding took place among these
dogs in the early days. Because the
Scottie came from the rocky area around
Aberdeen, Scotland, it was at first called
the Aberdeen Terrier. Like their short-
legged cousins, Scottish Terriers were
bred as earth dogs and were intended to
pursue foxes, ferrets, and other small
wildlife into their underground retreats.
The breed was was brought to this
country in 1883.
The Scottie has numerous friends and is
in fact familiar even to those who do not
know dog breeds. Franklin Roosevelt
propelled the Scottie to greater fame
when he took his beloved Fala to the
White House. Today the Scottie is a very
popular pet and show dog.

Recommendation
If you like an independent, self-assured
character, the Scottie may be for you. It
can prove to be too much dog for an
owner displeased by an occasional contest
of wills. The puppies are adorable, while
the adults are somewhat more dour. If
puppies have frequent contact with
people, they generally become pleasing
pets in later years.

Plate 36

Sealyham Terrier

Characteristics
Small and white
Wiry double coat
Rectangular head
Button ears
Shaggy eyebrows and
whiskers
Erect, docked tail

Personality
Anxious to please, with a sense of humor all its own. Outgoing, but has the ability to tell friends from intruders. Good with children. Males may fight each other.

Ideal Appearance
Resembles Wire Fox Terrier, but is heavier and has short legs. Males, about 10½" tall and 23 to 24 pounds; bitches, same height and slightly lighter. Compact, muscular body. Rectangular head with button ears. Shaggy, undivided eyebrows and long whiskers. Docked tail held stiffly erect. Harsh, wiry double coat. Permissible colors: always white, sometimes with tan, lemon, or badger markings on head and chest. Dark eyes.

Potential Health Problems
Generally healthy. May have allergic skin disease. Lens luxation and retinal dysplasia reported. Like most white dogs, may be subject to deafness as a result of recessive genes.

Care and Exercise
Regular grooming is essential to prevent coat from becoming matted. At least 2 or 3 grooming sessions a week with trimming at regular intervals will keep a Sealy presentable. Bathe as needed and pay routine attention to eyes, ears, teeth, and nails. Coat is generally hard, but on many dogs, soft hair is mixed in. To keep dog comfortable, strip or pluck hair. You can do this yourself, but first get a professional demonstration, as a special technique is involved.
Dog needs long walks on a leash as often as possible; such contact with its owner helps create a good personality. When supervised exercise cannot be provided, give the dog access to a fenced yard.

Puppies
Litters usually consist of 3 to 6 puppies, which exhibit their adult markings at birth. Should be trained early.

Comment
The Sealyham Terrier was developed in the late 19th century in Haverfordwest, Wales, by Captain John Edwardes, and was named for his estate. This dog was bred to have enormous courage; it tackled vermin from which other dogs would shrink, such as weasels and foxes. Among other breeds, the Fox, Bull, and Dandie Dinmont terriers may have been ancestors. Whatever their lineage, Captain Edwardes's dogs were, first and foremost, superb hunters.
Through the years, Sealies have become valued more as companions than as hunting dogs, although many still fiercely pursue game. Today the breed is very successful in the show ring. It is slowly making headway as a pet—a chance that it deserves, as it has evolved into a fine companion.

Recommendation
The Sealyham Terrier does well in any kind of environment—apartment, house, or farm. However, potential owners should keep in mind that its coat requires constant attention. Anyone who has ever owned one of these spunky dogs will tell you that it is well worth the effort. Sealies tend to be long-lived, but act perpetually youthful.

Plate 34

Skye Terrier

Characteristics
Very long body
Short legs
Long coat extends
to ground
Ears usually erect
Long, undocked tail

Personality
Reserved, and wary of strangers. An excellent watchdog and very protective of its family and property. With those it knows, the Skye is endearing and personable. Happy to please, but can be a bit stubborn.

Ideal Appearance
Very long and low to the ground. Males, 10″ tall; bitches, 9½″. Body should be twice as long as it is high. Although standard does not specify weight, males are usually about 25 pounds; bitches, approximately 23 pounds. Distinctive, 5½″-long double coat covers face, ears, and body, and touches the ground. Soft, woolly undercoat; hard, straight, and flat outer coat. Hair is parted from nose to root of tail. Either erect or drop ears. Long, undocked tail. Permissible colors: black, blue, cream, fawn, various shades of gray, or silver-platinum. Color must be uniform at the skin, but coat itself may show shadings. Black points on ears, muzzle, and tip of tail very desirable. Brown eyes.

Potential Health Problems
Healthy overall. Hypoplasia of the larynx and ulcerative colitis reported.

Care and Exercise
One look at a Skye and you know that magnificent coat demands considerable attention. Needs almost no trimming, but brushing and combing should be a daily ritual. Use a good pin brush and a strong metal comb. To set the part, some Skye owners use a knitting needle. As with all breeds, keep nails short and teeth clean. Check ears regularly to be sure that under the deep coat, the skin is free of infections; also check under tail for fecal accumulation. Bathe as necessary, but with proper attention to grooming, baths should not be needed too often.
Despite its ornamental appearance, the Skye needs a fair amount of exercise: It should either be taken for long walks on a leash or be allowed to run around in a secure yard—or both. Active games contribute to physical and emotional fitness. Supervise around other animals.

Puppies
Large litters of up to 9 puppies are not unheard of. Color of coat may change considerably between birth and adulthood. Ears usually become erect in 3 months or less.

Comment
Irrefutably one of the oldest terriers, the Skye was described by the celebrated Dr. Caius in the 16th-century book *Of Englishe Dogges*. According to this source, the Skye comes from the "barbarous borders northward" and, "by reason of lengthe of heare [hair], make show neither of face nor body." During the intervening centuries, Skyes in the Western Isles of Scotland, particularly the Isle of Skye, became known as the implacable foes of all vermin. The breed eventually traveled outside of the Hebrides to England, where the Skye Terrier developed a following that considered it a unique pet as well as an eye-catching show dog. Loved by high society and commoners alike, it was immensely popular for at least 200 years. One of the breed's staunchest supporters was Queen Victoria, whose Boz was often painted by Sir Edwin Landseer. The modern Skye Terrier still has many supporters.

Recommendation
A Skye Terrier can be a rewarding companion. It is a dog of great character, although it is sometimes stubborn. An owner should be prepared to devote time to grooming and to patient training. The Skye has powerful, punishing jaws. This is a breed for experienced, dedicated dog people.

Plate 35

Smooth Fox Terrier

Characteristics
Smooth coat
Button ears
Small, dark eyes
Erect, docked tail
Smart, alert
appearance overall

Personality
Friendly and outgoing. Very energetic; does best with active owner or family. Good with children and never tires of all sorts of games. A good watchdog, with a tendency to be vocal. Anxious to please. Clean in the home. Males may fight with one another.

Ideal Appearance
Males, up to 15½″ tall and 16 to 18 pounds; bitches, proportionately shorter and about 16 pounds. Button ears fold over top of skull. Docked tail carried stiffly erect. Coat is close and sleek, but dense and abundant enough to cover body all over. There should be no obvious bare areas. If allowed to grow unchecked, some coats will grow longer on tail, backs of hind legs and on sides of neck. Permissible colors: White should predominate with markings of black and/or tan on body.
Occasionally completely white. Black head with tan over eyes and on cheeks fairly common.

Potential Health Problems
Normally a healthy, boisterous breed, although deafness, lens luxation, glaucoma, and dislocated shoulders are sometimes reported. Subject to allergic skin disease, gait ataxia, congenital heart disease, and swallowing disorders.

Care and Exercise
Brushing with a natural bristle brush or a hound glove will promote a healthy coat and skin. Finish with a fine comb and, if you like, a chamois cloth for extra sheen. A stripping comb or thinning shears may be used to remove any longer hairs. Bathe the dog as needed, paying attention to ears, teeth and nails.
Fox Terriers are energetic and need plenty of exercise. A combination of long walks on a leash and off-leash play periods in a secure location is ideal. This dog enjoys playing ball and retrieving objects, so throwing games will furnish ample exercise while not taxing an owner who is not physically active. Keep alert for other animals during play to avoid possible dog fights or escape attempts.

Puppies
Litters usually contain from 3 to 6 puppies. Markings seen at birth are usually like those of adult dog.

Comment
The Smooth Fox Terrier is one of the most universally recognized and loved of all purebreds. Its global renown probably arose from the British custom of bringing their dogs to virtually every corner of the British Empire during the period of colonial expansion. Whatever the reason, this cosmopolitan breed was at first considered a sporting dog and was often used to accompany mounted fox hunters.
While still able to perform its original work, the Smooth is more often seen as a pet and show dog. This breed has a strong aptitude as a trick dog and has been used for this work in many performing dog troupes around the world. Even people who are totally unfamiliar with dog breeds know the Smooth from the famous "His Master's Voice" record trademark, which shows a Smooth Fox Terrier listening into an old-fashioned gramophone.
Until quite recently, the Smooth and Wire fox terriers were considered coat varieties of a single breed, but now are split into 2 distinct breeds.

Recommendation
A sedentary person who likes to sit back, relax, and listen to music would probably not enjoy a Smooth Fox Terrier. On the other hand, anyone who is on the go and likes to take his or her dog along should love this breed. The Smooth Fox Terrier is a hard-charging fellow that is happiest when active.

Plate 40

Soft-Coated Wheaten Terrier

Characteristics
Angular profile
Soft wheaten coat
Button ears
Small, dark eyes
Short, docked tail

Personality
Congenial companion that is excellent with adults and children of any age. Energetic, alert, and effective watchdog. Eager to please, and easy to train. Gets along well with other pets. Shows less aggressive behavior than many terriers.

Ideal Appearance
A sturdy, medium-size terrier. Males, 18″ to 19″ tall and 35 to 40 pounds; bitches, slightly smaller and lighter. Very similar to Kerry Blue, but has a broader, shorter skull. Button ears and small, dark eyes. Docked tail. Coat is distinctive feature: In adults it is a clear wheaten color, soft, and wavy. Coat is trimmed only to show outline, although fringe can be trimmed off ears. Permissible colors: wheaten; ears and muzzle may be shaded. Dark hazel or brown eyes.

Potential Health Problems
Usually robust and healthy. Colitis and progressive retinal atrophy reported. May have allergic skin disease.

Care and Exercise
Frequent grooming is necessary to keep a Wheaten clean and to avoid matting of its coat. Brush and comb 3 times a week, more often if possible. Use a good steel comb with long teeth and a wire slicker brush that will not rip out live hair. The Wheaten should be trimmed instead of plucked, using thinning shears. Examine ears, eyes, teeth, and nails regularly, cleaning or trimming as necessary. Check between paw pads for objects or small mats, and keep hair under tail short for hygienic purposes.
Long walks on a leash will keep a Wheaten in good physical condition, as well as promote a feeling of closeness between dog and owner. When walks are impractical, a fenced yard is advised. This breed appreciates a good game of fetch from time to time.

Puppies
Litters usually contain 5 or 6 puppies, occasionally more. Newborns are a red-wheaten color and have black masks. Although considerably darker than adults, they lighten to adult color in 18 to 24 months.

Comment
Terriers with soft coats have been present in Ireland for several centuries, although there are no reliable written records describing them. Like other terriers from Ireland, the Soft-Coated Wheaten Terrier was developed to be an all-purpose farm dog and is thought to have been an ancestor of the Kerry Blue Terrier.
The Wheaten has been recognized in Ireland since 1937, and in England since 1943. Although the first Soft-Coated Wheaten Terriers arrived in the United States in 1946, the breed was not recognized by the American Kennel Club until 1973. Today's Soft-Coated Wheaten Terrier is far more stylized than breed pioneers intended it to be, but it has the same endearing spirit.

Recommendation
If you want a medium-size dog that has a cheerful personality and is ready to do anything to make you happy, consider the Wheaten. It can be comfortable anywhere as long as it receives sensible care, including enough exercise and grooming.

Plate 92

Staffordshire Bull Terrier

Characteristics
Extremely muscular
Very broad, wedge-shaped head
Ears usually rose or half-prick
Smooth coat
Undocked tail

Personality
Friendly to people, and particularly good with children; tolerates both the mauling of toddlers and the rough play of older children. An alert watchdog and a protective companion. Needs a firm hand as a puppy, but is anxious to please. Must be supervised around other animals and strangers.

Ideal Appearance
Powerful, muscular build. Males, 14″ to 16″ tall and 28 to 38 pounds; bitches, proportionately shorter, and 24 to 34 pounds. Muscular, rather short neck and strong, short back. Heavy-boned legs set well apart. Very strong, wedge-shaped head with distinct stop. Dark eyes and either rose or half-prick ears. Undocked tail of medium length. Smooth coat. Permissible colors: red, fawn, white, black, blue; any of these colors in combination with white; or brindle in any shade with or without white. Black and tan or liver not allowed in shows.

Potential Health Problems
Strong and healthy. May get bilateral cataracts and mast cell tumors.

Care and Exercise
Smooth coat requires only vigorous brushing to keep it healthy and shiny. AKC standard specifically prohibits trimming of any kind and removal of whiskers. Use a natural, firm-bristle brush, and then rub down with a chamois. For a special gleam, spread a very small dab of brilliantine on your palms and massage into coat; brindles, in particular, will take on a tortoiseshell look. Pay regular attention to ears, eyes, teeth, and nails, and bathe only when needed.

Give a Staffordshire sufficient exercise to keep it fit and muscular. As with many terriers, long walks on a leash are best. Any off-leash activities should be provided under very secure conditions. Not only must the dog be unable to escape from the owner or the paddock, but other dogs should not be able to get in. No tie-out stakes or overhead trolleys.

Puppies
Litters average 4 to 6 puppies. Color depends on color and markings of parents. Puppies may have to be separated from each other at a fairly early age to prevent fights.

Comment
The Staffordshire Bull Terrier is a 19th-century form of a much older English dog that was bred for the sport of dogfighting: It combines the speed of the terrier with the tenacity of the Bulldog and the courage of both. Dogfighting became prominent after the 1835 abolition of bullbaiting and continued as a "respectable" diversion until more humane attitudes also prohibited this blood sport. However, the outlawing of dogfighting did not wipe it out completely; the practice merely went underground. Eventually British authorities forced fanciers of the sport to seek more peaceable ways of enjoying their dogs, and dog shows became the obvious answer. Unfortunately, although it is strictly illegal, these animals are still pitted against each other in battles to the death in clandestine arenas all over the United States.

Today the breed has many friends in Great Britain and the United States.

Recommendation
A firm hand is a must with a Staffordshire pup if it is to develop into a good companion showing all the best sides of the breed. Since the fighting instinct still remains, keep your dog away from other dogs. A lovely breed, but not for the unassertive or a first-time owner.

Plate 61

Welsh Terrier

Characteristics
Angular profile
Wiry double coat
Blanket pattern
Button ears
Small, dark eyes
Erect, docked tail

Personality
Intelligent, sensitive companion dog. Friendly with adults and children of any age. An alert watchdog, as game as any terrier, but less quarrelsome than most. Eager to please and quite trainable.

Ideal Appearance
Angular build of the Wire Fox Terrier type. Males, 15″ tall and about 20 pounds; bitches, slightly smaller and lighter. Has a wise expression created by long, wide skull and placement of eyes. Button ears. Thick, hard, wiry double coat. Erect, docked tail. Permissible colors: black or grizzle behind ears, down neck, and on body and upper side of tail; the rest, some shade of deep reddish-tan. Dark hazel eyes.

Potential Health Problems
Generally hardy. Prevent dry skin, or hot spots can develop. Sometimes allergic skin disease. Lens luxation and glaucoma reported.

Care and Exercise
Trimming is essential for typical tailored look. For show ring, hand stripping is necessary, but a pet may be clipped. Clipping, however, will eventually soften coat and alter its color permanently. Stripped or clipped, a Welsh Terrier should be brushed and combed at least 3 times a week. Bathe as needed; if a dog is groomed regularly, a bath once a month should suffice. Pay attention to ears, teeth, and nails. Long walks on a leash are especially good for the Welsh Terrier because it thrives on personal contact. Fetching games are great fun for both dog and owner. Exercise in a securely fenced yard is acceptable, but precautions should be taken against digging.

Puppies
Average litter contains 3 to 6 puppies. Almost solid black at birth, but dark color recedes quickly, leaving typical blanketed pattern at 3 to 4 months.

Comment
The Welsh Terrier is the modern version of a very old canine form. It is believed that its ancestors inhabited the British Isles several centuries ago. The Welsh Terrier was bred to hunt all sorts of small vermin—foxes, weasels, rabbits, and rats—and was expected to go to ground after its quarry. Since the dog had to be a useful working hunter, quarrelsome traits were discouraged. To this day, the Welsh Terrier is known as one of the most level-headed of all the terriers. First shown in Wales about a century ago, the breed appeared in the United States shortly thereafter and was recognized as a separate breed by about 1901. Of moderate popularity, the Welsh Terrier enjoys a following of faithful friends who enjoy its many virtues and who, wisely, have never attempted to exploit the breed.

Recommendation
The Welsh Terrier makes a pleasant companion and is at home in any setting. Nonetheless, it does require regular grooming and trimming to properly maintain its handsome appearance.

Plate 94

West Highland White Terrier

Characteristics
Small, compact body
Short, broad head
Erect ears
Harsh double coat
Short legs, but not
too low
Undocked tail

Personality
Light-hearted and outgoing. A wonderful family dog, although very small puppies and very small children are not always a good mix. An alert watchdog, keenly observant and vocal. Generally gets along with other pets, but more than one male in a household can become a problem. Some Westies tend to be diggers.

Ideal Appearance
Small and compact, with a short, broad head. Males, about 11" tall; bitches, approximately 10". Although standard does not specify weight, males usually weigh about 19 pounds; bitches, approximately 17 pounds. Considered a short-legged breed, but its legs are not really short in comparison to those of the Scottie or Dandie Dinmont. Small, pointed ears held stiffly erect. Dark, medium-size eyes radiate keen, active interest in surroundings. Erect, undocked tail. Harsh double coat about 2" long; abundant on head and face, shorter on neck and shoulders. Only pure white; jet-black nose.

Potential Health Problems
Usually healthy and robust. Subject to allergic skin disease. May have tear deficiency. Inguinal hernias, progressive neurologic disorder, craniomandibular osteopathy reported.

Care and Exercise
Must be groomed at least 2 or 3 times a week and trimmed at regular intervals to maintain appearance and promote healthy skin and coat. Show dogs must be plucked and stripped, but a pet may be clipped and trimmed with scissors if owner wishes. However, clipping will eventually promote a soft coat. Clean ears, eyes, and teeth regularly. Keep nails clipped. Area under tail should be trimmed for hygienic reasons. Hard coat sheds dirt, so keeping it clean is not difficult; baths needed once a month.

Long walks on a leash, running in a safe yard, and playing fetch are all beneficial forms of exercise that will keep a Westie fit and happy. Unsupervised, off-leash exercise is very unwise, and a yard should be escape-proof. An overhead trolley is also inadvisable, as it will cause a Westie to become frustrated and bark nonstop.

Puppies
Small to medium-size litters of 2 to 5 puppies. Always born pure white. Most newborns have pink noses and paw pads; these soon turn black. Ears come up by 8 weeks in most cases.

Comment
The West Highland White comes from the same family as the Cairn, the Scottie, and the other terriers of Scotland. These breeds were once just varieties of a single type, but branched out as serious breeding flourished. At one time, white puppies in Cairn litters were considered undesirable and were destroyed. Eventually, however, the white dogs were developed into the modern Westie. Recognized in the United States in 1908, the breed became immensely popular during the 1960s and is today one of the most beloved of all the terriers. Primarily a pet at the present time, it can still hunt small vermin with the best of the terriers.

Recommendation
The Westie is the sunniest of all Scotland's terriers. It requires a fair amount of regular grooming, and can be vocal. At home in any setting, this dog is happiest with a few well-chosen friends, human or canine, and preferably both. Its abundant charm and eye-catching appearance account for its universal popularity.

Plate 33

Wire Fox Terrier

Characteristics
Angular profile
Wiry double coat
Button ears
Small, dark eyes
Erect, docked tail

Personality
Gregarious and sociable. Filled with vitality and the sheer joy of living. Best appreciated by active people. A good child's dog that never refuses an invitation to play. Eager to please and clean in its household habits. A keen and vocal watchdog. Males can display aggressive behavior to other males.

Ideal Appearance
Males, up to 15½" tall and weigh 16 to 18 pounds; bitches proportionately shorter and about 16 pounds. Typical angular profile; long, rectangular head; button ears, and a stiffly erect, docked tail. Harsh, wiry coat, often wavy. Longer hair is usually left on eyebrows, muzzle, legs, and brisket. Permissible colors: White should predominate, usually with black and/or tan on body; rarely all white. Markings often differ from the Smooth Fox Terrier; for example, the Wire may have a tan head with black body patches, but such combinations are never observed in the Smooth Fox Terrier.

Potential Health Problems
Usually robust. Deafness, lens luxation, glaucoma, dislocated shoulders sometimes reported. Subject to allergic skin disease, gait ataxia, congenital heart disease, and swallowing disorders.

Care and Exercise
Regular brushing, with a natural bristle brush or hound glove and comb, is required. A terrier "palm pad" does a nice job; you can usually buy one from a dog show equipment supplier. The Wire Fox Terrier show dog must be hand-plucked or stripped to maintain the color and texture of its coat. A pet, however, may be clipped if it is never to enter the ring. Clipping eventually softens the coat texture and color but in no way adversely affects a dog's personality. Dog should also be bathed, and ears, teeth, and nails checked routinely. The Wire

Fox Terrier needs an abundance of vigorous exercise to keep really fit. Long walks on a leash, off-leash yard time playing ball, or other active games are all good for keeping it in shape. Watch for stray dogs, cats, or other distractions.

Puppies
Litters usually include 3 to 6 puppies, but fewer or more are common. A newborn with a predominately black head will become a nice tan well before its first birthday.

Comment
The Wire Fox Terrier shares with the Smooth Fox Terrier wide universal recognition. The 2 breeds were considered coat varieties until quite recently, when they were separated. Like the Smooth Fox Terrier, the Wire was a sporting breed, used to work with mounted hunters chasing the fox. Its background includes several breeds that assured its bravery and determination at work.
"Asta," the canine hero of Dashiell Hammet's detective series *The Thin Man,* is a Wire Fox Terrier who made many friends for the breed through books, movies, and television. Because of the breed's great style and showmanship, some people have called the Wire the "chorus girl of the dog world." Together with the Smooth Fox Terrier, it accounts for more Westminster Bests in Show than any other breed.

Recommendation
A clever, handsome pet, this energetic breed is a good choice for a family with children. It should be taught to respond to simple commands, such as "come," "sit," "stay," or "no." The Wire Fox Terrier responds well to a firm hand, love, and plenty of exercise.

Plate 38

Toys

A Royal Tradition

Although many of the toys are rather modern in origin in comparison with other breeds, some do have a long history. The Pekingese probably traces back to the eighth century, when it was the favorite of the Chinese imperial court. The Maltese is even older—Publius, the Roman governor of Malta during the time of the Apostle Paul, had a Maltese whose gentle, frolicsome nature was immortalized in an epigram by the great poet Martial. The Italian Greyhound, the smallest of the gaze hounds—and a favorite of Queen Victoria, Catherine the Great of Russia, and Frederick the Great of Prussia, among others—is believed to have originated over 2000 years ago. The Pug, one of the oldest of all toys, has been known since before 400 B.C. Throughout history these little dogs have captured the hearts of artists, poets, royalty, and just plain folk. Today the toy group comprises seventeen breeds of the AKC smallest dogs.

Types of Toys

Since toys are basically small dogs, and many are quite low to the ground, the different breeds in this group are best distinguished from each other by two characteristics other than height: the length of their muzzle, or foreface, and their coat type. In five breeds, the muzzle is approximately the same length as the skull: Italian Greyhound, Toy Manchester Terrier, Miniature Pinscher, Toy Poodle, and Silky Terrier. Most toys, however, have a short foreface. In the Chihuahua, the Maltese, the Papillon, the Pomeranian, and the Yorkshire Terrier, the foreface is somewhat shortened. But it is extremely short or blunt—to the point of looking pushed in—in the Affenpinscher, the Brussels Griffon, the English Toy Spaniel, the Japanese Chin, the Pekingese, the Pug, and the Shih Tzu.

Most of the toy breeds have long coats, some of which even trail to the ground or are tied in elaborate topknots on the head. The eleven toys with long coats are the longhaired Chihuahua, the English Toy Spaniel, the Japanese Chin, the Maltese, the Papillon, the Pekingese, the Pomeranian, the Toy Poodle, the Shih Tzu, the Silky Terrier, and the Yorkshire Terrier. Because of their luxurious locks, these toys usually require a lot of grooming. In contrast, the smooth-haired toys need little time spent on their coats; these breeds include the smooth-haired Brussels Griffon, the smooth-haired Chihuahua, the Italian Greyhound, the Toy Manchester Terrier, the Miniature Pinscher, and the Pug. Additionally, there are two wirehaired breeds: the Affenpinscher, sometimes called the monkey dog because of its amusing expression; and its descendant, the rough-haired Brussels Griffon.

Bred for Companionship

Unlike most dog breeds developed for a specific working purpose—hunting, herding, or guarding the home—many toy breeds were deliberately bred to be tiny companions without any other use than friendship.

The ladies and gentlemen of royalty, and even those of lesser social degree, were often reluctant to keep larger dogs in their palaces and homes, but instead wanted a tiny pet that could easily be held in the lap or carried about. Toys from the Orient were held in such high esteem by the nobility that they were given to distinguished visitors as gifts. Today toys are as popular as ever, especially among city-dwellers and the elderly. Small in stature, toys are bright, alert, and hardy. They are able to adjust to any climate and require little space.

Affenpinscher

Personality
Fun-loving, affectionate, and easily trained. Highly intelligent, a characteristic somewhat camouflaged by a comic monkey-face expression. Terrier-like in many ways, but not particularly aggressive. Good watchdog. Extremely loyal to those it knows; very reserved with others. Does have a mind of its own and a strong desire to be spoiled.

Ideal Appearance
Height under 10¼"; smaller dogs, if equal in quality, preferred. Although standard does not specify weight, Affenpinschers should not weigh more than 7 or 8 pounds. Large eyes, a mustache, and a tuft of hair on chin give dog a monkey-face expression. Short foreface, slightly undershot jaw, and cropped ears. Forelegs straight; somewhat unique hind legs without much bend at stifle. Docked tail. Harsh, wirehaired coat is short on body, longer on head and legs. Permissible colors: black preferred; black with tan, red, gray, or other mixture acceptable. Very light colors or white markings are show faults. Black eyes.

Potential Health Problems
Generally fairly healthy. Teeth require special care. Moisture will at times create some skin difficulties between stop and nose. Somewhat restricted breathing. Susceptible to eye ulcers and infections. Possible slipped stifle and fractures.

Care and Exercise
To preserve proper coat texture, hand-trimming is required. Although clipping is permitted for pets, it destroys the wiry texture. Bathing tends to soften coat, and should be restricted to legs and whiskers. A firm brushing with a medium to harsh brush 2 or 3 times a week can replace a bath. Ear, tooth, and nail care are required weekly. This breed needs minimal exercise, which it can get by itself in a small area. The Affenpinscher benefits, however, from outdoor exercise—either free runs in a confined, safe area, or walks on a leash once or twice a day. Avoid chills and harsh or wet weather, as with all of the toys.

Puppies
Litter of 2 to 6 very small puppies born approximately 63 days after breeding. At birth puppies are black, but color changes. If litter exceeds 4 puppies, care should be taken to see that enough nutrition is being provided. If any puppies are not doing well, consult your veterinarian.

Comment
Of European origin, the Affenpinscher was known in the 17th century. Some contend it is the ancestor of the Brussels Griffon. Although there seems to be little or no concrete evidence to support this theory, the breeds are somewhat similar in many respects and may reasonably be assumed to be related to some degree. Not the best known of the toys, the Affenpinscher has always had a relatively small but loyal following.

Recommendation
Hardy, affectionate, and reasonably easy to care for, the Affenpinscher makes a wonderful pet and—surprisingly for a dog of this size—an excellent watchdog. It adjusts well to apartment or country living. This breed requires little exercise, but can play for hours. A fine companion for people who are limited in their physical activities. Any necessary adjustments will be made by the dog—It copes well and fits in easily.

Plate 14

Brussels Griffon

Characteristics
Short-faced
Smooth or rough coat
Stocky body
Short back
Well-developed
hindquarters
Docked tail

Personality
Lively and independent. Asserts itself at every opportunity. A great bluffer: With much bluster and kicking of the legs, the Brussels will act as the aggressor toward dogs 10 times its size. Intelligent and extremely affectionate. Can be stubborn and is not easily trained. A typical toy.

Ideal Appearance
Small, compact, athletic build. Males and bitches usually weigh 8 to 10 pounds; should not exceed 12 pounds. Although standard does not specify height, dogs usually measure about 8″ tall. 2 coat varieties: smooth, with a straight coat; and rough, with a longer, harsh coat, similar to that of the Affenpinscher. Its large eyes with sharp, alert expression and its undershot jaw reflect independent attitude. Very short foreface. Ears cropped or natural. Stocky body with wide, deep chest; short back; and well-developed hindquarters. Docked tail. Permissible colors: reddish-brown; black and reddish-brown; or black—except in smooth coat, in which solid black is not allowed. Black eyes with black rims.

Potential Health Problems
A healthy toy breed. Breathing is somewhat restricted due to short foreface; respiratory infections may occur. Moisture at times creates skin difficulties between stop and nose. Susceptible to eye ulcers, which can be avoided with proper cleaning. Also susceptible to grass allergies. Possible slipped stifle.

Care and Exercise
Smooth-coated dogs require little or no grooming, aside from routine care of nails, teeth, and ears. Brushing twice a week with a medium-textured brush should suffice. Rough-coated dogs should be hand-stripped, a process requiring some expertise on the part of the groomer. Can be clipped, but this eliminates the highly desirable harsh texture.
Breed requires little supervised exercise; will keep fit on its own in a small area. Does enjoy a good run, but should never be let free unless protected by fencing.

Puppies
Bitches conceive on an irregular basis. Whelping is difficult because of puppies' head size. Litters small, from 1 to 3 puppies. Limited success in raising newborns to 2 to 4 weeks; approximately 60 percent survive. Life expectancy 8 to 10 years. Both rough-coated and smooth-coated dogs can result from the same mating.

Comment
"Personality plus" describes this little bundle of energy from Belgium. Little is known of its ancestry, although it is believed by some that the Affenpinscher, the Yorkshire Terrier, the Pug, the Black and Tan Terrier, and the Ruby Spaniel might have played a part in the breed's development.
Originally used as a ratter in stables and on farms, the Brussels Griffon now serves as a companion and watchdog. It was imported to Great Britain sometime in the late 1880s, and then to the United States.

Recommendation
The Brussels Griffon adjusts to any environment as long as it gets affection, attention, and tolerance of its whims. Exuberant and somewhat boisterous, this breed is not recommended for those who desire a quiet, reserved lapdog. It is easily spoiled and was always intended to be!

Plate 13

Chihuahua

Characteristics
Very small
Delicate looking
Domed skull
Large prick ears
Large eyes
Sickle tail

Personality
Charming, curious, alert, and clean. Extremely affectionate toward those it considers family; reserved with others. Prefers to be the head of the household, but will tolerate others, once adjusted. Can be very temperamental.

Ideal Appearance
Very small; tiniest dog breed. Should not weigh more than 6 pounds, with 2 to 4 pounds preferred. Although standard does not specify height, dogs usually measure about 5″ tall. Apple-domed skull, with or without molera (soft spot on top of head where bones have not joined). Large ears. Back is slightly longer than height. Long sickle (looped) tail. 2 coat varieties: Smooth-coated dogs have soft, close-fitting hair with ruff on neck; long-coated dogs (roughs) have soft, long hair with fringe on ears and feathering on legs and tail; either variety can have undercoat. Permissible colors: any color in any combination, from sand-white to blue, mole, or black; tan markings acceptable. Eyes usually dark; light eyes acceptable with light coat.

Potential Health Problems
Fairly healthy overall. Moves rather uncertainly. In some dogs, soft spot in skull does not close; a blow in this area can produce serious damage or death. Bones are easily broken. Low blood sugar. Some older dogs subject to heart disease, arthritis, bleeding disorders, gum ailments, slipped stifle, and epilepsy.

Care and Exercise
Ears, nails, and teeth must be attended to weekly. For both coat varieties, brushing with a medium or soft brush twice a week will make frequent bathing unnecessary.
Minimal exercise needed; allowing dog to move about freely in apartment or room is sufficient. Avoid overexposure to extreme weather conditions, since this breed lacks the resistance of larger dogs.

Puppies
Small litters, generally from 1 to 4 puppies. Bitches often have difficulty whelping. Warmth should be provided for puppies, such as from a heating pad covered by a towel or blanket. As with all toy breeds, puppies develop very rapidly.

Comment
The history of the Chihuahua is quite speculative. The modern breed, discovered in about 1850 in the state of Chihuahua, Mexico, is believed to have descended from a small dog known to the Toltec Indians of Mexico in the 9th century. Some authorities think the Aztecs developed the Chihuahua by crossing a breed called *techichi* with a small, hairless dog that came to Mexico from Asia. Others trace the breed to the Spanish dogs that accompanied Hernando Cortes and his armies in 1519.
According to Indian legends, these little dogs had great religious significance. Archeologists working in Mexico and the southern United States have in fact unearthed dog bones buried in graves alongside their masters. It is said that dogs with blue coats were sacred, while those with red coats were sacrificed on the funeral pyre in the belief that the sins of their masters would be transferred to the dog, allowing the soul to make the trip to the hereafter untarnished.

Recommendation
The ultimate lapdog, this breed responds well to comfort and companionship. It is definitely not an outdoor dog, although it does like a short run in warm weather. Quick to learn, and easily paper-trained. Because it is fragile, the Chihuahua is not for small children.

Plates 17, 18

English Toy Spaniel

Characteristics
Large body
Big head
Turned-up nose
Large, wide-set eyes
Colorful coat
Feathering
Docked tail

Personality
Affectionate, playful companion that enjoys comfort. Attentive but not demanding. Gets along well with other dogs. Needs to be treated with respect. Good little watchdog.

Ideal Appearance
One of larger toys, weighing 9 to 12 pounds. Although standard does not specify height, males usually measure about 10″ tall; bitches, approximately 9″. Large, well-rounded skull. Turned-up, short, black nose, and distinct stop between large, dark, wide-set eyes. Square, deep muzzle; tongue should not protrude. Long, low-set ears with abundant feathering. Short body with wide chest, broad back, and sturdy bones. Docked tail. Long, soft, thick wavy coat on ears, chest, backs of legs, and feet. 2 color varieties, solid and mixed (broken). Solid red dog, called Ruby, is chestnut-red overall with small amount of white, allowed only on chest. Another solid-colored variety, called King Charles, has black on most of its body, with tan over eyes, and on muzzle, chest, and legs; a few white hairs are allowed on chest, but a white spot disqualifies it from show. A 2-color mixed variety in red and white, called Blenheim, is white with red on ears and cheeks, and a dime-size red blaze on forehead. A tricolor mixed variety in white, black, and tan, called Prince Charles, has white ground; large black markings; and tan over eyes, on chest, legs, and feet, and lining ears and vent; lacks red forehead blaze.

Potential Health Problems
A hardy toy. Moisture may cause ear infections, eye irritations, and inflammation of stop. Possible retention of first teeth, dislocation of joints, and respiratory problems.

Care and Exercise
Daily brushing required to prevent long hair from matting. Bathe once a week, taking care to keep soap from entering eyes, and water out of ears. Needs immediate, thorough drying.
This breed requires limited exercise. Should not be exposed too often to cement or blacktop, since legs and feet stain. Avoid long grass and brush, which damage long coat.

Puppies
Whelping can be difficult. Normal litter of 2 to 4 puppies, which gain strength quite rapidly. Puppies mature by 2 years of age.

Comment
Although a favorite lapdog of British royalty for over 300 years, the English Toy Spaniel did not originate in England, but probably came there from Japan—or perhaps China—by way of Spain. No one really knows for sure. The Asian imports were most likely crossed with the Springer Spaniel and other small cocker types, which explains the breed's lingering hunting instincts. Regardless of its ancestry, the Toy Spaniel was always intended as a companion animal. Mary, Queen of Scots, is said to have kept several English Toy Spaniels, and even died with one by her side. The names of the 4 color types all derive from English nobility, with the King Charles variety being in honor of the 17th-century Charles II. The 4 types are identical except for their coloring.

Recommendation
Despite its somewhat dour expression, the English Toy Spaniel is sturdy, fun-loving, and happy. It adjusts very well to either city or country environments and—unlike many toy breeds—is hardy enough for small children. An alert little watchdog, this toy is tougher than it looks.

Plates 9, 10, 11, 12

Italian Greyhound

Characteristics
Slender build
Long, narrow head
Graceful, arched neck
Arched back
Long tail
Regal but fragile look
High-stepping action

Personality
Very affectionate and playful with those it knows; reserved toward others. Sensitive to the point that a harsh word is the only reprimand needed for correction. May be difficult to housebreak. If left alone, can be vindictive.

Ideal Appearance
Very slender and finely made, like the Greyhound, although smaller. Males and bitches, 13″ to 15″ tall. Although standard does not specify weight, both sexes weigh up to 15 pounds—usually 8 pounds, but sometimes as little as 5 pounds. Long, narrow head with dark nose and dark, intelligent eyes. Small, rose-shaped ears. Long, graceful, well-arched neck. Medium-length back with definite curve starting at loin, dropping off to long tail. Short, glossy coat. Permissible colors: any; all markings acceptable except those that are brindle or tan.

Potential Health Problems
A fairly healthy breed. Slender legs may break or wrench. Very susceptible to chills and must be protected. Low blood sugar. Joints easily dislocated, particularly the knee. May experience deterioration of ball of the hip.

Care and Exercise
If coat is brushed twice a week and rubbed down with a damp towel, only infrequent bathing required. Minimal exercise necessary and is best given on a leash because, like all hounds, the Italian Greyhound tends to run at top speed, without regard to safety, when given the opportunity for a chase. Should never be exposed to drafts or inclement weather.

Puppies
Generally 3 to 5 very small and fragile puppies in a litter. Whelping usually with little or no difficulty. Puppies retain birth color, although colors other than white sometimes change a shade.

Comment
A prized breed in Renaissance Italy, the Italian Greyhound was known throughout continental Europe and in England. These dogs were painted along with their aristocratic masters by such celebrated artists as Giotto, Carpaccio, Bosch, and David. Yet this breed's noble lineage goes back much further—to about 2000 years ago: In the area that now comprises Greece and Turkey, archeologists have discovered tiny skeletons of Greyhound-like dogs.
The modern breed was developed in Italy —hence its name. A fine pet and companion, the Italian Greyhound was never used for hunting game, at least in its modern form. It has always had a regal look; indeed, it has shared more than one throne.

Recommendation
The Italian Greyhound prefers a warm, comfortable resting place near its human companions, rather than excessive fondling or cuddling. This breed is a good choice for a person who seeks a mild-mannered, small, and elegant dog without the spoiled nature of some toys.

Plate 52

Japanese Chin

Characteristics
Compact body
Large, broad head
Small, hanging ears
Long hair
Fluffy tail
Self-satisfied look

Personality
Perky, sensitive little aristocrat that carries itself with pride. Intelligent, with a mind of its own—can be obstinate. Very playful with those it loves, reserved with others. Never aggressive. Receptive to training, although little is required as it seems to be born with impeccable manners.

Ideal Appearance
Compact build. 2 sizes: 7 pounds and under and those over 7 pounds, with smaller dogs preferred. Although standard does not specify height, Japanese Chins are usually about 9″ tall. Large, broad head with short muzzle, wide-set eyes, and small V-shaped ears. Square body, with tail carried over back. Long, straight, silky coat, with a ruff at neck and feathering on ears, thighs, and tail. Permissible colors: black and white, or red and white (red includes all shades of sable, brindle, lemon, or orange). Nose color should match markings. Dark eyes.

Potential Health Problems
A fairly healthy breed. Breathing difficulties, particularly when overheated. Susceptible to irritation at stop if not kept dry and clean. Weather extremes can be dangerous or even fatal. Eyes susceptible to irritation and inflammation. May dislocate joints, particularly the knee. Low blood sugar. Sometimes retention of first teeth and failure of skull to close.

Care and Exercise
Light brushing required, with particular attention to longer hair to prevent tangles. Bathe when needed, which should not be often, taking care to dry completely. If paper-trained, requires little outdoor exercise, although the Japanese Chin does enjoy running and playing.

Puppies
Whelping can be difficult. Litters average from 1 to 3 puppies, which develop quite rapidly. Care must be taken for the first 2 to 3 weeks after birth. Puppies of various colors can appear in same litter.

Comment
Formerly called the Japanese Spaniel. There is little doubt that this breed was first developed in China, long before it was brought to England and America from Japan in the mid-1880s by Commodore Matthew Perry (who gave a pair of Japanese dogs to Queen Victoria). For various reasons, later importations to America became limited, and further development of the breed took place in England. Perhaps this accounts for current differences in size and coat texture.

The breed name was officially changed in 1977, because many felt the old name was deceiving since there is no spaniel blood in the Chin's ancestry. The name "spaniel" has often been misused, but in this case it has been corrected.

Recommendation
This lively, clean little dog thrives on affection and pampering. It does well in all home situations and readily accepts new environments if not uprooted from its family. It likes children, but will not tolerate rough handling. This is an ideal dog for those that desire a quiet, obedient companion.

Plate 7

Maltese

Characteristics
Very small
Long, silky coat
Long hair on head
and tail
Short body
White

Personality
Joyful little extrovert. Lively and active. Insists on being involved in all family activities. Can be very strong-willed. Resents being forced, but will respond well to patient insistence. Owner must make peace with the individual dog's personality or there will be a stand-off.

Ideal Appearance
Very small dog with long, silky hair reaching to ground. Dogs should weigh under 7 pounds, with 4 to 6 pounds preferred. Although standard does not specify height, dogs usually measure about 5″ tall. Somewhat rounded skull with long hair on head, round eyes, and close-hanging, feathered ears. Short body has level topline. Tail carried over back, covered with long hair. No undercoat. Permissible colors: pure white; light fawn or lemon allowed on ears, though not desirable. Dark eyes with black rims; black nose.

Potential Health Problems
A generally healthy toy. Eyes tear a lot and require constant care. Conversely, may have inadequate tear production. Teeth should be watched carefully, and a balanced diet should not be seriously varied. Frequently allergic to grass. Possible slipped stifle, and respiratory and skin problems.

Care and Exercise
Coat needs a great deal of attention. It stains easily, particularly around eyes and mouth. Bathing essential at least once a week. Brushing unclean hair is detrimental, making it harder to keep dog clean later. Coat may discolor. For show purposes, hair on head may be done in topknot and tied with a ribbon, or it may be left hanging; it should be brushed out and redone every day. Nonshow pets can be trimmed, but some of the dog's beauty is lost with trimming.
Breed requires little exercise and in fact should not go outdoors in bad weather, but be paper-trained. Indoor play provides sufficient exercise. Avoid excess heat and chills. Low body bulk leaves all toys vulnerable to the effects of weather.

Puppies
From 2 to 4 puppies in a litter. Some are born with light fawn markings about the ears, which normally turn white within 2 to 4 months. Eye rims and noses darken with age. Life expectancy is from 9 to 11 years.

Comment
One of the oldest dog breeds, the Maltese comes from the Island of Malta, or Melita, which was settled around 1500 B.C. by the Phoenicians. Literature and paintings dating to Greek and Roman times indicate that a small white dog resembling today's breed was carried about as a pet and companion. By the time of Queen Elizabeth, this tiny dog was so highly prized by ladies of the court that it is said that Maltese were selling for the equivalent of thousands of dollars. The Maltese is probably related to the spaniel family, but definitely not to the terriers, as has been suggested.

Recommendation
This breed is recommended for owners interested in an alert, busy little dog that requires more than average coat care. Does not mix especially well with other pets. It is easy to spoil, although not particularly a lapdog.

Plate 6

Toy Manchester Terrier

Characteristics
Smart, clean look
Narrow, wedge-
shaped head
Erect ears
Smooth coat
Slightly arched back
Whiplike tail

Personality
Inquisitive, alert, and active. Must investigate any sound or movement. Good watchdog: will alert its master if things are amiss. Fond of comfort, affection, and play. Likes to hunt if given the opportunity. May be overly aggressive toward other animals.

Ideal Appearance
Miniature version of Manchester Terrier. Toy variety is often separated into dogs 7 pounds and under and those over 7 pounds but under 12. Should not exceed 12 pounds. Although standard does not specify height, Toy Manchesters usually measure about 6″ or 7″ tall. Long, narrow, wedge-shaped head. Level or scissors bite. Naturally erect, close-set ears, with pointed tips. Slim, graceful neck. Forechest is narrow between the legs, with deep brisket. Broad rib cage, medium-short body, with slight arched back. Straight forelegs. Moderately long whiplike tail, thick at base, tapering to point, carried straight off back. Short, smooth, shiny, thick coat. Permissible colors: jet black, with mahogany markings over eyes, on cheeks and chest, and under tail; tan on lower part of legs. Black lines on toes, black nails, and black thumb mark on foreleg between pastern and knee. White in any area is undesirable; only a white spot less than ½″ is allowed. Dark eyes.

Potential Health Problems
Fairly healthy, but sensitive to cold and damp weather. Some eye problems may occur. Teeth should be carefully monitored, and good balanced diet must be maintained faithfully. May experience deterioration of the ball of the hip. Possible skin ailments, fractures, and slipped stifle.

Care and Exercise
Little coat care required aside from regular brushing with a natural-bristle brush twice a week. Bathing is rarely needed. Exercises itself well in a small area but enjoys a run when possible. If not in country setting, needs long walks as part of its routine.

Puppies
Litters consist of from 3 to 5 puppies. They develop quickly, maturing at just over 1 year. Life expectancy is 10 to 11 years.

Comment
The Toy Manchester Terrier is a derivative of the standard variety of the Manchester Terrier, which was known in England before the 16th century as the Black and Tan Terrier. Although the breed could be found throughout England, it became associated with Manchester, which was the breeding center in the late 19th century.
The toy and the standard varieties were considered separate breeds until 1959, but are now registered as one breed with 2 varieties and are judged by the same rules. The only distinction is in size and in the ears: the larger dog's ears may be erect, button, or cropped, and its weight is over 12 pounds, while Toy Manchesters may not have cropped ears and must be under 12 pounds.

Recommendation
This intelligent, responsive pet does well either alone or paired with a Toy Manchester of the opposite sex. This breed is not for those interested in a quiet lapdog, as it is a terrier in a very small package. The Toy Manchester adapts perfectly well to apartment life and is a good, alert watchdog.

Plate 51

Miniature Pinscher

Characteristics
Small, wedge-shaped head
Square body
Level back
Deep chest
Smooth, shiny coat
Short, docked tail

Personality
Vibrant, vivacious, and perky—always on the go. Affectionate and playful. Tends to be aggressive in spite of its size. Can be destructive if left alone too long. A very proud and dynamic little dog.

Ideal Appearance
Resembles small Doberman. Males and bitches must be between 10″ and 12½″ tall for competition; 11″ to 11½″ is preferred. Although standard does not specify weight, males usually weigh about 10 pounds; bitches, around 9 pounds. Wedge-shaped head. Ears may be natural or cropped. Square body with deep chest and firm topline that slopes slightly toward rear. High-set, docked tail; short tail and level back immediately distinguishes this breed from the Toy Manchester. Smooth coat. Permissible colors: solid red, black with tan markings, or chocolate with rust markings. Dark brown or black eyes; black nose except in chocolates, which have chocolate-colored noses.

Potential Health Problems
Overall perhaps the hardiest of the toy breeds. Teeth must be checked regularly for dietary problems. Tends to dislocate joints, particularly the knee.

Care and Exercise
Bathing not required. Instead, brush once or twice a week and rub down with damp cloth. Nails and ears must be attended to weekly.
Once a day, walk on a leash or let loose in an escape-proof area for a short time to enable it to release abundant energy. Male has a tendency to mark its territory, as do all breeds that are of an aggressive nature. Care must be taken during cold weather since it has little coat protection.

Puppies
Generally from 2 to 4 puppies in a litter. Puppies become very active in 3 to 4 weeks. They reach maturity within 2 years. Life expectancy is 10 to 11 years.

Comment
Developed in Germany, the Miniature Pinscher is very similar in appearance to the Doberman Pinscher. It is at times mistakenly referred to as the Miniature Doberman, although the 2 breeds are not related, and the Miniature Pinscher is actually a few centuries older.
This breed was brought to the United States in the 1920s, where it soon became quite popular both as a pet and as a watchdog. The Minpin, as it is affectionately known, has also appeared on the stage. Its intelligence, smart appearance, and fearless self-assurance make it an appealing companion.

Recommendation
An excellent, hardy dog for the lively, fun-loving family. The Miniature Pinscher is good with children and adjusts quickly to new situations. It should not be left to its own devices too long. Rather noisy, but makes an excellent watchdog. It does not care for excessive pampering. This breed will soon run the home if not stopped.

Plate 20

Papillon

Characteristics
Large, wide,
feathered ears
Pointed muzzle
Particolored coat
Long, flowing hair on
chest and tail
Breeches on hind legs

Personality
Bright, active, and extremely alert.
Interested in everything that goes on.
Thrives in the company of human
companions and other pets. Can be
snippy if it feels put upon or threatened.
Will readily take on much larger animals
—does not seem to know it is small.

Ideal Appearance
Small dog with wide ears. Males and
bitches, 8″ to 11″ tall; over 12″
disqualifies. Weight should be in
proportion to height. Although no
standard has been set, males usually
weigh about 10 pounds; bitches,
approximately 8 pounds. Small skull,
somewhat rounded between large ears
with rounded tips; ears either upright or
drop. Muzzle is pointed and much
thinner than skull. Body slightly longer
than high, with level topline. Long,
high-set tail carried over back in arch.
Long, silky coat, profuse on tail and
chest; feathering on backs of forelegs
forming breeches on upper hind legs. No
undercoat. Permissible colors: always
parti-colored; white ground with patches
of any color covering ears and extending
over eyes. Coats that are all white or
have no white disqualify. Dark eyes;
black nose.

Potential Health Problems
Overall a healthy toy. May have
inadequate tear production and low
blood sugar. Subject to slipped stifles,
fractures, and deterioration of ball of
hip.

Care and Exercise
Light brushing twice a week. Coat stains
easily, particularly on feet and legs.
Bathe occasionally using baby shampoo.
Coat may be blow-dried once the dog is
conditioned to it. No trimming
necessary. Ears should be kept very
clean. Easily paper-trained.
Required exercise can usually be
accomplished by allowing dog to run
loose indoors. This is an active, playful
breed that will exercise itself with
another dog or even a cat.

Puppies
Whelping is normal. From 2 to 4
puppies in a litter. For the first 2 or 3
weeks, puppies must be kept warm and
well-nurtured. Life expectancy is 10 to
12 years. Both ear types can appear in
the same litter.

Comment
Because its large, feathered ears and
patched face markings resemble a
butterfly's outstretched wings, this breed
was named Papillon (which is French for
butterfly). The Papillon's country of
origin is unknown; however, the French
are given credit for the development of
the breed. Some trace its ancestry to the
16th-century dwarf spaniel that became
highly fashionable with the French
court, after having traveled from Spain
via Bologna, Italy. Both Madame de
Pompadour and Marie Antoinette are
said to have kept these smart-looking,
dainty dogs. From France the Papillon
was imported to England and then to the
United States, where it gained
recognition by the American Kennel
Club in 1935.

Recommendation
An exceptionally fine companion, the
Papillon adjusts easily to different
climates and to changes in environment.
It does well in country or city and in
large or small family situations. This
breed likes to be pampered and seems to
have been created to be spoiled. It is,
however, a serious little dog and will
assert itself.

Plate 5

Pekingese

Characteristics
Lionlike mane
Large, broad head
Short, wrinkled muzzle
Broad chest
Bowed forelegs
Long coat

Personality
Lovable, comic companion, yet independent and strong-willed. Insists on having its own way. Can be aloof toward strangers. A happy, inquisitive breed that can be very possessive of its owner and its territory.

Ideal Appearance
Lionlike mane on small dog. Males and bitches, up to 14 pounds; medium-size dogs preferred. Although standard does not specify height, males usually measure about 9″ tall; bitches, approximately 8″. Large, broad, wide head. Broad, short nose; large, round, dark eyes; and heart-shaped ears with feathering that extends below short, broad, wrinkled muzzle. Broad-chested body. Short, bowed forelegs. High-set tail carried over back. Long, flat coat with thick undercoat; feathering on neck, legs, tail, and toes, heaviest on neck. Permissible colors: any, including black, red, fawn, black and tan, sable, white, brindle, and parti-colored. Black mask and spectacles around eyes, with lines to ears, desirable.

Potential Health Problems
Generally hardy toy. Susceptible to eye injuries and infections. Extra care must be taken when handling the eye area, since pressure can easily force the eye out of the socket. Immediately call a veterinarian under these circumstances. Skin infections and breathing difficulties during hot weather. Kidney stones, herniated discs, and slipped stifles are possible. Sometimes inadequate tear production.

Care and Exercise
Needs frequent brushing, at least 3 or 4 times a week. Avoid bathing because it breaks coat down. Instead, lightly dust coat with cleansing powder, such as corn starch or baby powder, then dampen lightly with water using an atomizer. Trimming not required.

Normal indoor activity is sufficient, but young dogs do like some outdoor exercise and play. Eyes must be cared for daily. Consult veterinarian about possible use of eye salve.

Puppies
Litter of 2 to 4 puppies after difficult whelping. Life expectancy of 10 to 12 years.

Comment
Highly regarded by the Chinese imperial family and even believed to be sacred, the Pekingese has an ancient Chinese lineage, with written records dating from the T'ang Dynasty of the 7th and 8th centuries. It probably existed much earlier. This breed's distinctive appearance inspired numerous unusual names—among them Lion Dog, because of its massive front and profuse mane; and Sleeve Dog, because very small dogs were carried inside their owners' sleeves (this practice is still known today). The breed is surrounded by all sorts of romantic legends. Supposedly robbers were punished by death if they stole a royal pet, and the Pekingese was intentionally bred with short, bowed legs to prevent straying. The story of the Pekingese's arrival in the West is equally colorful—apparently a few dogs were stolen during the British plundering of the royal palace in 1860. To prevent the soldiers from seizing more, the remaining pets were all slaughtered by the Chinese. The breed gained AKC recognition in 1909. Today it is one of the most popular toys.

Recommendation
Not for owners that demand instant response. A hardy breed, it adjusts well to change and gets along well with adults. Not recommended for small children.

Plate 2

Pomeranian

Characteristics
Foxlike head
Frill of hair on chest
Short body
Curled, bushy tail
Feathering on forelegs
and hindquarters
Sled-dog build

Personality
Pleasant, friendly, and somewhat excitable. Intelligent and alert. Can be inquisitive to the point that it may become annoying. Tends to be noisy. A dog with pride, style and tenacity. Cannot be left out of a game.

Ideal Appearance
Small sled-dog look. Males and bitches, 3 to 7 pounds, ideally 4 to 5 pounds for show. Although standard does not specify height, males usually measure approximately 7″ tall; bitches, about 6½″. Foxlike, wedge-shaped head with dark, almond-shaped eyes; small, erect ears; and definite stop. Frill of hair below neck on chest. Short back with level topline. High-set tail carried flat over back. Double coat: soft undercoat, and harsh outer coat in which hair stands out off body. Abundant feathering on backs of forelegs, on hindquarters, and on tail. Permissible colors: any solid color, with or without shading in same color or in sable or black; white and any solid; sable; or black and tan. Black nose, dark eyes, eye rims, and area around eyes.

Potential Health Problems
Fairly healthy toy. Susceptible to tooth decay, tooth loss at early age, and gum disorders. May get tear stains under eyes or have inadequate tear production. Prone to skin hormonal disorders. Soft spot on skull may fail to close. Low blood sugar, epilepsy, progressive retinal atrophy, tracheal collapse, and congenital heart disease possible.

Care and Exercise
Daily brushing is essential to maintain thick, bushy coat, particularly in summer when shedding. Avoid bathing because it destroys the coat; it is essential to blow-dry after bathing. Lightly sprinkle baby powder into the coat and dampen lightly with water from an atomizer while brushing. Requires weekly dental care to prevent mouth disorders. Wash eyes daily. Minimal exercise required. With patience, can be easily trained.

Puppies
From 1 to 3 puppies in a litter after normal whelping. Color at birth often changes as puppies grow. They mature early in 1 to 1½ years. Full coat may take 2 years to develop. Life expectancy is 9 to 11 years.

Comment
Originally a much larger dog used for herding, this breed was first noticed in Pomerania—hence its name. It is considered a member of the Spitz family, a group of Northern sled dogs that includes the Samoyed, the Norwegian Elkhound, the Chow Chow, and other Arctic breeds. In England, through careful breeding, the Pomeranian was reduced in size from a huge 30-pound working breed to the diminutive 4- or 5-pound toy affectionately called the Pom. Recognized in America in 1900, the breed has since undergone further size reduction.

Recommendation
This fine family companion thrives in a busy atmosphere. Despite its small stature, it is a capable watchdog. It adjusts well to climatic changes and new situations, and is an excellent apartment dog for people who do not like walking at night or in bad weather, as it can be paper-trained. The Pomeranian is happy in almost any situation, as long as it is pampered by its family.

Plate 16

Toy Poodle

Characteristics
Tiny
Long, lean head
Square build
Curly or corded coat
Fancy clip
Docked tail

Personality
Pert, lively, and playful. Highly intelligent and willing to please. This most popular of the toy breeds is easily trained. Vain about its smart appearance.

Ideal Appearance
Toy size variety of Poodle. Males and bitches, 10″ or under. Although standard does not specify weight, Toy Poodles usually weigh 5 to 7 pounds. Long, lean head; moderately rounded skull with chiseling under its dark, oval-shaped eyes. Long, wide, heavily feathered ears, set just below eye level. Square body with level topline; slight hollow just behind withers. Small, oval feet. High-set, docked tail, carried up. Harsh, dense coat may be curly or corded. Accepted show trims: puppy (under 1 years old), English saddle, continental, and sporting (the latter in noncompetitive classes only). Permissible colors: all solids; combinations of colors not permitted.

Potential Health Problems
Generally a healthy toy. Susceptible to early tooth loss. May get tear stains under eyes. Ears tend to become infected due to poor air circulation; hair should be plucked from ear canals. Possible eye problems such as degeneration of the retina. Other potential difficulties include low blood sugar, congenital heart disease, epilepsy, slipped stifles, and tracheal collapse.

Care and Exercise
Requires weekly bathing and brushing, particularly if has fancy show coat. Blow-dry while brushing after bath. Needs professional clipping and trimming every 3 to 6 weeks, because—unlike other breeds—hair grows fast and has no natural maximum length. Ears must be cleaned frequently. Teeth should be checked regularly for loosening. Check with a veterinarian for instructions and help.

Requires a good daily run in an area free of long grass or brush, unless coat is in pet trim. If a run is impossible, substitute long walks on a leash.

Puppies
Litter of 2 to 5 puppies after normal whelping. Birth color changes as puppies grow. Early physical maturity, at 1 to 1½ years, but full coat may take 2 years to develop. Life expectancy is 9 to 11 years.

Comment
An all-time favorite, the Toy Poodle is not a distinct breed, but is instead a size classification of the Poodle, along with the standard and the miniature. Although the larger, standard Poodle—which is over 15″ tall—is generally accepted as the oldest type, there is little question that toys were the well-established, pampered pets of royalty during the 18th century in both England and France. Highly intelligent and easily trained, all sizes of the Poodle were used in dog acts throughout Europe. Unlike the standard, the Toy Poodle was never a sporting dog; it was developed exclusively as a companion animal. This small version retains all the other attributes of its larger ancestors.

Recommendation
The Toy Poodle makes an excellent family dog, as it adjusts to any situation and responds well to other pets and children. Like the other toy breeds, it is ideally suited for apartment life, although it does require some exercise—either daily walks on a leash or runs in a protected park. This breed is only for those who are willing to devote considerable time and expense to coat care. A superb pet breed. One of the most intelligent of all dogs.

Plate 15

Pug

Characteristics
Large, deeply
wrinkled head
Black mask
Short, pushed-in
muzzle
Broad chest
Curled tail

Personality
Impish and good-humored—the jester of the toy breeds. Always friendly and playful, the Pug is ready to frolic at all times. Learns quickly, but responds to commands only when it is good and ready. Headstrong, but it is difficult to remain angry with a Pug.

Ideal Appearance
Longest toy. Males and bitches, 14 to 18 pounds. Although standard does not specify height, Pugs usually measure about 10″ or 11″ tall. Large, massive, deeply wrinkled head with black mask; short, square muzzle. Small, thin, button or rose ears. Large, dark, round eyes have soft expression. Short body with broad chest. Tail curled tightly over hip. Soft, fine coat. Permissible colors: black, silver-fawn, or apricot-fawn; fawn requires a black line, called a trace, from occiput to tail.

Potential Health Problems
Overall a fairly healthy toy. Breathing difficulties when overheated and other respiratory difficulties due to short foreface. Prone to heart problems, eye injury, and irritation of the stop. Possible disc disease, slipped stifle, and demodectic mange.

Care and Exercise
Requires brushing at least twice a week, bathing when necessary. Sheds heavily. Some trimming required for show. Stop must be kept clean and dry. Needs to have its eyes washed every other day. Can be a picky eater unless its owner is insistent.

Requires more exercise than most toys, preferably an outdoors walk at least once a day. Must be watched closely in hot weather to monitor possible breathing problems. Snores when asleep.

Puppies
Litter of from 2 to 5 puppies. Whelping can be difficult. Puppies mature at 2 to 3 years. Life expectancy is 9 to 11 years.

Comment
Thought to have originated in China sometime before 400 B.C., the Pug was the favorite pet of Tibetan monks and became popular in Japan. During the 16th century, the breed was adopted as a mascot by the Dutch House of Orange after a Pug reportedly warned the prince of approaching Spanish invaders. By the late 1700s, the popularity of the Pug spread throughout Europe.

In later centuries, its popularity declined to such a degree that some believed the breed would become extinct. Since being imported to the United States, however, the number of Pugs has increased steadily.

Recommendation
The Pug is a fun-loving, impulsive little creature that enjoys life and those with whom it resides. It responds well to other pets and children, but this varies from dog to dog. At home in an apartment or a house, it adjusts well to any situation. It is easy to spoil.

Plate 42

Shih Tzu

Characteristics
Long, flowing coat
Long mustache
Square muzzle
Looks like a small
Lhasa Apso

Personality
Lively and gay—charming manner wins the hearts of all. Thrives on human companionship. Friendly, but will tolerate no nonsense. Proud and stately. Somewhat stubborn, although very receptive to training. Easy to spoil.

Ideal Appearance
Small dog with luxurious, flowing coat. Appears to have a pronounced mustache. Males and bitches, 8″ to 11″ tall and 9 to 18 pounds; ideal size, 9″ to 10½″ and 12 to 15 pounds. Broad, round head. Square, short, unwrinkled muzzle with pronounced stop. Dark, large, appealing round eyes. Large, long, hanging ears. Body slightly longer than high, with level topline and broad, deep chest. Rather large, firm feet, with hair between pads. High-set tail carried over back. Long, dense coat with undercoat may be wavy but not curly. All colors permissible. Black nose, except in dogs with liver markings, which may have liver nose.

Potential Health Problems
Fairly healthy toy. Subject to breathing difficulties, respiratory infections, eye injury and irritations, and inadequate tear production. Tendency toward bad teeth and retention of first teeth; teeth need weekly care. Kidney problems and slipped stifles are common. Possible allergic skin disease and ear problems.

Care and Exercise
Requires weekly brushing and bathing for show purposes. Must be blown dry after bath. No trimming needed, but cute pet trims are available. Check eyes daily. Head hair should be kept up with a rubber band or a barrette, which helps prevent eye irritations. Attend to ears weekly and check teeth routinely. Needs minimal exercise. If dog has very full coat, paper train and keep indoors to maintain show elegance. Avoid weather extremes of any kind.

Puppies
From 2 to 4 puppies in a litter. Whelping sometimes difficult. Coat color changes after birth. Dogs mature at 1½ to 2 years. Life expectancy 10 to 12 years.

Comment
The Shih Tzu—whose name means "lion" in Chinese—is believed to be of Tibetan origin and could be related to the Pekingese, but this is not certain. During the 7th century, these tiny dogs with long, flowing locks captivated the Chinese imperial court and were immortalized in countless sculptures and paintings. Up until the revolution, the breed remained one of the favorite house pets of Chinese royalty.

Imported into England from China in about 1930, the breed was brought to the United States after World War II by returning servicemen and was accepted by the American Kennel Club registry in 1969. Since then the Shih Tzu's popularity has grown rapidly.

Recommendation
Very affectionate and hardy, the Shih Tzu gets along well with children, if not handled roughly. It loves the outdoors and likes to play in all weather; for show purposes, however, it must be kept indoors to protect its coat. Quick-moving, the Shih Tzu responds well in a family situation. An owner should be prepared to spend time on grooming this stylish breed.

Plate 28

Silky Terrier

Characteristics
Resembles Yorkshire,
but larger with
shorter hair
Long, low-set build
Docked tail
Fine, silky coat
Robust

Personality
Mentally and physically quick. Feisty
and independent like a true terrier. Can
be rather aggressive toward other pets.
Not particularly friendly toward
strangers. Possessive of home territory.
Somewhat noisy. Despite all these
seeming shortcomings, this breed's
following is intense and growing in size.

Ideal Appearance
Males and bitches, 9″ to 10″ tall and 8 to
10 pounds; very small size is not
desirable. Moderately long, wedge-
shaped head. Flat skull, somewhat
longer than foreface, not too wide
between ears. Erect, V-shaped ears.
Small, piercing, dark eyes. Body longer
than high, with level topline dropping
slightly over loins. Moderate angulation
of bone between stifle and hock in rear.
High-set tail, docked and carried
upright. Small, round feet with dark
nails. Fine, silky, flat coat is rather long
on body; profuse on top of head; short on
face, ears, and legs from knee and hock
joints to feet. Hair parted on head and
down back to root of tail. Permissible
colors: tan and various shades of blue
(silver-blue, pigeon-blue, or slate-blue).

Potential Health Problems
Overall a robust dog. Eyes and teeth
must be monitored to catch developing
problems.

Care and Exercise
Brush every day and bathe once a week.
Coat mats easily if not cared for.
More active than most toy breeds, the
Silky needs daily runs or walks on leash.
Will chase other animals without regard
for its own safety if allowed to run free.

Puppies
Litters of from 3 to 5 puppies after
normal whelping. Mature at 1½ to 2
years. Life expectancy of 10 to 12 years.

Comment
Developed in Sydney, Australia, by
crossing the Australian Terrier with the
Yorkshire Terrier, the Silky Terrier was
originally known as the Sydney Silky. It
was quite popular, both as a city pet and
as a ratter on poultry farms. Stories of its
use as a mine guard are unlikely but
amusing. Imported into the United
States in the early 1950s, the Silky
Terrier was accepted by the American
Kennel Club in 1959.

Recommendation
Active, spirited and energetic, the Silky
Terrier tolerates children if handled
properly. It is bent on doing things in
its own way at all times, and objects to
variations in routine. Inclined to be
noisy, it makes a good watchdog. This
breed should have obedience training, to
which it responds well. If training is not
provided, the Silky will take over the
household, which it generally tries to do
most of the time.

Plate 4

Yorkshire Terrier

Characteristics
Tiny
Compact, low-set
build
Docked tail with long
fall of hair
Long, silky coat
Very stylish look

Personality
The ultimate pampered pet. Assertive and affectionate. A Yorkie expects to sit on someone's lap or to be taken along, no matter what the plan. If left behind for a time, may misbehave. A bundle of energy. Eager to express its point of view. Good watchdog despite its size. Very intelligent.

Ideal Appearance
Tiny. Yorkshires weigh up to 7 pounds, but can be as light as 2 or 3 pounds. Although standard does not specify height, dogs usually measure 6″ to 7″ tall. Small head with rather flat top. Dark eyes with dark rims. Small, erect, V-shaped ears. Compact body with level topline. Round feet with black nails. Glossy, fine, silky coat hangs evenly to ground; is straight, not wavy. Coat is very important; is parted on face and from head to docked tail. Permissible colors: steel-blue on back and tail; golden tan on head, chest, and legs. Black nose.

Potential Health Problems
Generally healthy overall. Susceptible to eye irritations and inadequate tear production. Tendency toward early tooth loss and bad breath. Low blood sugar, epilepsy, slipped stifles, liver disease, and progressive retinal atrophy possible.

Care and Exercise
Needs daily brushing to keep long coat in finest condition, and periodic professional grooming. Usually long topknot is tied with a ribbon in center of head. Some alternative nonshow trims are often used to reduce the task of grooming a Yorkie. Bathing should be done with great care to avoid chills. Blow-dry after bath. Requires almost no exercise; running about inside an apartment or house is sufficient. Paper-train and keep indoors rather than expose a Yorkshire Terrier to bad weather and the risk of chills.

Puppies
Usually 3 puppies in a litter. Very tiny bitches may have trouble delivering even 1 or 2 pups; indeed some are too small to risk breeding. Puppies are born black, with tan markings over eyebrows and on chin, chest, and feet. Mature in 2 years.

Comment
Developed in Yorkshire, England, during the Victorian period, this tiny toy derived from a mixture of terrier breeds, not all of which have survived. Originally a workers' dog—and a particular favorite of British weavers—the Yorkie was soon adopted by all classes. This breed has been shown in the United States since 1878. Like the toy poodle, it is now a status symbol. Good Yorkshires can be expensive.

Recommendation
The Yorkshire Terrier is an excellent pet for those who want to fuss and to be cared about in return. Easily trained, it can learn almost anything, although most people spoil their Yorkies. The breed is fine with children as long as they are not rough; it also gets along well with other pets, including cats. Be careful when closing doors—a Yorkie can be killed if hit by one. Potential owners should beware of poor puppy-mill examples, buying only from specialized breeders.

Plate 3

Non-Sporting Dogs

An Unusual Variety

Unquestionably the most diverse group, the catchall non-sporting-dog category includes twelve breeds. Its members are from all over the globe—China, Tibet, Europe, and America—and vary greatly in size, shape, color, and personality. The term "non-sporting dogs" was adopted to describe breeds that were not developed for a specific purpose, as well as those that are no longer used in the same way they originally were. For example, the Poodle and the Dalmatian, once hard-working hunting dogs, are now bred more for appearance than for their usefulness in the field. Similarly, the Bulldog developed as a fierce fighting animal, but today is a friendly and gentle pet. Other members of the non-sporting-dog group, such as the Lhasa Apso and the Bichon Frise, seem to have always served as companions, appreciated for their stylish looks.

Some breeds in this group are considered symbols of their presumed nations of origin. The Bulldog, the Poodle, the Boston Terrier, the Chow Chow, and the Tibetan Terrier are typically identified with England, France, the United States, China, and Tibet, respectively.

Many Choices

The non-sporting-dog group offers a future dog owner an unusual variety of breeds from which to choose. Large or small, long or short hair, almost any shape or color—all are represented here. There are city dogs and country dogs; breeds requiring minimal coat care, and some that need substantial professional grooming.

The characteristic that seems to link these twelve breeds is the inability to fit them into any other group. But however catchall the category may be, it includes some of the most popular breeds in the United States, such as the standard and miniature Poodles, and the Boston Terrier.

Bichon Frise

Characteristics
Small
Poodle-like
Long, flowing hair on
drop ears and tail
Topknot
Curly outer coat

Personality
Playful, affectionate, and happy. A gentle and obedient companion, although this breed can be stubborn. Pleasant with children and easygoing with other pets. Altogether a most appealing breed, wonderful as a pet.

Ideal Appearance
Small dog with poodlelike appearance. Males and bitches, preferably 9½″ to 11½″ tall, with ½″ beyond either limit allowed. Although standard does not specify weight, dogs usually weigh about 7 to 12 pounds. Body is slightly longer than tall. Head size proportionate to body. Long, flowing hair on drop ears and tail; hair on head forms a topknot. Double coat: profuse, silky, and loosely curled outer coat, 2″ or longer; short, soft undercoat. Permissible colors: white alone, or white in combination with buff, cream, apricot, or gray; distinct markings or black hair undesirable. Large, dark brown or black eyes and prominent, round, black nose.

Potential Health Problems
Generally healthy. Subject to ear and skin ailments, cataracts, progressive retinal atrophy, and low blood sugar.

Care and Exercise
Coat requires considerable grooming to keep it fluffy and elegant (show trim calls for a "powder-puff" look); brush about 30 minutes a day. Occasional professional trimming necessary. Needs little exercise and is thus a highly suitable breed for apartment life. May be hard to housebreak.

Puppies
Average litter, 3 to 5 puppies. Adult coloring appears by about 6 months. Puppies are slower developers than some breeds. Like all dogs, they should get used to people at an early age.

Comment
Bichon-type dogs, descendants of the Barbet, or Water Spaniel, were known in the region surrounding the Mediterranean during the Middle Ages. Then as now, these friendly little dogs were valued for their appealing personalities. Seafarers took them on voyages and often used them as articles of trade. In the 14th century, Italian sailors are said to have found the breed on the Canary Island of Tenerife and taken it home to Europe, where the Bichon, or Teneriffe, became the prized pet of both the Italian and French nobility. The breed won further popularity in the English court during the reign of Henry II, and it is featured in the paintings of the Spanish masters, including several of Goya's works. By the end of the 19th century, however, its status declined to that of an ordinary street dog.

The Bichon Frise's popularity rose once again after World War I, when a small group of French enthusiasts began to reestablish the breed's bloodlines. The breed's present name was adopted in 1933, and the Bichon Frise was admitted to the French Kennel Club in 1934. A French family brought the first Bichon Frises to America in 1956, and the breed has enjoyed a loyal following in this country ever since. In 1973 it was recognized as an AKC non-sporting dog.

Recommendation
This attentive, charming breed is exceptionally good with children. It is intelligent and cheerful, and has a stylish appearance and confident manner. Because of the breed's burgeoning popularity, would-be owners should shop with care, as unscrupulous breeders may sell poor-quality animals. The Bichon Frise is an excellent city pet for an owner that is willing to provide the daily coat care required.

Plate 26

Boston Terrier

Characteristics
Square, wrinkle-free
head
Short, square muzzle
Erect ears
Broad chest
Short tail
White markings

Personality
Dapper, gay, and highly intelligent. A delightful family companion. Ideal with other pets and children. One of the most affectionate of all breeds. Responds well to training and attention.

Ideal Appearance
Males and bitches, up to 25 pounds; usually considerably smaller. Divided into 3 weight classes: under 15 pounds, 15 to under 20 pounds, and 20 to 25 pounds. Although standard does not specify height, males usually measure about 17″ tall; bitches, 16″. Head appearance is crucial: it should be square, flat, and wrinkle-free, with abrupt brow and well-defined stop. Short, square, wide muzzle has broad, square jaws. Large, round, wide-set dark eyes. Erect ears placed near corners of skull; sometimes cropped. Broad chest and short back. Short, low-set tail may be straight or screw. Smooth, short, shiny coat. Permissible colors: brindle and white preferable; also black and white; should have white muzzle and white blaze on head, neck, chest, forelegs, and below hocks of hind legs.

Potential Health Problems
A generally healthy breed. Subject to respiratory problems and eye injuries and infections. Tends to wheeze and snore. Possible cataracts, fold dermatitis, pattern baldness, mast cell tumors, Cushing's disease, and demodectic mange.

Care and Exercise
Minimal coat care required. A good brisk buffing with an old, rough face cloth is generally sufficient. Rarely needs bathing. Provide daily, but not necessarily lengthy, exercise. Ball-fetching is always popular with this breed. May be hard to housebreak because of stubbornness; this is a small aristocrat. Actually can learn anything, including toilet manners, in a day or so.

Puppies
Average litter, 3 to 4 puppies. Whelping very difficult; cesarean section usually recommended. Newborns have color of mature dogs. Hyperactive puppies; obedience training at 6 to 8 weeks.

Comment
Descended from the Bulldog and the English Terrier, the Boston Terrier is one of the few truly American breeds; it is widely recognized as the national dog of the United States. The breed was given full recognition in 1893. Through selective breeding, size has been greatly reduced—from the 32 pounds common in the late 19th century to 25 pounds or smaller today. Although called a terrier, it is not one at all; it is not a fighter like the true terriers are.

Recommendation
This is a long-lived, affectionate breed and an alert watchdog. An excellent family pet, the Boston Terrier is gentle and full of fun, and adapts to any home environment—whether in the city, the suburbs, or the country. An easy dog for even the relatively inexperienced owner to manage.

Plate 59

Bulldog

Characteristics
Low, heavy build
Massive head
Rose ears
Wrinkles from head
to chest
Short, wide-set legs
Short tail

Personality
Gentle, easygoing, and companionable. Although generally pleasant with other pets, its behavior may be unpredictable until it establishes dominance. Possessive about food; should never be fed in the presence of other animals. Very affectionate with people; an ideal pet for children.

Ideal Appearance
Heavy, thick, low build. Males, about 50 pounds; bitches, about 40 pounds. Although standard does not specify height, males usually measure about 15″ tall; bitches, 14¼″. Massive head with short face, round cheeks, and enormous jaws with lower jaw protruding. Small, high-set rose ears. Large, dark eyes. Broad, deep-set nose. Skin is loose, especially from head to chest, where it should hang in 2 huge wrinkles. Broad shoulders on heavy body. Short, thick forelegs set wide apart; powerful hind legs. Short, straight or screw tail. Short, smooth, fine coat lies flat. Permissible colors: brindle, preferably red; or solid white, red, or fawn, but not black; piebald. Brown or liver unacceptable.

Potential Health Problems
Usually healthy. Very susceptible to heat stroke in hot weather. Also prone to respiratory problems, and may snore loudly. Possible allergic skin diseases, eyelid abnormalities, tear deficiency, congenital heart disease, hip dysplasia, and some other ailments. Short-lived: 9 to 10 years is a long life.

Care and Exercise
Required coat care and exercise are both minimal. Use a rough cloth routinely on the coat. Better to exercise too little rather than overexercise. This breed likes walks in cool weather. Beware of overheating; in summer try to keep in an air-conditioned environment. Never leave a dog in a car with the windows closed.

Puppies
Average litter, 4 puppies; cesarean section usually required. Color at birth is same as that of adult dog. Easy to train and care for. Wonderful with children.

Comment
A descendant of the powerful Mastiff, the Bulldog is recognized as a national symbol in Britain. Its name derives from the sport of bullbaiting, for which it was bred for centuries: Bulls were leashed to stakes and the dogs attacked them by grabbing on to their noses. After the decline of this inhumane sport, the Bulldog had a brief career as a fighting dog until dogfighting was banned in England in 1835. Thereafter, breeders began eliminating the Bulldog's ferocity. Today the Bulldog is a gentle and very loving pet.

Recommendation
A delightful companion requiring little exercise. Because of the potential for health problems, this breed must be purchased from a reputable kennel. It is extremely sensitive to heat and must never be left in a hot, poorly ventilated area, such as a car. When food is present, Bulldogs may be aggressive toward other animals.

Plate 57

Chow Chow

Characteristics
Full, brushlike coat
Frowning expression
Enormous head
Small, erect ears
Short, compact build
Blue-black tongue

Personality
Aloof at times, even standoffish. Very much a one-person dog. Generally not the best choice for a household with children, and can be unpredictable with other animals. Can be stubborn. This breed is a guard dog by nature.

Ideal Appearance
Massive, short, compact body with lionlike ruff around head. Although standard specifies neither height nor weight, males usually measure 17″ to 20″ tall and weigh 55 to 70 pounds; bitches, 16″ to 18″ and 45 to 55 pounds. Enormous, broad, flat head with short, broad muzzle, and large black nose. Small, stiff, erect, and slightly rounded ears. Dark oval eyes. Unusual blue-black tongue. Frowning expression or scowl. Strong neck set on muscular shoulders, and broad chest. Forelegs and hind hocks are straight and heavy, giving dog an unusual, stilted gait. Bushy tail carried high over back. Dense, brushlike double coat: coarse outer coat; soft, woolly undercoat. Permissible colors: any solid color, with lighter shade on ruff, tail, and breeches; often red or black. Red tongue or one with pink spots not allowed for show.

Potential Health Problems
Hardy overall, but subject to hot spots, ear infections, eyelid abnormalities, and hormonal skin disease. Not a good breed for very hot, humid climates.

Care and Exercise
Significant grooming, at least twice a week, is essential to avoid matted coat. Use a rake brush to remove undercoat and a pin brush to groom coarser outer coat. This breed sheds a great deal in the summer. Although inactive indoors, the Chow requires a fair amount of outdoor exercise, so is not a highly suitable breed for city life.

Puppies
Usually 3 to 6 puppies. Many Chow Chows have whelping problems, and cesarean deliveries are not uncommon. Puppies should become accustomed to people, other dogs, and different environments. Can be housebroken at 8 weeks. Needs obedience training early.

Comment
Possibly one of the oldest recognizable breeds of dogs, dating back at least as far as 150 B.C., the Chow Chow originally came from northeastern Asia, but no one knows its exact history. Some people believe it may have originally come from the Arctic Circle and then traveled to Mongolia, Siberia, and China. It may be traceable to the Northern sled dogs—perhaps it is kin to the Akita or Samoyed. Its unique blue-black tongue is truly puzzling.
Whatever its origin, for centuries the Chow Chow was used in China as a hunting dog. A 7th-century T'ang Dynasty emperor is said to have kept 2500 pairs of dogs resembling the Chow Chow. The breed was noted for its strong scenting abilities, cleverness, speed, strength, and stamina. In the markets of Manchuria and Mongolia, Chow skins were sold as clothing and the flesh eaten. The first Chow Chows were imported to England during the 1880s; English sailors are said to have named them after the term used for miscellaneous cargo or bric-a-brac. The breed was first exhibited in the United States in 1890. Today the Chow Chow is quite popular in the show ring.

Recommendation
The Chow Chow is not an easy, cuddly breed nor appropriate for every household. It has a tendency to be haughty, but makes a loyal guard dog. This breed is for the experienced, serious dog owner. It is a unique, intelligent, and dignified companion.

Plate 111

Dalmatian

Characteristics
Long head
Long, arched neck
Deep chest
Muscular build
Long, thin tail
White with dark spots

Personality
Lively, spirited, and willing. Intelligent; a quick learner. Loves to participate in all activities. Stylish by nature, and seems to accept the role of being both decorative and a pleasing companion.

Ideal Appearance
Males and bitches, 19″ to 23″ tall (disqualified over 24″). Although standard does not specify weight, both sexes usually weigh 55 to 65 pounds. Rather long head with flat, broad skull. Round, widely spaced eyes, and fine, thin, high-set ears carried close to head. Long, graceful, arched neck set into very muscular shoulders. Deep chest, not too wide. Powerful back. Straight, heavy forelegs and muscular hind legs. Long tail, ideally reaching to hocks. Short, hard, dense coat. Permissible colors: black or liver-brown markings set against pure white ground. Spots are very important: should be round and well-defined without intermingling; may be as large as silver dollars. Rims around eyes must match spot color. Eyes of black-spotted dogs are dark black, brown, or dark blue, while noses are black; liver-spotted dogs have light brown, golden, or light blue eyes and brown noses. Variation in color or patches is not allowed for show.

Potential Health Problems
Generally hardy. Subject to cataracts, deafness, allergic skin disease, and urinary stones. Puppies' hearing should be checked before purchase.

Care and Exercise
Required coat care is minimal, but daily brushing will help prevent shedding. This is a very active breed, both indoors and out; it needs plenty of exercise. If confined to the city, long, vigorous walks are essential.

Puppies
Litter of 8 to 10 puppies. Normal whelping. Puppies are born all white and gradually develop spots at about 10 days to 2 weeks. Teach puppies to be calm and not timid by exposing them to people and different situations.

Comment
An ancient breed of long-disputed and unknown origin, the Dalmatian has served as dog of war, watchdog, shepherd, hunter, controller of vermin, and coach dog. Its name comes from its first proven home, Dalmatia, a coastal province formerly in Austria, but now included within the borders of Yugoslavia. It is also known by various nicknames: the English coach dog, spotted Dick, and the fire house dog. In the United States, it is indisputably the mascot of the firehouse, as well as a frequent circus performer. Its high-stepping style made it the choice of privileged aristocrats during the 19th century.

Recommendation
The Dalmatian is an intelligent, playful breed, and is very responsive to training. As a family dog, it is reserved with strangers and can be unpredictable with other dogs. It may be too excitable for small children. Because of an inherited tendency toward deafness, a Dalmatian's lineage should be checked carefully, and dogs should be purchased only from a very reputable breeder. Not for sedentary owners, the Dalmatian is instead for people who enjoy regular workouts, long runs, and a lively pet.

Plate 77

French Bulldog

Characteristics
Large, square head
with flat top and
domed forehead
Bat ears
Short, muscular build
Deep chest
Short tail

Personality
A clean, quiet, easygoing breed. Highly
suitable for city life. Occasionally
stubborn, but a quick learner. Ideally a
one-person dog, the French Bulldog does
not have much tolerance for children,
but is an excellent companion for elderly
people.

Ideal Appearance
2 classes: under 22 pounds, and 22 to 28
pounds. Although standard does not
specify height, both males and bitches
usually measure about 12″ tall. Large,
square head with domelike forehead and
flat top. Round, dark eyes set far apart
and deep in skull. Broad, deep muzzle
with well-defined stop. Short, black
nose. Broad, square lower jaw turned up.
Erect ears are batlike and set wide apart.
Short body with broad, deep chest. Back
is wide at shoulders and narrows toward
rear. Widely spaced forelegs are straight,
short, muscular, and slightly shorter
than the hind legs. Short, fine coat.
Permissible colors: all brindles, as well as
white, fawn, or brindle and white; black
and white, black and tan, liver, mouse,
or solid black are unacceptable.

Potential Health Problems
Healthy in general, but subject to
respiratory problems, eye injuries, and
cataracts. Very sensitive to heat stroke.

Care and Exercise
Virtually no coat care is required, except
a brisk rub with a rough cloth. Although
fairly active, both indoors and out, does
not need a great deal of exercise. It
should be kept in a well-ventilated
environment and not be subjected to
closeness. Avoid overheating.

Puppies
Average litter, 2 to 5 puppies.
Occasionally whelping is difficult,
requiring a cesarean delivery. Usually
puppies are extremely healthy. They
require normal training and adjustment
to people.

Comment
The English and French disagree about
the derivation of this little dog. While
the English maintain that they exported
it when it did not suit their fancy, the
French claim the breed as an original.
The truth is probably somewhere in
between. The English Bulldog is no
doubt a strong ancestor of this French
breed. But the French Bulldog has been
present in France since the 17th century,
when it was bred by artisans in Paris as a
fighting dog. The first official
organization for the breed was the French
Bulldog Club of America, founded in
1898.

Recommendation
Best suited to an individual rather than a
family, the French Bulldog thrives on a
one-to-one relationship. It is an alert
little watchdog that does well in the
city. In a family situation, it behaves
like a child, in that it tends to compete
with other pets or children. An ideal dog
for the right family or a single owner.
Demands a great deal of personal
attention and interaction; needs fussing
over.

Plate 58

Keeshond

Personality
Loving, gentle, and loyal. A perfect house dog. An alert watchdog, but tends to like everyone. Exceptionally good with children, and an aristocrat with other animals. Learns quickly, is occasionally stubborn, but makes a delightful companion of high style.

Ideal Appearance
Northern sled dog type. Males, 18″ tall; bitches, 17″. Although standard does not specify weight, males usually weigh about 40 pounds; bitches, around 36 pounds. Length of body should equal height. Spectacular bushy coat and relatively short back. Wedge-shaped head with foxlike face; smart expression. Medium-long muzzle. Small, erect, high-set ears are triangular. Appears to have spectacles, which show as linear markings slanting upward from outer corners of eyes to lower corners of ears. Almond-shaped, dark brown eyes. Thick feathering on forelegs and hind legs looks like breeches. Fairly long plume tail tightly curled over back. Double coat: long, straight, abundant outer coat that stands off body; thick, downy undercoat. Head is covered with short, soft hair; ears feel velvety. Permissible colors: undercoat, pale gray or cream; outer-coat hairs, a mixture of gray and black, tipped in black; legs and feet, cream; tail, light gray when curled back, with a black tip. Markings are characteristic.

Potential Health Problems
Healthy overall. Some skin problems possible. Possible congenital heart disease and epilepsy. Does not do well in hot, humid climate.

Care and Exercise
Abundant coat should be brushed against the grain about twice a week for 45 minutes. Should not be bathed unless it is essential, because bathing softens this breed's glamorous coat. Use dry shampoo. Although dogs need a fair amount of exercise, this breed does well in an urban setting. Bred to be a companion, it should not be locked in backyard away from its family. If it must be kept there, a 6-foot fence around the yard is essential to prevent escape.

Puppies
Usually 3 to 8 puppies in a litter. At birth, puppies are black to seal-brown, becoming pale white to cream by 4 months, and developing markings sometime between 5 and 18 months of age. Accustom puppies to grooming at least once a week during the 6-week to 8-month period.

Comment
A longtime resident of Holland, the Keeshond became the mascot of the antimonarchistic patriots in the 18th century. Its name comes from the leader of this group, Kees de Gyselaer, who owned a dog that was also called Kees. When the Prince of Orange came to power, the breed—the symbol of the opposing party—all but disappeared. However, riverboat captains and farmers quietly kept the dog in its original form through careful breeding. Over the last 2 centuries, the Keeshond has hardly changed. Despite its solid Dutch lineage in modern times, the Keeshond probably traces back to some northern sled dog, perhaps an ancestor it shares with the Samoyed, the Norwegian Elkhound, and the Pomeranian.

Recommendation
This is an almost ideal breed for any household. It is affectionate and attentive, naturally a watchdog, and lovely in the show ring. A moderate amount of coat care will keep the Keeshond looking handsome and stylish. It can be a loving companion for an elderly person who wants a pet.

Plate 102

Lhasa Apso

Characteristics
Long, flowing coat
hides face and body
Hanging ears
Whiskers and beard
Plume tail carried
high over back

Personality
Playful and affectionate with owners, but reserved with strangers. Bold and frequently quick-tempered. Despite its cuddly appearance, not an ideal lapdog, nor is it usually tolerant of young children.

Ideal Appearance
Males, about 10″ to 11″ tall; bitches, slightly smaller. Although standard does not specify weight, males usually weigh about 15 pounds; bitches, around 14 pounds. Body longer than tall, with straight forelegs. Narrow head has a medium-length muzzle. Well-feathered screw tail is carried high over back. Small body and head completely hidden in long hair: Hair covering face forms whiskers and a beard; abundant hair present on hanging ears; legs and feet also covered with hair. Long, straight, heavy, and dense coat should be hard, not silky. Permissible colors: any—gold, sand, honey, dark grizzle, slate, smoke, black, parti-color, white, or brown; golden or lion colors preferred, with dark tips on ears and beard. Dark brown eyes; black nose.

Potential Health Problems
Hardy overall. Subject to kidney ailments, allergic skin disease, eye injuries and tear deficiency.

Care and Exercise
Considerable coat care is imperative. Daily brushing, plus about 1 hour of real grooming twice a week, will keep the Lhasa Apso's coat in glorious condition. Active indoors and out, dog needs a fair amount of exercise. Long walks are not essential, but should be exercised on a routine basis.

Puppies
Average litter, 4 to 5 puppies. Color at birth varies; usually born slightly darker than adult color. Obedience training recommended at 6 months. Begin grooming at 8 to 10 weeks.

Comment
One of 4 native breeds from the Tibetan mountains, the Lhasa Apso was kept as a watchdog. For centuries this small dog commanded considerable respect. It is said that the Tibetan monks believed that, upon death, their souls entered the Lhasas' bodies. The breed was a popular pet in homes and monasteries. Like the other 3 Tibetan breeds—the Mastiff, the Tibetan Terrier, and the Tibetan Spaniel —the Lhasa Apso has long, thick hair, which protected it from the freezing mountain air.

The breed was first exhibited in a London show in 1929. Its hardiness, cheerful disposition, and keen hearing are as evident today as they were long ago in the mountains of Tibet.

Recommendation
The Lhasa Apso should be purchased carefully, from a reputable breeder. Homes with younger or inconsiderate children are not ideal environments for this breed. The Lhasa is suited only to owners willing to take care of its long, abundant coat.

Plate 27

Poodle

Characteristics
Elegant appearance
Long, lean head
Hanging ears
Square build
Curly or corded coat
in fancy clip

Personality
Highly intelligent and responsive. Loyal and gentle, though assertive. Standard Poodle is bold but easygoing, and a very alert watchdog. Miniature Poodle may be too excitable for young children, but it makes an excellent pet for apartment-dwellers.

Ideal Appearance
3 sizes: standard, miniature, and toy. Standard size is over 15″ tall (disqualified in competition if 15″ or under); males, preferably 24″ to 26″ tall, and bitches, 22″ to 24.″ Miniature size, above 10″ to 15″ (disqualified if over 15″ or if 10″ or less). Toy size, 10″ and under (see Toy Poodle, page 219). Although AKC standard does not specify weight, standard-size males usually weigh about 55 pounds; bitches, around 50 pounds. Miniature-size males usually weigh approximately 16 pounds; bitches, about 15 pounds. All sizes have square build, with proud carriage. Moderately round head with a small but definite stop and long, straight muzzle. Long, wide ears hang close to head and are thickly feathered. Short back; deep chest; and broad, muscular loins. Straight, parallel forelegs; very muscular hind legs with well-bent stifles. Docked tail carried high and straight. Harsh, dense coat. Accepted show trims: puppy clip (under 1 year old), sporting, English saddle, or Continental. Face, throat, feet, and base of tail are shaved close. Permissible colors: only solids, including black, white, cream, apricot, café au lait, brown, silver, gray, or blue; parti-color not permitted; some shading allowed.

Potential Health Problems
Healthy overall, especially standard size. Subject to progressive retinal atrophy and runny eyes. May be susceptible to hip dysplasia, cataracts, gastric bloat, and epilepsy. Miniature variety is prone to numerous metabolic disorders, heart disease, and several other ailments.

Care and Exercise
Amount of coat care depends on size, but at least 2 to 5 hours a week of grooming are necessary for either size. Trimming and shaping should be done by a professional every 4 to 6 weeks. Standard Poodles should have a fair amount of outdoor exercise. Miniatures are very active both indoors and out, but require less outdoor exercise. Both adapt to urban life.

Puppies
Average litter, 8 to 10 puppies. Begin brushing and shaving at 3½ weeks. Begin obedience training at about 6 months.

Comment
The Poodle's exact origin is unknown. Although it probably came from Germany or Russia, it has been the national dog of France for years. The English word "poodle" comes from the German word *puddeln,* which means "to paddle or splash": This reflects the fact that the standard-size dog, the first size variety to be developed, was employed as a water retriever. The now-familiar trimmed coat with shorn areas was originally intended to help the dog swim faster. Trims later became universally adopted as a symbol of fashionable elegance. In Russia, large, usually black, standard poodles were used to pull milk carts. Breeders in France are credited with developing the miniature as a companion dog.

Recommendation
This fine dog should only be purchased from the most reputable breeders, because its immense popularity has led to puppy-mill breeding of bad-tempered, excessively nervous dogs. A well-bred Poodle is a fine pet. It does not shed and is one of the few breeds that some allergy sufferers can live with. The Poodle is the perfect dog to fuss over or to jog with.

Plates 25, 87

Schipperke

Characteristics
Foxlike face
Erect ears
Short, thick-set build
Thick double coat
Docked tail
Black only

Personality
A small but tough breed. Loyal and responsive, yet stubborn. A very alert watchdog. May be quick-tempered and territorial. Very much a family dog; fond of children. With proper training, makes a wonderful house pet.

Ideal Appearance
Males and bitches, up to 18 pounds. Although standard does not specify height, males usually measure about 13" tall; bitches, approximately 12". Fairly wide face, narrowing at eyes, is almost foxlike. Medium-length muzzle. Small, erect, high-set ears are triangular. Short, strong, slightly arched neck. Deep, broad chest. Straight back and forelegs; muscular hindquarters; round rump. Docked tail should be no longer than 1". Abundant double coat: short, dense undercoat; slightly harsh outer coat. Permissible color: only solid black allowed. Small, dark brown, oval eyes; small, black nose.

Potential Health Problems
Very few ailments reported. An exceptionally long-lived breed; many live up to 20 years.

Care and Exercise
Minimal coat care required: Give a good, quick brushing twice a week. Regular, brisk walks are all that is needed to keep the Schipperke happy and healthy. Fine in urban or suburban settings. Responds to obedience training, which is recommended.

Puppies
Average litter, 3 to 7 puppies. Puppies are ready to be trained by about 6 weeks. Should become accustomed to people at an early age.

Comment
Despite the similarity in appearance, the Schipperke does not derive from the northern sled dogs, but comes instead from the Flemish provinces of Belgium.

It is descended from the Belgian Sheepdog and the "Leauvenaar." Its name is Flemish for "little captain," a reference to the breed's career as a watchdog on the barges and canals of northern Europe. In 1885 the queen of Belgium purchased a Schipperke, making it a fashionable pet almost overnight.

In 1888 the breed first appeared in the United States. It has never been very popular in this country, but it has a devoted following. A natural performer in the show ring, it is also a bold, affectionate family pet.

Recommendation
This easy-to-care-for breed is generally quite long-lived. Give early and ongoing training, for it is stubborn and occasionally quick-tempered. The Schipperke has long been noted for its devotion to children; it readily becomes their permanent protector.

Plate 50

Tibetan Spaniel

Characteristics
Small
Small, dome-shaped head
Hanging ears
Long back
Long, abundant coat
Plume tail

Personality
A happy, outgoing, and highly intelligent little dog. Lively and enthusiastic, but aloof with strangers. Assertive. Small in size, but big in personality.

Ideal Appearance
Males and bitches, about 10″ tall and ideally 9 to 15 pounds. Slightly longer than tall. Head small in proportion to body. Moderately wide skull is slightly dome-shaped. Medium-length muzzle with deep, wide chin. Medium-size, high-set hanging ears. Ideally, mouth should be slightly undershot. High-set plume tail carried over back. Silky-textured double coat is moderately long and smooth on face and front of legs; and very long or feathered on ears, backs of forelegs, tail, and rear. Permissible colors: any color or assortment of colors. Dark brown eyes with black rims. Black nose.

Potential Health Problems
No known difficulties, because of breed's newness in the United States. Beware of overheating, as with all short-muzzled dogs.

Care and Exercise
Only moderate coat care is necessary: Brush a couple of times a week. This lively breed loves to romp outdoors and does best with lots of exercise; it needs routine walks and runs. Stubborn, so may be hard to housebreak. Should receive obedience training and not be allowed to take over household.

Puppies
Average litter about 2 to 4 puppies. Like all dogs, puppies benefit from handling by people at an early age.

Comment
Used for centuries by the monks of Tibet as a "prayer dog," this breed dates back to at least 1100 B.C. Tibetan Spaniels were trained to work small treadmills that turned prayer wheels containing parchment scrolls, It was believed that with each turn, the prayers ascended closer to heaven. The Tibetan Spaniel was a treasured dog that was frequently given as a gift to the emperors of China. It was one of the first Tibetan breeds to reach the West: It arrived in Britain around 1900 looking very much like a Pekingese. Careful breeding resulted in the lengthening of its muzzle, making it more distinguishable. The Tibetan Spaniel was probably one of the Pekingese's ancestors, but the origins of both ancient far eastern breeds are vague.

Recommendation
Alert and keenly aware of all goings-on, the Tibetan Spaniel loves to play, both outdoors and in. If given a fair amount of exercise, it is quite suited to urban life. It is happiest when being pampered and fussed over. Not a true spaniel at all, this breed is not a hunter. It is a new breed, having been recognized by the American Kennel Club only in 1984.

Plate 8

Tibetan Terrier

Characteristics
Long, abundant hair
over body and face
Beard
Hanging ears
Square build
Plume tail curled over
back

Personality
An affectionate companion with a lively personality. Initially aloof with strangers, but gentle with everyone. Alert watchdog. A born participator and very adaptable. Good with other animals. Loves to travel.

Ideal Appearance
Males and bitches, 14″ to 16″ tall, and usually 22 to 23 pounds, but may weigh as much as 18 to 30 pounds. Medium-length skull with a marked stop in front of eyes. Compact, powerful body as tall at withers as it is long from shoulder to tail. Head covered with long hair that conceals large dark eyes; small beard hangs from lower jaw, and hanging, V-shaped ears are heavily feathered. Legs and large, round feet also covered with hair. Medium-long tail set high up, curled over back. Thick double coat: fine woolly undercoat; outer coat is profuse and fine, but not silky or woolly. Fur is long and straight or wavy. Permissible colors: any color or combination of colors.

Potential Health Problems
As a rule, healthy. Watch for developing skin conditions, such as hot spots. Possible eye disorders.

Care and Exercise
Coat requires quite a bit of care: Brush about 1 hour twice a week to avoid tangles and mats, and give baths periodically. May be hard to housebreak because of stubbornness. Actually easy to keep. Suited to urban life, but should get plenty of exercise.

Puppies
Average litter of 5 to 8 puppies. White dogs born white; puppies that are light at birth will gradually change to gold, brindle, or silver.

Comment
Nicknamed "the holy dog of Tibet," the Tibetan Terrier was highly treasured by the Tibetan lamas of ancient times; they thought this little dog would bring luck to those who owned it. Dogs of this breed were given to special friends or dignitaries as tokens of esteem or gratitude; they were never sold. Anything that might reduce the luck of this breed—such as crossbreeding—was avoided.

In the 1920s, an Indian doctor, A. R. H. Greig, received one of these valued dogs as a gift after he treated the wife of a Tibetan nobleman. Dr. Greig began to breed Tibetan Terriers in India and eventually established the renowned Lamleh Kennel in England.

The first Tibetan Terrier was imported to the United States in 1956 and was admitted to the non-sporting-dog group in 1973. Despite the name, this breed does not have any terrier blood.

Recommendation
The Tibetan Terrier is an affectionate and intelligent companion. It is a healthy dog, probably because it has been carefully bred. It seems suited to any climate or environment. Does very well in both apartments and houses.

Plate 84

Herding Dogs

Early Guard Dogs and Shepherds

Since the Neolithic Era, people have recognized the importance of dogs in helping them to survive in a difficult and hostile world. Unquestionably, people's primary interest at first was in the dog's value as a hunter, a guardian, and a shepherd. Only secondarily did the dog serve as a companion.

In earlier days, herding was performed by a variety of dogs all referred to as herding dogs. With the assistance of four or five herders, a farmer or rancher could control a large number of sheep, cattle, or other livestock. The physical appearance of these dogs was unimportant; their value was instead measured according to their utility—their ability to survive long, hard days in every kind of weather and to sustain constant running at a full trot.

As farming tasks became more specialized, so did the varieties of herding dogs, through selective breeding. Over time, the breeds evolved into those we have today. The American Kennel Club recognizes fourteen herding breeds. One of these—the Collie—is also recognized by the United Kennel Club under the name Scotch Collie.

Types of Herding Dogs

Herding dogs tend their flocks in two different ways, each related to the size of the dog. The larger breeds—Belgian Malinois, Belgian Sheepdog, Belgian Tervuren, Bouvier des Flandres, Briard, Collie, German Shepherd, and Old English Sheepdog—bark loudly and slowly circle the herd, keeping strays in line by virtue of their size and strength. They can direct an entire herd to a new location when necessary. These dogs move more slowly than their smaller counterparts. Long ago, when wolves roamed the European countryside, such large breeds protected the livestock from predators; dogs engaged in battle to the death to save the herd.

The smaller breeds—Australian Cattle Dog, Bearded Collie, Puli, Shetland Sheepdog, Cardigan Welsh Corgi, and Pembroke Welsh Corgi—work quickly. They dart in and out of the herd, nipping at the heels of the livestock, dodging their kicks, raising a ruckus with their barking, and, in this different manner, accomplishing the same task the larger dogs do. Unlike the other breeds, the Puli can also jump over the backs of animals to control them.

Modern Uses of Herding Dogs

On farms throughout the world, herding dogs are still used in the fields, but modern ranching methods have greatly reduced the need for them. Some herding dogs protect flocks that are preyed upon by wild animals.

Other breeds, such as the Bouvier des Flandres and the German Shepherd, serve as guide dogs for the blind, a function to which they have adapted readily. And the German Shepherd's work with police is legendary. Many herding breeds primarily function as companions and guardians of the home.

Care of Herding Dogs

In order to become useful home companions, herding dogs need to be around people from the time they are puppies. As soon as possible, they need to be introduced to outside noises and situations in order to allow them to overcome any timidity, which can turn into viciousness if the dogs are kept isolated.

Herding dogs should be patiently trained with love, not fearful punishment, if they are to learn to take their places as family members. Because these breeds are naturally active, they must be exercised routinely, as well as bathed, brushed, and generally kept happy and healthy. If you cannot devote time to a dog, a herding breed is not the right companion for you.

Australian Cattle Dog

Characteristics
Muscular build
Broad head
Erect ears
Short, rough coat
Natural tail
Mottled blue or
speckled red

Personality
An active, alert working dog. Outgoing with its family, but reserved and sometimes aggressive toward strangers. Good with children it knows; but will snap at other children if mistreated. Wary of other dogs. Learns quickly. An obedient dog, though quite bold. Good watchdog.

Ideal Appearance
Sturdy, compact, medium-size dog. Males, 18″ to 20″ tall; bitches, 17″ to 19″. Although standard does not specify weight, both sexes usually weigh 40 to 45 pounds. Square, muscular build; strong neck and deep chest. Broad head with deep, powerful muzzle. Dark eyes and erect ears. Low-set tail. Rough, moderately short double coat. Permissible colors: mottled blue, with or without markings in black, blue, or tan; or speckled red, with or without darker red markings on head.

Potential Health Problems
Generally robust. Subject to hip dysplasia and, occasionally, deafness. Should be X-rayed by a veterinarian before breeding.

Care and Exercise
Brush about 15 minutes a week. Sheds an average amount. An active herding dog by nature, this breed requires vigorous daily exercise to work off excess energy; long walks on a leash are essential. In its native Australia, it is reared as a hardworking breed. It needs outside activity.

Puppies
Litter averages 4 to 8 puppies. Born completely white, puppies gain adult coloring as they mature. Relatively easy to housebreak and train.

Comment
As its name suggests, the Australian Cattle Dog was developed in Australia to round up and drive cattle on the range.

Because cattle are among the most difficult livestock to herd, the dog that herds them has to be bold, tough, and a biter. When the cattle kick, the dog must move quickly out of the way with lightning-fast reflexes and then drop flat to the ground to avoid injury.

The first records of the breed date from around 1840 or 1850. It was known alternately as the Blue Heeler, the Queensland Heeler, and the Australian Heeler.

The Australian Cattle Dog's popularity has been growing slowly in the United States since the breed was recognized by the American Kennel Club in 1979. Its alert and suspicious nature makes it a good guardian of the home.

Recommendation
Two factors should be kept in mind when considering the Australian Cattle Dog: The dog requires good, brisk exercise, such as walking on a leash once or twice a day; moreover, although it can be an excellent family dog, it must become accustomed to people from the time it is a puppy. Learning to be with people and having sufficient exercise will reduce any aggressive behavior. This breed's protectiveness and loyalty to its family prevent it from being overly friendly toward strangers.

Plate 100

Bearded Collie

Characteristics
Resembles Old
English Sheepdog,
but smaller and
thinner
Shaggy coat
Hanging ears
Quizzical expression

Personality
Outgoing and lovable. Full of fun.
Accepting of its surroundings. A gentle,
intelligent dog. Generally responds well
to training, affection, and its
environment.

Ideal Appearance
Medium-size dog; resembles a smaller,
thinner Old English Sheepdog. Males,
21″ to 22″ tall, bitches, 20″ to 21″.
Although standard does not specify
weight, both sexes usually weigh about
50 pounds. Shaggy, double coat with
long, rough outer coat and soft
undercoat. Arched eyebrows and wide-set
eyes give dog a quizzical expression.
Hanging ears. Long, lean body. Low-set,
medium-length tail. Permissible colors:
black, brown, reddish-fawn, blue,
sandy, or many shades of gray, silver, or
slate; touches of white on head, neck,
chest, legs, feet, and tip of tail. Eyes
harmonize with coat color.

Potential Health Problems
Healthy overall, but subject to hip
dysplasia. Tends to be fragile.

Care and Exercise
Abundant coat will cause problems if not
brushed regularly. Brush for 30 minutes
twice a week to avoid matting and excess
accumulation of dirt. With proper care,
shedding is normal. Since the Bearded
Collie should have a natural look, it does
not need professional grooming. Must be
exercised every day on a long leash so
that it can really move around. Requires
long walks or outside games involving a
lot of activity, such as fetch.

Puppies
Average litter of 4 to 8 puppies.
Newborns are black, blue, brown, or
fawn; puppies assume final coloring as
they mature. Should be around people
from an early age. Easy to housebreak.

Comment
The Bearded Collie was bred to herd
sheep in the mountainous Scottish
Highlands and the gentle hills of the
Lowlands. Although little is known of
the breed's history prior to this century,
the dog was undoubtedly an early
herding dog that was first known as the
Highland Sheepdog.
The Bearded Collie became well known
in the British Isles within the last 60 to
70 years. Slow to be accepted in the
United States, the Bearded Collie was
recognized by the American Kennel Club
in 1976.

Recommendation
This breed is an outstanding companion
for the family, even in cities and
suburbs, as long as it gets plenty of
exercise. A wonderful clown, it is
outgoing with those it knows, but
reserved with strangers.

Plate 85

Belgian Malinois

Personality
Intelligent and questioning. Cautious
with strangers, but affectionate and
protective of its family. A vigilant guard
dog, especially if caring for children.
Fearless. Needs to be trained early.

Ideal Appearance
Square build. Males, 24″ to 26″ tall;
bitches, 22″ to 24″. Although standard
does not specify weight, both males and
bitches usually weigh 70 to 80 pounds.
Large head with flattened top and
moderately pointed muzzle. Erect ears.
Powerful neck and muscular body. Long,
bushy tail. Short, straight coat,
especially short on head, ears, and lower
legs. Permissible colors: rich fawn to
mahogany, with black tipping; black
mask and ears. Brown to dark brown
eyes.

Potential Health Problems
Generally healthy. Subject to hip
dysplasia, so should be X-rayed by a
veterinarian before breeding.

Care and Exercise
Short coat requires little care, only 15
minutes of brushing a week. With
regular brushing, shedding is minimal,
except in spring and fall, when dogs
should be brushed daily. Like its Belgian
relatives, the Malinois needs plenty of
hardy exercise daily—at the very least,
long walks on a leash. Do not allow it to
run free around other animals.

Puppies
Litters contain 6 to 10 puppies. To
prevent aggressive behavior in adult
dogs, give puppies daily contact with
people as soon as possible. Also expose
them to strangers and unfamiliar noises.
Obedience training at an early age is
recommended to discourage aggressive
tendencies.

Comment
The Belgian Malinois is identical to the
Belgian Sheepdog and the Belgian
Tervuren except for its short coat and
mahogany coloring. Like these other 2
herding breeds, it descended from the
European herding dogs of the Middle
Ages.

The American Kennel Club recognized
the Belgian Malinois as a distinct breed
in 1959. In Europe and Great Britain,
however, it is still considered a coat
variety of the Belgian Sheepdog.

Recommendation
This is a no-nonsense dog that must be
taken seriously by its owner. Obedience
training and exercise are essential. The
Belgian Malinois is for devoted,
preferably experienced, dog people.

Plate 107

Belgian Sheepdog

Characteristics
Square build
Long, wedge-shaped head
Muscular body
Erect ears
Long, harsh coat
Usually all black

Personality
Alert and active. Responsive to those it knows, but possessive; wary of strangers. Can be aggressive; needs to be trained and carefully managed. Very intelligent; learns quickly.

Ideal Appearance
Square build and elegant carriage. Males, 24″ to 26″ tall; bitches, 22″ to 24″. Body should be as long as it is tall. Although standard does not specify weight, both sexes usually weigh 70 to 80 pounds. Long, wedge-shaped head with erect ears. Outstretched neck tapers into sturdy, muscular body. Long, full tail. Moderately long, straight, slightly harsh coat lies close to body. Permissible colors: usually completely black; small amounts of white allowed. Brown to dark brown eyes.

Potential Health Problems
Healthy and strong. Subject to hip dysplasia, so should be X-rayed by veterinarian prior to breeding.

Care and Exercise
Coat requires about 30 minutes of brushing once a week. If dog is brushed out as suggested, shedding is normal except in spring and fall, when this breed sheds heavily and must be brushed every day.
Must at least have daily exercise on a long leash, and preferably some active games as well. To offer less is unfair.

Puppies
Usually 6 to 10 puppies in a litter. Can be house-trained readily. Puppies should become accustomed to the presence of people, including strangers, at an early age; they need direct contact every day. They should also be introduced to different places and strange noises. Natural aggressive tendencies require obedience training at an early age.

Comment
In most parts of the world, the Belgian Sheepdog, the Belgian Malinois, and the Belgian Tervuren are regarded as 3 coat varieties of a single breed. The dogs originated in Belgium, where they were used for centuries to herd sheep and cattle in the fields. The farmers who bred them were more concerned with their ability to perform their tasks for long hours than with the type of coat.
It was not until the turn of the 20th century that breeders began to separate the varieties of Belgian dogs. In the United States, the American Kennel Club has considered them 3 distinct breeds since 1959.

Recommendation
The Belgian Sheepdog is a good guard dog—very possessive of its family, especially children. When a dog is caring for children, it is very suspicious of approaching strangers, so caution should be exercised. The best dogs are those raised with children since puppyhood.

Plate 106

Belgian Tervuren

Characteristics
Square build
Long, wedge-shaped
head
Muscular body
Erect ears
Long, harsh coat
Black tipping

Personality
Lively and eager to please those it knows well. Faithful companion and earnest worker. Courageous. Suspicious of strangers. A good guard dog, but will not attack if unwarranted. Needs obedience training. Temperament similar to that of the Belgian Sheepdog and the Belgian Malinois.

Ideal Appearance
Square build and elegant, sturdy look. Males, 24″ to 26″ tall; bitches, 22″ to 24″. Although standard does not specify weight, both males and bitches usually weigh 70 to 80 pounds. Long, wedge-shaped head and erect ears. Long, muscular neck. Deep chest and muscular body. Full tail. Long, straight, moderately harsh double coat lies close to body: dense undercoat; long outer coat. Permissible colors: rich fawn to russet-mahogany, with black tips; gives impression of black overlay. Black mask. Brown to dark brown eyes.

Potential Health Problems
Strong and healthy, but susceptible to hip dysplasia. Needs to be X-rayed by veterinarian before breeding. Possible loss of color in skin and hair.

Care and Exercise
Long coat needs about 30 minutes of brushing once a week to keep shedding to a minimum. Sheds heavily in spring and fall, when it requires daily brushing. Requires strenuous daily exercise: at the very least, walks on a long leash; runs in a fenced-in area are even better. Natural aggressive tendencies require obedience training at an early age.

Puppies
Usually litters of 6 to 10 puppies. Easily housebroken. Puppies need daily contact with people—with strangers as well as friends—from an early age. Exposure to different faces, noises, and places can prevent dogs from becoming overly possessive or aggressive.

Comment
Only in the United States is the Belgian Tervuren considered a distinct breed; nearly everywhere else it is viewed as a long-haired, black-tipped variety of the Belgian Sheepdog. It was developed as a vigilant guard dog, originally used to keep wolves and wild dogs from attacking farmers' flocks. Today, the Tervuren is still a superb watchdog.

Recommendation
Like the Belgian Sheepdog and the Belgian Malinois, the Belgian Tervuren is not for every household. This superb guard dog takes its job seriously: Highly protective of its family, it may attack unless commanded not to. It should be trained early and well. Because the Tervuren needs a lot of exercise, it is best suited to country or suburban homes.

Plate 105

Bouvier des Flandres

Characteristics
Large and rugged
Large head
Long eyebrows
Full beard and mustache
Rough coat
Docked tail

Personality
Docile. An ideal family companion; attentive to children. Wary of other dogs. May appear aloof, but actually very aware of its surroundings. Its herding instincts keep it close to home. Good watchdog.

Ideal Appearance
Large and rugged-looking. Males, 24½" to 27½" tall; bitches, 23½" to 26½". Although standard does not specify weight, both sexes usually weigh 75 to 95 pounds. Large head with flat skull. Dark brown eyes covered with long eyebrows. Full beard and mustache. High-set ears, natural or cropped. Powerful, square build with short, broad back and muscular legs. Docked tail. Tousled coat, about 2½" long, is rough to the touch. Permissible colors: fawn to black, including brindle, gray, and salt-and-pepper; small white star on chest is acceptable. White, chocolate, or parti-colored coat penalized in shows.

Potential Health Problems
Generally healthy, but subject to hip dysplasia, bloat, and laryngeal paralysis. Should be X-rayed by a veterinarian before breeding.

Care and Exercise
Keep coat 2½" long over most of the body, and brush for 30 minutes each week. If brushed, shedding is normal. Exercise dog twice a day, either taking it for a good, brisk walk on a long leash, or allowing it to run in an open area. Can live in an apartment if exercised well, but that is not its ideal setting.

Puppies
Average litter of 5 to 10 puppies. If cropped ears are desired, this should be done by a veterinarian at 8 to 12 weeks. Puppies mature by about 2½ years. Easy to housebreak and train.

Comment
The Bouvier des Flandres originated in the Flanders area of Belgium and in northern France, where it was used to herd cattle, and later, to pull milk carts. The word *bouvier* means cowherd or ox driver. In World War I, much of Flanders was almost destroyed, and the breed nearly disappeared. A few dogs were saved by a Belgian army veterinarian, who then started breeding them. In the 1930s, movie producer Louis de Rochemont brought the Bouvier des Flandres to the United States. Because of its impressive appearance, this large dog serves well as a watchdog. However, its docile temperament does not allow it to be a guard dog, like the Doberman or the Rottweiler. Still an excellent farm dog, the Bouvier has also been used for many other tasks—for example, as a guide dog for the blind, and as a police dog.

Recommendation
Given some exercise, the Bouvier will adjust to most environments, although it does best in a country or suburban home. It is basically docile, yet because of its size, this breed is not recommended for cramped quarters.

Plate 113

Briard

Characteristics
Large and powerful
Long, coarse, shaggy
coat
Long head
Mustache and beard
High-set ears
Long, feathered tail

Personality
Has a mind of its own; stubborn and independent, with an instinct for guarding. Reserved, both with strangers and other dogs. A quick learner, it remembers well what it has been taught. Good with children it knows.

Ideal Appearance
Large, powerful dog. Males, 23″ to 27″ tall, bitches, 22″ to 25½″. Although standard does not specify weight, males and bitches usually weigh 75 to 90 pounds. Body is slightly longer than high. Long head with mustache and beard. Large, wide-set eyes. High-set, natural or cropped ears. Shaggy, coarse double coat falling in slightly wavy locks, 4″ to 6″ long. Permissible colors: black or various shades of gray or tawny. White hairs or a white spot on chest not more than 1″ in diameter is acceptable. Nose, any color other than black. Black or black-brown eyes; yellow or spotted eyes are show faults.

Potential Health Problems
Generally robust. Prone to hip dysplasia, so should be X-rayed prior to breeding. Susceptible to bloat, some ear problems, and progressive retinal atrophy.

Care and Exercise
Brush for about 2 hours twice a week, or coat will quickly become matted and dirty, as long coat picks up and retains leaves, grass, and other small particles. If the dog is brushed regularly, it will not shed too much.
The Briard does not need as much exercise as some herding dogs, but should have ample opportunity to stretch. At the least, it needs daily walks on a long leash; runs in an open area will make for a happier dog.

Puppies
Litters average 8 to 10 puppies. Colors in a litter may vary from the color of the parents. If cropped ears are desired, the procedure should be done several weeks after birth by a veterinarian. Puppies are easy to raise, but should get used to people at an early age.

Comment
Although probably descended from the many herding dogs present in Europe hundreds of years ago, the modern Briard can be traced to 19th century France. Originally it may have guarded flocks from wolves and other intruders, but more recently the breed has been used for herding. Because of its large size and protective nature, the Briard makes an impressive guard dog.

Recommendation
If this dog becomes accustomed to people as a puppy, it will make an excellent family dog and a good companion for children. Otherwise it can become antisocial and overprotective to the point of being aggressive. Because of its large size and its need for considerable brushing and exercise, the breed is best suited to a large home, preferably one with a yard. However, the Briard can adapt to city apartments, although it does not like to be left alone for long periods.

Plate 112

Collie

Characteristics
Lean, wedge-shaped
head
Distinctive semi-
prick ears
Hard, muscular build
2 coat varieties
Natural tail

Personality
Intelligent. Sensitive and outgoing with those it knows, but reserved with strangers. Obedient and gentle. Proud. Wonderful with children. Friendly and loving. Nostalgic or wistful expression. Can be noisy, but this trait can be corrected with obedience training.

Ideal Appearance
One of the most beautiful dogs. Males, 24″ to 26″ tall and 60 to 75 pounds; bitches, 22″ to 24″ and 50 to 65 pounds. Lean, smooth, wedge-shaped head. Distinctive ears break naturally at about three quarters of the distance from the base. Trim, hard, muscular body with deep chest. Moderately long tail. 2 coat varieties: Rough variety has straight, harsh outer coat and full, soft undercoat; smooth variety has short, hard, flat coat. Permissible colors: sable and white; tricolor (black with white markings and tan shading); blue merle; or white (mostly white with sable, tricolor, or blue-merle markings). Dark eyes.
UKC differences:
Somewhat shorter and lighter: males, 22″ to 24″ tall and 45 to 65 pounds; bitches, 20″ to 22″ and 40 to 50 pounds.

Potential Health Problems
Basically a healthy breed, although subject to hip dysplasia, various eye diseases and infections, and skin diseases. Possible congenital eye defects and congenital heart disease. Sensitive to some drugs. Subject to deafness. Possible Gray Collie syndrome, a serious problem in puppies.

Care and Exercise
All Collies tend to shed a lot, especially in spring and fall. If not brushed regularly, shedding can be a problem. Rough coat needs brushing twice a week for 30 minutes. Smooth coat requires only 15 minutes of brushing once a week.
Regular daily exercise—such as brisk walks on a long leash or, even better, outdoor games—is a must to keep this breed healthy and happy.

Puppies
Litters usually consist of 6 to 10 puppies. Color sometimes becomes richer as puppies mature. Easy to raise. Housebreaking is relatively easy.

Comment
Made famous on television by the beloved Lassie, this breed originated in Scotland centuries ago and at one time was known as the Scotch Collie. Because of the breed's great intelligence and, some claim, telepathic power, Collies were used in the Scottish mountains to control flocks of sheep.
Although early English colonists probably brought their dogs with them to America, the modern breed was introduced in the United States only in the late 19th century. One of the first breeds to be recognized by the American Kennel Club, the Collie was registered in 1885. The United Kennel Club registered the breed as the Scotch Collie in the 1920s.
Few breeds are as attractive and graceful as the Collie. Although not as well known, the smooth variety possesses all of the qualities of the rough-coated Collie, and is becoming increasingly popular, especially since it requires less grooming.

Recommendation
The Collie is a fine family dog. It is exceptional with children and, although aloof with strangers, will welcome them as it gets to know them. An alert watchdog, the Collie should not be used as a guard dog: It will make friends rather than attack. Best suited to a home with room to exercise, but adaptable to apartment living, provided it gets long walks daily.

Plates 141, 142, 143

German Shepherd

Characteristics
Long, wedge-shaped muzzle
Erect ears
Muscular build
Short, harsh, dense coat
Bushy tail

Personality
Extremely smart. Excellent watchdog and guard dog. Can be trained to perform almost any task. Reserved with strangers, but completely devoted to its family, including children. Looks stern, but is loving toward those it knows. Can be sharp with strange dogs, especially small ones. Must receive thorough obedience training early. Very responsive.

Ideal Appearance
Muscular dog. Males, ideally 24" to 26" tall, sometimes up to 28"; bitches, 22" to 24". Although standard does not specify weight, both sexes usually weigh between 65 and 90 pounds. Strong, agile build, longer than high. Sharply defined, tapering skull, and strong, long, wedge-shaped muzzle. Erect, high-set ears. Relatively long, muscular neck. Deep chest and straight back. Bushy, slightly curved tail. Short, straight, harsh, dense coat lies close to body. Permissible colors: black, tan, tan and black, or gray; white not allowed. Dark eyes.

Potential Health Problems
Generally hardy but can be subject to several problems: hip dysplasia, skin diseases and infections, bloat, congenital heart disease, nervous conditions, Von Willebrandt's disease, and some other disorders, including dwarfism.

Care and Exercise
Coat tends to shed and should be brushed 3 times a week for 10 minutes each session. Exercise is very important: this breed needs daily exercise of long walks on a leash at the very least. Daily runs in an open area are even better. Because of its energy and keen mind, dog can become troublesome if inactive. Idle dogs can become timid, nervous, or even dangerous. Continual contact with people from the time dog is a puppy will make a wonderful pet. Start obedience training early.

Puppies
Litters average 5 to 10 puppies, which mature in 18 to 24 months. Each puppy should receive daily individual contact with people.

Comment
A native of Germany, the German Shepherd traces its ancestry to the early herding dogs of Europe several hundred years ago. In England and other countries in the United Kingdom, it is called the Alsatian, because the English wanted to protect the animal from anti-German sentiment following World War I.

The German Shepherd loves working with people. It has been used as a police dog, a guide dog for the blind, an army patrol dog, and a guard dog. American soldiers returning from Europe brought German Shepherds home. The breed is now the most popular herding dog registered with the American Kennel Club.

Recommendation
The German Shepherd can be a most loyal and intelligent companion if trained properly. It must have regular companionship with people and plenty of room to be active. This breed should not be left alone for long hours with nothing to do, nor should it be tied up or restricted. A pet should not be trained to attack or to be more territorial than it is naturally.

Plate 140

Old English Sheepdog

Characteristics
Shaggy coat
Head appears round
Hanging ears
Tail very short or absent
Round feet

Personality
Lovable, sensible, and affectionate. Responsive to people. Especially exuberant at a young age. Consequently a somewhat slow learner, but nontheless readily trainable. Becomes a member of the family.

Ideal Appearance
Shaggy, compact dog. Males, 22″ tall or more (up to 24″); bitches, slightly less. Although standard does not specify weight, dogs usually weigh 65 to 90 pounds. Shaggy double coat covers eyes, giving head a rounded, distinctive look. Large head with large, black nose. Medium-size hanging ears carried flat against head. Short body. Small, round feet. Very short natural tail, or one docked to 2″ or less. Permissible colors: any shade of gray, grizzle, blue, or blue merle, with or without white markings. Dark eyes.

Potential Health Problems
Usually healthy. Subject to hip dysplasia, congenital eye defects, cataracts, and some skin disorders. Possible respiratory and bleeding problems.

Care and Exercise
Coat requires attention, but, if properly cared for, will not be too great a problem. Although show dogs often have very long coats, pets' coats can be trimmed to a more manageable length. Soft undercoat collects dirt easily and should be combed out weekly. Brush for at least 30 minutes each week. Brush from the tail forward. With proper care, shedding is moderate. Bathing is required only when dog gets dirty. The Old English Sheepdog needs plenty of daily exercise, such as several long walks on a long leash. Obedience training is required.

Puppies
Usual litter consists of 5 to 8 puppies. Often tails are docked within a few days of birth, giving the breed the nickname "bobtail." Puppies mature in about 2 years. They should become accustomed to people from the beginning on a daily basis.

Comment
Originally a herding dog in western England, the Old English Sheepdog is not an old breed; it was first encountered in its present form about 150 years ago. Although cuddly and docile-looking, this sheepdog was a hardworking breed, quick to retrieve and drive straying sheep. It was without peer on the farm. The breed has long been a familiar character in paintings and literature, most prominently as the beloved Nana in J. M. Barrie's *Peter Pan*. At one time, combings from these dogs' coats were used to make wool garments in England, but this practice has been discontinued on a commercial basis.

Recommendation
Although its coat requires considerable care, the Old English Sheepdog makes a fine, companionable family pet. Like all dogs, it deserves attention. As it grows older, its exuberance lessens. Devoted to its family, the Old English Sheepdog makes a good watchdog. It does best in a large home with a good yard. Not an ideal first dog, this breed is recommended for experienced dog people.

Plate 109

Puli

Characteristics
Resembles
Komondor, but much
smaller
Unusual, corded coat
falls to ground
Solid color

Personality
Happy, bustling, and tirelessly energetic. Reserved with other dogs and strangers. Good watchdog. May bark excessively. Fine with its family, including children with which it has been raised.

Ideal Appearance
Resembles miniature Komondor. Males, about 17"; bitches, about 16" (1" over or under acceptable for both). Although standard does not specify weight, both males and bitches usually weigh about 30 pounds. Slightly domed head with hanging ears. Muscular neck, sloping shoulders, and deep chest. Tail carried low with end curled up when relaxed; carried over back when alert. Unusual, natural, corded coat reaches ground. Permissible colors: solids, usually black, rusty black, shades of gray, or, rarely, white. Dark brown eyes.

Potential Health Problems
Robust overall. Subject to hip dysplasia, so should be X-rayed by a veterinarian before breeding.

Care and Exercise
Long coat requires regular bathing and brushing. Takes longer to dry than shorthaired breeds. Brush once a week for 45 minutes. Cords can be brushed out if desired, for pets. Sheds very little. This active, bouncy dog needs ample daily exercise: walks on a leash at least; strenuous games are even better. Territorial by nature, it should be given obedience training.

Puppies
Litters generally made up of 4 to 7 puppies, which mature in 15 to 18 months. Puppy's coat is tufted, but as dog matures, undercoat tangles into top coat, forming the cords. Puppies should be handled by people from birth.

Comment
Known in Hungary since the Magyar invasion of the 10th century, the Puli has a unique herding style: It can stop suddenly and leap straight up over the backs of the animals it is tending, which makes it a most effective drover. Moreover, the breed's unusual, thick, corded coat helps it withstand the most rugged weather. Still used to guard sheep in Hungary, the breed is rarely put to work in this country.

The Puli is a small but excellent watchdog, as it is fearless, energetic, and a loud barker. With its fast, short-stepping strides, the Puli always appears to be going someplace in a hurry. The breed was brought to the United States in the 1930s.

Recommendation
This quick learner is an alert family dog. It must learn early to be accepting of other dogs and strangers; otherwise it may become aggressive when approached by them. The breed's intelligence makes it readily trainable. Best suited to an active outdoor lifestyle.

Plate 86

Shetland Sheepdog

Characteristics
Resembles miniature
Collie
Long, wedge-shaped
head
Semi-prick ears
Long, full tail
Long double coat

Personality
Good-natured and eager to please. Alert but not aggressive; in some instances, somewhat shy. Tends to be standoffish with strangers, but good with other dogs. Very gentle. Usually quite active. Good with children. Noisy.

Ideal Appearance
Resembles rough-coated Collie. Males and bitches, 13″ to 16″ tall. Although standard does not specify weight, both sexes usually weigh about 20 pounds. Long, wedge-shaped head with dark eyes. Small, high-set, semi-prick ears break forward three quarters of the distance from base. Arched, muscular neck. Level back and compact body. Tail quite long. Double coat: long, straight, harsh outer coat; dense undercoat. Permissible colors: black, blue merle, or sable, marked with varying amounts of white and/or tan.

Potential Health Problems
Generally healthy, but some dogs subject to eye problems, skin disorders, hip dysplasia, polyarthritis, or congenital heart problems. Possible bleeding disorders and epilepsy.

Care and Exercise
Brush twice a week for 15 minutes each time. This breed sheds heavily in fall and especially spring; otherwise, normal shedding.
Exercise daily on a leash. Requires less exercise than larger herding dogs. Excessive barking should be discouraged.

Puppies
Average litter, 4 to 6 puppies, which mature in 15 to 18 months. Puppies require no special treatment, only daily contact with people.

Comment
Often referred to as the "miniature" rough Collie, this breed originated in the Shetland Isles of Scotland, which are also famous for miniature ponies, cattle, and sheep. Perhaps the somewhat bare, rugged, and hostile nature of these islands, where little food and space was available, encouraged the breeding of the miniature animals. Both the Sheltie and modern Collie trace back to a common ancestor, a small, Collie-like sheepdog. By crossing several small dogs—including spaniels, small herding breeds, and the larger rough Collie—breeders eventually developed the Shetland Sheepdog we know today.
Despite its diminutive size, the Sheltie is an impressive herder, able to work the flocks for long hours with great tenacity, nipping at the sheep's heels. In this country, the breed has become an immensely popular pet.

Recommendation
The Shetland Sheepdog is an excellent companion and family dog, good in a suburban home or an apartment. Because some dogs are extremely shy, it is important to acquire one with an outgoing personality and then to make it comfortable with people and noise while still young. Shelties thrive on exercise, but this need be nothing more than a long daily walk. However, prospective owners should bear in mind that this little dog requires considerable grooming to maintain its elegant look.

Plate 49

Cardigan Welsh Corgi

Characteristics
Bushy tail
Long, low body
Very short legs
Large, erect ears,
larger than
Pembroke's

Personality
Bright, alert, and moderately active. Unaware of its small size; behaves like a much larger dog. Can be quite reserved with strangers. Good watchdog.

Ideal Appearance
A small, sturdy, low dog. Both sexes, 10½″ to 12½″ tall and 36″ to 43″ long from nose to tip of tail. Males weigh 30 to 38 pounds; bitches, 25 to 34 pounds. Very short legs. Main differences from Pembroke are presence of low-set, bushy tail and shape of head: Muzzle is not as tapered, and erect ears are larger and set well apart. Dense, harsh, medium-length coat lies close to body. Permissible colors: red, sable, brindle, blue merle, or black with or without tan or blue brindle points; all colors usually with white on neck, chest, feet, face, under body, or on tip of tail. Dark eyes.

Potential Health Problems
Generally a healthy breed. Because of long back, prone to back problems, but usually these are not serious. Possible eye disorders and bleeding tendencies.

Care and Exercise
Coat requires little care, only brushing for 10 minutes twice a week. Shedding is normal. Loves to run about and should be given daily exercise on a leash.

Puppies
Litters average 5 to 7 puppies, which mature in 12 to 15 months. As with all breeds, puppies should be handled by people daily from an early age. Puppies are easy to raise and train.

Comment
The Cardigan Welsh Corgi originated more than 3000 years ago in the high country of Wales known as Cardiganshire, where it was an excellent cattle drover. Fast, low, and fearless, the breed could also be used to chase small game, including weasels, foxes, and rats. Undoubtedly, the Cardigan's ancestors came from the same family as the Dachshund's. The breed has not achieved the popularity of the Pembroke Corgi.

Recommendation
An excellent companion, the Cardigan Welsh Corgi can do well in either apartments or the suburbs if exercised regularly. This playful breed requires little care, but great amounts of love. Given the attention it needs, the Cardigan will become your most devoted friend. Cardigans do very well in pairs.

Plate 56

Pembroke Welsh Corgi

Characteristics
No tail
Long, low body
Very short legs, shorter than Cardigan's
Medium-size erect ears

Personality
More outgoing and restless than Cardigan Welsh Corgi. High spirited and fun-loving. Friendly with other dogs and strangers. Quite bold, but obedient. An alert watchdog.

Ideal Appearance
A low, long, tailless dog. Both sexes, 10" to 12" tall. Males, up to 30 pounds, ideally 27; bitches, up to 28 pounds, ideally 25. Foxlike head with oval eyes and medium-size, erect, high-set ears. Very short legs. No tail, unlike Cardigan. Straight, medium-length coat lies flat; is harsh to the touch. Permissible colors: red, sable, fawn, black, or tan, with or without white markings; too much white disqualifies for show. Brown eyes.

Potential Health Problems
Robust and long-lived. Tends to have back problems, but these are not usually serious. Possible eye disorders and bleeding tendencies.

Care and Exercise
Coat requires about 10 minutes of brushing twice a week. Normal amount of shedding. Like all herding dogs, this Corgi loves to run. It is full of energy and should be exercised daily on a leash.

Puppies
Average litter, 5 to 8 puppies, which mature in 12 to 15 months. Puppies should become accustomed to people soon after birth.

Comment
Considerably younger than the Cardigan Welsh Corgi, the Pembroke traces its origin to the 12th century. It comes from Pembrokeshire, Wales. Despite a striking physical resemblance to today's Cardigan, the Pembroke did not originally have any ancestors in common with the Cardigan. It descended from a northern sled dog-type rather than from the Dachshund family. However, during the 19th century, the Cardigan and the Pembroke were interbred, a practice that is no longer allowed.

Today the 2 Corgis are regarded as separate breeds. The Pembroke is far more popular than the Cardigan, possibly because the English royalty has owned the breed for several generations. Starting in 1936, King George VI gave Pembroke Welsh Corgis to his daughters, Margaret and Elizabeth; today the queen still owns Pembroke Corgis.

Recommendation
This breed apparently does not know it is a small dog; it behaves like a giant. Bold and fun-loving, the Pembroke Welsh Corgi makes a great family dog. With care and attention, it will bring many happy hours to its family. Many owners like to have pairs of these dogs.

Plate 55

United Kennel Club Breeds

Working Dogs

The ten breeds described in this section are recognized by the United Kennel Club but not by the American Kennel Club. All are working dogs, except the tiny Toy Fox Terrier, which is a lapdog. The five coonhounds described here are hunting dogs that track game using their keen sense of smell. Hunters use these dogs to trail and tree large animals such as bears, mountain lions, and bobcats, as well as the smaller raccoons and oppossums. These outdoor dogs hunt either individually or in packs of several hounds and are usually kept in kennels. The UKC hunting dogs are the Bluetick, English, Redbone, and Treeing Walker coonhounds, and the Plott Hound. Three breeds are herding dogs used on the farm or ranch: the Australian Shepherd, the English Shepherd, and the Border Collie. These dogs herd cattle and sheep. Their thick coats enable them to endure the most rugged weather and conditions, while their sturdy builds give them great endurance for long days of work. Some of them make good guardians for children. The American Eskimo is essentially a guard dog; it does well in both country and city homes as long as it has enough exercise.

The last member of this group, the Toy Fox Terrier, makes an ideal apartment pet, as it requires little exercise or care.

Dual Registration

Four additional UKC breeds are referred to in the AKC sections. These dogs include the American Pit Bull Terrier (see American Staffordshire Terrier), Arctic Husky (see Siberian Husky), American Black and Tan Coonhound (see Black and Tan Coonhound), and Scotch Collie (see Collie). The United Kennel Club registers seventy-one additional breeds, which are identical to those recognized by the American Kennel Club.

American Eskimo

Characteristics
Resembles Samoyed,
but smaller
Lionlike mane
Wedge-shaped head
Prick ears
Long, white coat
Plume tail

Personality
An exceptionally alert, robust, companionable dog. Remarkably intelligent. Playful and eager to please. Normally a one-family breed; wary of strangers. An excellent watchdog.

Ideal Appearance
Member of northern sled-dog family, resembling a small Samoyed. 2 sizes. Miniature: male, 12″ to 15″ tall and 12 to 20 pounds; bitches, slightly smaller and 10 to 18 pounds. Standard: males, 16″ to 20″ tall and 20 to 35 pounds; bitches, slightly smaller and 18 to 32 pounds. Wedge-shaped head with prick ears. Sturdy, muscular build forms square: Distance from withers to ground equals distance from brisket to rump. Long coat with lionlike mane. Permissible colors: white or biscuit-cream; darker shade is undesirable. Black to dark brown eyes with white eyelashes. Black to dark brown nose, mouth, and rims of eyes.

Potential Health Problems
Healthy and strong. If not groomed routinely, may get skin ailments. Does not do well in heat and humidity.

Care and Exercise
Normally needs only weekly brushing, but brush more frequently in spring and summer, when dog sheds heavily. Bathe once a month or as needed: The white coat contains a natural oil that repels soil, and this breed does not have the odor problems of many longhaired breeds, so bathing is not required as often as one might think.
The American Eskimo enjoys active exercise and roughhousing. Daily runs in a fenced-in backyard are sufficient. If kept in a city, dog needs long walks on leash and occasional free runs in the country.

Puppies
Litters usually contain about 5 puppies. Newborns resemble little polar bears.

Ears should become erect by 10 to 12 weeks. Black nose, mouth, and eye rims usually appear within 10 weeks.

Comment
Among the oldest dog breeds, the American Eskimo belongs to the group of northern sled dogs that descended from the peat dog, a breed that lived among the New Stone Age lake dwellers. Remains of these dogs, dating back some 6000 years, have been found in the Soviet Union, Finland, Lapland, Scandinavia, and Germany. The strong hunting instinct of most of the other Nordic breeds has been replaced in the American Eskimo by a guarding ability. The United Kennel Club first recognized the American Eskimo in 1913. For many years it was relatively rare, but in the last decade it has grown in popularity and number.

Recommendation
The American Eskimo's keen wit and gentle temperament make it an excellent, obedient dog. It learns quickly. While playful with children, it will bark aggressively to announce intruders. The Eskie enjoys cold weather better than warm, but is adaptable to almost any region. As long as it is near its family, it will be happy either in an apartment or on a farm.

Plate 103

Australian Shepherd

Characteristics
Collie-like build
Full, medium-length coat
Natural or docked tail

Personality
Attentive and animated. Strong and agile, with great stamina. A working dog that is both a herder and a guard dog. Performs all tasks with style and enthusiasm. An aggressive, authoritative, and tireless worker. This exceptional companion is reserved with strangers, but not shy. Intelligent and easily trained.

Ideal Appearance
Collie-like build. Males, 20″ to 23″ tall and 50 to 65 pounds; bitches, 18″ to 21″ and proportionately lighter. Strong head with slightly tapering muzzle. Body slightly longer than tall, with level topline. Low center of gravity. Double coat is medium length and straight to slightly wavy. Backs of forelegs feathered, forming breeches on rear legs. Moderate mane. Permissible colors: blue merle; red (liver) merle; solid red; and solid black, with or without white markings and/or tan (copper) on face, ears, legs, and tail. White splashes not allowed. Blue, brown, or amber eyes; any variation acceptable.

Potential Health Problems
Healthy overall. Watch for skin hot spots.

Care and Exercise
Brush about twice a week. This active breed requires a lot of exercise. Running alongside a bicycle will keep an Aussie in top physical condition. Ideal workout is routine herding on a farm or ranch. This dog should not work cattle until approximately a year old. Obedience training recommended.

Puppies
Litters average 5 to 8 puppies. Owner should establish dominance early so that puppies can easily be trained to accept commands when herding. Without training, puppies tend to heel to their mother or littermates and do not accept commands.

Comment
Despite this breed's name, the Australian Shepherd's origins extend beyond Australia; it is undoubtedly a composite of various herding dogs from several countries. The Spanish are said to have brought their own herding dogs to New Zealand and Australia, where the dogs mixed with English and Scottish breeds, ultimately developing a new herding dog, which is now called the Australian Shepherd. The breed was recognized by the United Kennel Club in 1979.

Recommendation
The Australian Shepherd should have a large yard or live in the country. While it may adapt to apartment living, it cannot live a sedentary life nor stand being left alone for long hours. This dog enjoys being with people and makes an ideal baby-sitter for children, a result of its herding instincts. However, the Aussie is really a herding breed, meant to work cattle or sheep.

Plate 97

Border Collie

Characteristics
Broad skull
Semi-prick ears
Dense double coat
Mane
Feathering on legs
Bushy tail

Personality

A fast, strong, working breed. Used to handle livestock, especially sheep. Quick to learn and exceptionally intelligent. Reserved with strangers. Very aware of surroundings and a good watchdog. Quite territorial. Usually stays on own property. Can be stubborn.

Ideal Appearance

Males, 17″ to 21″ tall and 30 to 50 pounds; bitches, usually smaller. Body is slightly longer than tall. Head like that of old-fashioned Collie, with broad skull, slightly blunt muzzle, and moderate stop. Fairly large, dark eyes set wide apart. Medium-size, half-prick ears, broad at base and tapering to tip. Deep chest. Straight back from withers to loin, with slight rise over loin. Straight, muscular forelegs with muscular forearms. Long, wide-set hind legs. Bushy, low-set tail carried low with slight upward swirl. Dense and curly or slightly wavy double coat: harsh outer coat; soft undercoat. Feathering on legs. Full mane. Permissible colors: black, gray, or blue merle, with white on face, ears, legs, and tail; or black, white, and tan. Markings on face, collar, feet, breast, and tip of tail. Dark eyes.

Potential Health Problems

Usually robust, but watch for progressive retinal atrophy and possible skin ailments.

Care and Exercise

Brush at least once a week. Bathe as needed. If kept as a working dog in a kennel, the Border Collie exercises itself. It loves to run free in a fenced yard. Thrives when working. Can be exercised by running next to you, but it may nip other bikers' or joggers' heels, since it takes territorial guarding seriously. May chase cars if not corrected early and well.

Puppies

Litters average 6 to 8 puppies. Tails of newborns are not docked.

Comment

Very little is known about the Border Collie's history, except that it traces back to the 1700s. Originally called Colly, after the Colly Sheep, the Border Collie may be a mixture of the Scotch Collie and the Bearded Collie. The integrity of this working breed was almost destroyed when it became a favorite of the English gentry in the 19th century. Yet despite the tendency at that time to transform the dog into a pet, some breeders strove to maintain its working abilities.

The Border Collie was registered by the United Kennel Club in 1961. Although the American Kennel Club does not include the breed in its stud registry, it is part of the AKC miscellaneous class.

Recommendation

The Border Collie is happiest at work and outdoors. It is not well suited to apartment living. The breed's instinct to herd makes it an outstanding, obedient dog and a great baby-sitter and watchdog.

Plate 99

Bluetick Coonhound

Characteristics
Muscular hound build
Long, hanging ears
Tail carried high
above back
Mottled blue

Personality
Typical working hound, although somewhat more aggressive than the American Black and Tan Coonhound. Energetic and very persistent; has great endurance. Gets along fairly well with other animals and people. Loud, bawling bark. Some dogs may become very aggressive after years of pursuing big game. Not a house dog. Usually works alone.

Ideal Appearance
Males, 22″ to 27″ tall and 55 to 80 pounds; bitches, up to 25″ and a maximum weight of 65 pounds. Has a pleading hound expression, which is neither wild nor cowering. Head carried high. Straight tail carried gaily above back. Muscular body is generally slightly higher at shoulders than at hips, never lower. Short, neat, glossy coat. Permissible colors: dark blue, thickly mottled with variously shaped black spots on back, ears, and sides; preferably more blue than black on body. Black on head; tan dots over eyes and on cheeks; dark red ticking on feet and lower legs. Markings not required. Blue ticking should prevail over white in body coat. Dark brown, black, or hazel eyes.

Potential Health Problems
A strong breed. Internal parasites, such as hookworms, whipworms, roundworms, and heart worms, pose the greatest threat to health of this working breed; dogs should be checked by a veterinarian routinely.

Care and Exercise
A rough-and-ready hound, equally at home in swamps, mountains, or desert landscapes, the Bluetick Coonhound requires little special care. Removal of ticks, thorns, or briars from feet, and seeds from eyes, may be necessary after nocturnal trips in the field. Regular dipping in a reliable stock dip helps keep external parasites in check.

This is basically an outdoor dog that needs regular exercise to maintain the top physical condition necessary for hunting. Kennel should contain a warm, dry box with adequate room for exercise during times when a lot of outdoor activity is not possible.

Puppies
Litters average 6 to 12 puppies, but sometimes contain more. At birth puppies are white with black spots; they usually develop adult's mottled, ticking coloration before weaning time. Loud, bawling voice at an early age. Puppies tend to bark a lot. May learn slowly at first.

Comment
The Bluetick probably descended from the English Foxhounds and the various French hounds that were used for hunting mountain lions and bears. In addition, some Bloodhound is almost certainly in its background.
This breed was originally registered with the United Kennel Club as a variety of the English Coonhound. In 1946, at the request of Bluetick fanciers, the Bluetick Coonhound was recognized as a separate breed.

Recommendation
Primarily used to hunt animals that climb trees, the Bluetick Coonhound trails raccoon, bear, mountain lion, and bobcat. This breed's strong, melodious voice can be heard for miles. The Bluetick is a hard-going, rugged breed that easily adapts to different terrains.

Plate 70

English Coonhound

Characteristics
Muscular hound build
Deep chest
Slightly arched back
Long, hanging ears
Natural tail

Personality
A working hound. Milder in temperament than the Bluetick Coonhound; otherwise similar to other coonhound breeds. Quick to please. A good all-around hunting dog. Usually hunts individually.

Ideal Appearance
Strong, sleek body. Males, 22" to 27" tall; bitches, up to 25". Although standard does not specify weight, males range from 50 to 80 pounds; bitches, from 40 to 65 pounds. Deep "barrel" chest. Strong, slightly arched back. Slightly higher at shoulders than at hips. Short, glossy coat. Permissible colors: any hound colors; ticked color; or tricolored, with black saddle. Dark eyes.

Potential Health Problems
Not particularly susceptible to usual canine abnormalities, such as hip dysplasia. May, however, get bloat or gastric torsion, which can be fatal if not tended to immediately. Check for internal parasites.

Care and Exercise
Requires a complete and balanced daily ration of commercial food, with plenty of water, which should be changed daily or dog will reject it. A proper feeding schedule and close observation can be helpful in preventing gastric torsion and bloat. Overfeeding during periods of little exercise, such as summer months, will lead to weight gain. Inspect dog carefully after each trip in the field for external parasites, and check with a veterinarian routinely. Provide warm, dry sleeping quarters and keep kennel area clean. These dogs do not need to be pampered: A good, commonsense approach to care, feeding, and shelter is advised.
Like all working hounds, the English Coonhound needs a routine of hardy exercise to stay in prime condition. Long runs in a field are a must.

Puppies
Litters usually contain 6 to 12 puppies. Blue-ticked, red-ticked, and tricolored puppies may occur in same litter. Keep bitch and litter in warm, draft-free environment. Eyes of newborns open at 2 weeks. English Coonhound puppies can usually take solid food when just a month old.

Comment
Like all coonhounds except the Plott Hound, the English Coonhound's ancestry is deeply rooted in the English Foxhound. It is also related to the Virginia hounds raised by George Washington.
The English Coonhound was first registered by the United Kennel Club in 1905 under the name English Fox and Coonhound, because in England the dogs had been used primarily to hunt fox. However, the breed was gradually adapted to the much rougher American terrain and climate through careful breeding, and was trained to hunt raccoon, opossum, cougar, and bear. Breed standards are more lenient for the English Coonhound than for other coonhound breeds; hunting ability comes first, and appearance is only secondary. English Coonhounds have excelled in both the field and the show ring.

Recommendation
An easily handled hunting dog with excellent treeing instincts, the English Coonhound is an expert hunter of many types of game. It is strictly a working breed.

Plate 71

English Shepherd

Characteristics
Collie-like build
Long, heavy nose
Bushy tail
No mane

Personality
Energetic, intelligent, very active, and courageous. Dominant and protective. A natural heeler, loyal to its master. A versatile herding dog. Responds almost at once to working commands around farm stock. Works well with cattle, sheep, hogs, and poultry. A wonderful companion and watchdog, but inclined to chase cars, joggers, and bicyclists.

Ideal Appearance
Collie-like build. Males, 18″ to 22″ tall and 40 to 50 pounds; bitches, slightly smaller and 35 to 45 pounds. Head and neck carried slightly raised. Wide skull, flat above dark eyes and broad between ears. Long, heavy muzzle about 4″ long from tip to stop. Semi-prick ears are wide at top and narrow to point. Deep, wide chest. Bushy tail, carried slightly higher than back with only a slight curve. Heavy, glossy coat is straight or curly, abundant over body. No mane. Slight feathering on legs. Permissible colors: black and white; black and tan; black, white, and tan. White allowed on chest, in ring around neck, on tip of tail, in blaze on face and lower legs; tan dots over eyes; sable feet.

Potential Health Problems
A healthy breed, relatively free from genetic weakness. Watch for temporary skin conditions.

Care and Exercise
Full coat requires very little care; brush about twice a week. An active breed, the English Shepherd needs a good deal of exercise, such as running alongside a bicycle. But this herding dog may be inclined to chase or "herd" joggers and cars; this tendency must be discouraged at an early age. Best exercise is routine work as a farm or ranch dog.

Puppies
Litters average 5 to 8 puppies. An owner should establish dominance at a very early age so that dogs can be easily trained to accept commands when herding.

Comment
Stock dogs of the shepherd type have been carefully bred on the British Isles for centuries. As is true of most dogs from the Highlands or in the rough border country between England and Scotland, this breed's history is highly conjectural; little is known for certain. The English Shepherd was introduced in the United States by the early settlers and has come down to us practically unchanged in type and temperament.

Recommendation
The English Shepherd is primarily an outdoor dog. Although it can adjust to apartment living, it is happiest on the farm or ranch.

Plate 98

Plott Hound

Characteristics
Very muscular hound build
Head carried high
Deep chest
Slightly arched back
Saberlike tail
Always brindle

Personality
Warm, friendly, and gregarious with people, but fierce and aggressive toward wild game. A working hound. Has a sharp, high-pitched bark. Can be a loyal guardian of children. Hunts both in packs and individually.

Ideal Appearance
Males, 22″ to 27″ tall and 50 to 75 pounds; bitches, slightly smaller and 40 to 65 pounds. Head is carried high. Medium-length ears, set moderately high, are generally shorter than those of other hound breeds. Deep chest; slightly arched, muscular back. Moderately heavy, saberlike tail. Glossy, fine to medium-coarse coat of short or medium length. Permissible colors: brindle, or black with brindle trim; no solid colors accepted. Some white allowed on chest and feet, but not elsewhere; gray allowed around muzzle. Coat should have a streaked or striped effect. Dark eyes.

Potential Health Problems
Hardiest of all coonhound breeds. Rare cases of hip dysplasia observed. As in all large working dogs, susceptible to bloat. Needs to be checked routinely by a veterinarian for internal parasites.

Care and Exercise
Little grooming required: After hunts, check dogs for burrs, ticks, and other external parasites. Plott Hounds are ravenous eaters and should be given moderate servings of complete and balanced commercial dog food. Do not allow them to become obese.
Needs plenty of exercise to keep muscle tone, especially before the hunting season. Many big game hunters exercise their dogs by releasing 1 or 2 at a time in front of a car on an untraveled road. This allows the dogs to run several miles on the stone or gravel surface, which hones their feet and legs, preparing them for the sharp surfaces they will encounter when chasing bears and other big game.

However, unless you live in a deserted area, this method of exercise is not recommended.

Puppies
Litters of 6 to 12 puppies. Newborns that appear black usually become lighter, and light-colored ones turn to darker shades of brindle as they mature. Brindle hair can be detected in very young puppies by rubbing the hair backward in the light. Eyes open at 12 to 14 days.

Comment
Unlike the other UKC hounds, the Plott Hound has no English background; instead it traces back to Germany, where its ancestors hunted wild boar for centuries. The American breed is largely credited to Jonathan Plott, who emigrated from Germany to the mountains of North Carolina in 1750, bringing a few hounds with him. Plott used his dogs to hunt bear.
The all-purpose Plott Hound met the requirements of the early settlers in the Appalachians, the Blue Ridge Mountains, and the Great Smoky Mountains. Known for its stamina, courage, and hunting instinct, the Plott Hound is said to have also served as a patient nursemaid for pioneer infants while their mothers tended to chores. During the late 18th century, the Plott Hound was bred with a strain of "leopard-spotted bear dogs" in Georgia, and other crosses possibly took place around 1900.
The Plott Hound was registered with the United Kennel Club in 1946.

Recommendation
The Plott Hound can hunt both small game such as raccoons and big game like bear. Hunters should note that it does not have the loud, bawling voice common to most hounds. Thus the breed can also be used as a farm or stock dog.

Plate 69

Redbone Coonhound

Characteristics
Muscular hound build
Deep chest
Slightly arched back
Long ears
Natural tail
Red

Personality
Easygoing. Compatible with people and other dogs. Even-tempered; slower to excite than some hound breeds. A fine hunter with a sweet hound voice. Does well in packs or individually.

Ideal Appearance
Muscular build. Males, 22″ to 27″ tall; bitches, up to 25″. Although standard does not specify weight, males weigh from 50 to 80 pounds; bitches, from 40 to 65 pounds. Moderately broad head with fairly low-set ears. Deep, broad chest. Strong, slightly arched back. Slightly taller at shoulder than at hips. Straight, well-boned legs. Medium-length tail with slight brush. Permissible colors: solid red preferred; small amount of white allowed on brisket or feet. Brown to hazel eyes; dark eyes preferred.

Potential Health Problems
No known inherited weaknesses. Susceptible to gastric torsion and rarely hip dysplasia. Should be checked routinely by a veterinarian for internal parasites.

Care and Exercise
A complete, balanced diet of good commercial food is essential. During periods of reduced activity, lessen food intake. Cut toenails to reduce splitting and injury to feet. Give dogs warm, dry sleeping quarters and plenty of fresh water. Keep ears dry and free of fungus and parasites. Frequent, periodic dipping for external parasites is a must, especially in the South. Seeds should be removed from eyes after trips afield. Proper exercise is necessary for top performance as a hunter.

Puppies
Litters average 6 to 12 puppies. At birth puppies appear tan; they darken as they mature. Full height and weight usually reached by 10 months, but sometimes not until 2 years of age.

Comment
Years ago, most coon hunters referred to any red dog of unknown ancestry that could track and tree raccoons as a Redbone. A few serious breeders decided to produce a superior coonhound that would always breed true to this type in both color and body build. The foundation stock for the modern-day Redbone came from George F. L. Birdsong of Georgia, a noted breeder in the 1840s.

Like most of the other coonhound breeds, the Redbone derived from the English Foxhound. It is believed that at one time these dogs were crossed with the Bloodhound and, later, Irish hounds. The Bloodhound gave the breed its sweet voice and fine nose, while the Irish hounds account for its white chest and feet markings.

In 1902 the Redbone became the second coonhound breed to be registered with the United Kennel Club, 2 years after the American Black and Tan. Used primarily to hunt raccoon, the Redbone can also trail and tree bear, cougar, and bobcat. It is a favorite hound in the South.

Recommendation
Equally at home hunting alone or in a pack, the Redbone is predictable and reliable. Its agility allows it to hunt either in fenced country or on steep, rocky ground, and Redbones are also known to make excellent water dogs. Although the breed is not as competitive as some other coonhounds are, the Redbone Coonhound compensates with its excellent treeing instincts and tracking ability.

Plate 72

Treeing Walker Coonhound

Characteristics
Resembles English
Foxhound
Muscular hound build
Slightly arched back
Long, hanging ears
Natural tail
Tricolor

Personality
A high-energy hunting breed. Fast, with remarkable endurance. Alert and ready, but sometimes hyperactive. Strictly an outdoor dog. Works well in packs or alone.

Ideal Appearance
Males, 22″ to 27″ tall; bitches, up to 25″, but higher at the shoulders in proportion to body length than males. Although standard does not specify weight, males weigh from 50 to 80 pounds; bitches, from 40 to 65 pounds. Slightly domed head. Muscular build with slightly arched back and sloping shoulders. Saberlike tail carried up. Smooth, fine coat. Permissible colors: Preferably tricolored—white, black, and tan, with black or white predominating; white with tan spots or white with black spots acceptable. Dark brown or black eyes.

Potential Health Problems
Usually healthy. Occasionally gets canine bloat. Rare instances of hip dysplasia reported. Some dogs are hyperactive as a result of breeding for performance in competition events.

Care and Exercise
During periods of activity, feed a complete and balanced commercial food that is high in protein and fat; reduce protein and fat content when dog is receiving less exercise, especially during the summer.

Tends to look lean, even gaunt—even when well cared for—due to continuous activity. Thrives on exercise in large doses, and should be given ample opportunity to run and romp. Exercise by taking it on frequent trips to a field. The great speed of the Treeing Walker makes it prone to injury from fences, briars, and other obstacles at night.

Puppies
Litters average 6 to 12 puppies, but larger litters are not uncommon. Most newborns are white with black spots; tan appears as the dogs mature. Overfed puppies tend to mature faster, but excess weight at an early age may present problems later. Mature height reached before 1 year.

Comment
A descendant of the English Foxhound, the Treeing Walker Coonhound traces its lineage to the Virginia Hound of the Colonial period. Thomas Walker of Virginia is said to have imported a pack from England in 1742, and George Washington, an avid foxhunter, had several hounds brought over from England in 1770. From this foundation stock, George Washington Maupin and John W. Walker (descendants of the original Walker and Washington) developed the Walker Hound, now known as the Treeing Walker Coonhound. At least one major cross made in the 19th century influenced the modern breed; strangely, it was with a stolen dog of unknown origin from Tennessee, called Tennessee Lead. Although Lead did not resemble the Virginia strain of the English Foxhound existing then, it had an exceptional hunting instinct and plenty of drive and speed.

Treeing Walker Coonhounds were first registered by the United Kennel Club as part of the English Coonhound breed. In 1945, at the request of Walker breeders, the Treeing Walker Coonhound was recognized as a separate breed.

Recommendation
Adept at trailing big game, this breed reigns as the most popular raccoon hound. They do well in UKC night-hunt events, as well as in the field. However, their wide-ranging hunting style and independent spirit may not appeal to all hunters.

Plate 74

Toy Fox Terrier

Characteristics
Foxlike head
Small
Square build
Natural or docked tail
Satiny coat

Personality
Energetic, spirited, and intelligent. Easily trained to perform tricks. Playful. Enjoys the company of its owner. Initially wary of strangers, but brave for its size. Good playmate for older children. Can be noisy unless trained.

Ideal Appearance
Miniature version of Smooth Fox Terrier. Both males and bitches, up to 10″ tall, and 3½ to 7 pounds. Foxlike head with erect ears. Muscular, streamlined build with deep, broad chest and strong, straight back. Square body: Distance from feet to withers equals that from withers to rump. Natural bobtail, or docked tail. Short, satiny, full-textured coat, with slightly longer ruff. Permissible colors: black and white with tan trim, or tan and white; maltese, chocolate, or solid coats not acceptable. Dark eyes and black nose; brown or pink-spotted nose not allowed.

Potential Health Problems
Healthy overall. Cannot withstand long exposure to cold temperatures. Possible eye problems.

Care and Exercise
Brush and bathe occasionally. This active little dog does not require a lot of space to exercise, but it does enjoy going for walks and scouting different neighborhoods. Should wear a sweater in very cold weather.

Puppies
Litters of 2 to 4 puppies. Due to the small size of dams, a veterinarian may be necessary to assist in deliveries.

Comment
The Toy Fox Terrier was developed in the mid-1920s from the Smooth Fox Terrier and is a miniature version of that dog. The original English breed probably includes the Black and Tan Terrier, the Greyhound, the Bull Terrier, and the Beagle as its ancestors.

The Toy Fox Terrier was at first developed to rid its owners' premises of vermin. In recent years, the Toy Fox has evolved into a house or apartment dog. The breed was officially recognized by the United Kennel Club in 1936.

Recommendation
This is an ideal pet for an elderly owner because it does not need a great deal of exercise and its coat requires little care. It is not recommended for very young children; the Toy Fox Terrier often does not trust small children and cannot take their abuse and roughhousing. However, it does well with adults and older children. This breed also trains easily for obedience trials and the show ring.

Plate 19

Health Care

Before You Purchase a Dog

If given proper care from the time they are born, dogs are basically healthy animals. Nevertheless, when you purchase a dog, you want to be sure that there are not any health problems. Because some illnesses may not be immediately apparent, the bill of sale from a reputable breeder, kennel, or pet shop should include an option to return the dog within fourteen days. A full refund or replacement should be guaranteed if a veterinarian certifies that the animal has a valid health problem. This two-week period covers the incubation time for most common infectious diseases. Any illness that develops after two weeks should not be blamed on the breeder, since it probably was contracted some time after purchase. Certain breeds may be prone to inherited health problems. Maladies such as congenital heart defects, hip dysplasia, retinal (eye) degeneration, or demodectic mange may not be evident until weeks or months after a dog is purchased. Some breeders will replace puppies that develop inherited health problems, but these arrangements are usually voluntary, and the breeders involved are truly interested in the improvement of their breed. Of course, after several weeks of ownership, most people have fallen in love with their pet and do not want to trade it. The seller may therefore insist, by prior agreement, that affected dogs be neutered so they cannot reproduce and pass on undesirable traits.

Before purchasing a dog, it is wise to read as much as you can about the breed you are considering. Check the Potential Health Problems section in each breed account and, at the end of this chapter, refer to the list rating the seriousness of health problems. It is important to ask a breeder about the history of a dog's parents. Talk with breeders, other owners, or veterinarians to see if there are any serious problems with this breed.

At the time of purchase, ask the seller what you should do if your puppy develops some inherited problem. Certain congenital abnormalities, such as extra toes, a bent tail, or unusual coat or eye color, may disqualify the dog from breeding and show, but they do not affect its health or detract from the dog's suitability as a pet. To prevent future health difficulties, it is essential to take your dog for a complete veterinary examination within a few days of purchasing your pet.

Dog Beds and Dog Houses

Once you have taken your puppy home, you must decide where it will sleep. A household pet needs only a padded box or basket to call its own—a comfortable refuge for rest and seclusion. Put the box in an out-of-the-way corner of a room or a part of the house that is acceptable to you. As tempting as it might be to allow your cute puppy to sleep on your bed, remember that all too soon it will be an adult dog expecting the same privilege. The habits a dog forms as a puppy will last a lifetime.

A dog kept outdoors—a healthier situation—requires a tight, dry house to protect it from wind and weather. The house should be big enough for your pet to stand up and turn around in easily, but not so large that its body heat will not keep it warm. Loose bedding and a cloth flap over the door can help keep your dog snug in cold weather. The house should be built for easy cleaning and treating with insecticides to control parasites. Except in very rural areas, an outdoor dog should be confined to a pen or leashed to a trolley wire, which allows exercise but protects it from injury from cars, other animals, poisons, or exposure to the elements. The pen or trolley wire should always have fresh, clean water nearby.

Choosing the Right Dog Food

Selecting a dog food can be extremely

confusing, since there are so many types as well as brands available. Contrary to some advertising promotion, dogs do not need flavor variety in their food. And although they are classified as carnivores, dogs do not do well on an exclusive diet of meat. Their wild ancestors ate a balanced diet by consuming the entire carcasses of the game they caught—meat, bone, hair, and the vegetable matter their prey had eaten earlier—but modern dogs cannot.

Today dogs still require a balanced diet, and the best dog foods provide a lot of different ingredients, carefully supplemented with all the required amino acids (protein), fats, and carbohydrates, as well as essential vitamins and minerals. Commercial foods are far superior to diets composed of ingredients found in our own kitchens. Many families have cooked table food left over, especially if the household has children or finicky eaters. These leftovers can be used if limited to no more than twenty percent of the dog's diet. Most of the dog's meal should be a proven, balanced and complete commercial dog food.

Dog foods are sold either as complete and balanced diets or as special treats that are not complete. Always use the balanced diet as the basic food. If treats or snacks are also given, a single day's supply of the treat should be calculated as part of the dog's daily food consumption. The best way to control the quantity of snacks is to place a day's supply in a dish out of the dog's reach. Reward your dog with these tidbits until the dish is empty, and do not offer any more for the rest of the day. If you follow a consistent feeding plan, your dog will not be overfed and it will not become obese.

Each basic type of commerical dog food has special characteristics. Some dogs like dry and crunchy food; others prefer it sloppy and moist. Some owners want their dogs to feed themselves; others seek an inexpensive, easy-to-store product; and still others like to pamper their pets with different foods. One type of commercial dog food will probably meet both your needs and those of your dog. However, if your dog has particular problems with its diet and is very thin or very fat, or has frequent digestive upsets, you should seek veterinary advice.

Dry Dog Foods

These foods contain eight to ten percent water and are a mixture of cereals, meat by-products, and vegetable protein (soy) combined with vegetable and animal fats, vitamins, and minerals. Not only are dry dog foods the least expensive products, but also their dry, rough texture helps keep the dog's teeth and gums in good condition.

Some dry products come as loose flakes, resembling breakfast foods. Although these products are the most inexpensive, they contain high amounts of cereal and vegetable fats, and have a dry texture that is not especially palatable to a dog. Dry flake products may also contain poor-quality ingredients.

The best dry foods are expanded foods—compressed, small, irregular cubes or puffs that are sprayed with fat. Unlike the dry flakes, expanded foods have a high content of animal protein, animal fat, and moisture, and these improve the palatability or flavor. Because dogs taste the fat on the outside, they like it better; they also feel full sooner because the food is bulky but has fewer calories per ounce than denser foods, so there is less tendency to overeat. Many owners prefer the expanded food, since a big bag is relatively lightweight for the volume it contains.

Only slightly more expensive than dry flakes, expanded dry foods are very suitable as a base diet if you want to add meat scraps or leftover table foods. Moreover, they can be used for self-feeding schedules in which a dog essentially feeds itself when hungry. To accustom a dog to self-feeding, place a very large pan or pail of food before the dog just after it has been satiated by a regular feeding. Eventually the dog will nibble at its new food and then eat a small amount fifteen or twenty times a day. You must never let the food dish become empty. Since there are no leftovers, this method does not waste food, and the dog will not beg and bark at feeding time because there is none: food is available at all times. Although a few self-fed dogs overeat and become obese, most adjust their food intake to balance their energy needs for exercise, keeping warm, and maintaining their ideal body weight.

Semi-moist Foods

These foods contain twenty-five to thirty percent water and are usually packaged in cellophane or plastic pouches in the form of meat cubes, hamburgers, or steaklike patties. They are all balanced, high-protein foods and, although they look like meat, are composed mostly of meat by-products, textured soybean meal, cereals, and chemical agents added to prevent spoilage and keep the product moist. Semi-moist foods no longer have the high levels of salt or sugar that were used to prevent spoilage in the first products.

Because semi-moist foods are rich in calories and protein and are highly palatable, they are good for tempting fussy eaters, feeding puppies, or encouraging weight gain. Normal dogs may overeat when given these foods unless you watch the amount carefully. Semi-moist foods can be added to dry kibble to enhance palatability. Once the plastic seal of the packaging is broken, some of these products dry out rapidly, become less palatable, and spoil. They cannot be used for self-feeding. However, semi-moist food is useful for feeding young puppies or ill animals if it is broken up with milk or water to make a gruel.

Canned (Moist) Foods

This type of food contains seventy to eighty percent water and is highly palatable; it is also very expensive, especially for large dogs. Canned foods cannot be used for self-feeding and do not promote good teeth and gum condition. Many canned foods are classified as gourmet foods and contain ingredients such as chicken, liver, kidney, or shrimp, with special sauces or flavorings. Some are not balanced, complete foods. These products cater to the owner rather than the dog and are not recommended, especially as a staple. They may look as if they are composed entirely of muscle meat, but in reality they contain a variety of animal by-products with textured vegetable protein dyed red to look like meat. Always check the label for contents.

If a product is balanced and complete, the label will say so. In contrast to the so-called gourmet foods, complete canned foods resemble meat pudding and contain animal by-products (with cereals or soy meal as binders) as well as vitamins and minerals to meet dogs' nutritional requirements. Because of their excellent palatability, they are good for fussy eaters. However, if you are not careful, normal animals may become obese by overeating.

Homemade Diets and Dietary Supplements

Food prepared at home is rarely balanced and adequate for a dog. Homemade dishes should not be used routinely for long periods unless they are carefully formulated by a nutritionist. Even then, most people do not have the discipline to prepare baked potatoes, toast, eggs, hamburger, and/or other special items every day. The best advice here is not to use a homemade diet.

Healthy dogs rarely need dietary supplements. Rather than helping your pet, these foods may upset the ratio of nutrients in carefully balanced commercial diets. Extra does not mean better. Too much supplementation may cause serious problems in growing puppies. Vitamin and mineral powders, vitamin tablets, natural food products, and other supplements are usually a waste of money. Use them only if directed by your veterinarian to meet your pet's special needs.

Special Diets

At certain times in its life, a dog may require a special diet. Some foods are designed especially for growth, pregnancy and lactation, or weight loss. Others are intended to treat special diseases that must be managed in part by modifying or regulating food intake. Growth or weight-loss foods are designed to fulfill special physiological needs; they can be purchased from a grocery store or your veterinarian. Disease-treatment products are available only from veterinarians. They serve as part of a medical treatment and, although expensive, are worth the cost. Some are used for only a few weeks; others may be needed for the pet's lifetime. For example, a recently introduced diet has been extremely effective in causing dissolution of one common type of bladder stone.

Feeding Schedule

How often and how much should you feed your dog? When you bring your new dog home—whether puppy or adult —do not try to change its diet drastically. Feed the dog the same food on the same schedule it was on before. Later you may want or need to change this program, but do it gradually or over a period of several days.

Soon after you bring your new dog home, weigh it. You will want to watch the weight gain in a puppy or to make sure the weight of a full-grown dog is constant. Your veterinarian can give you a growth chart showing the ideal weight for your breed at different stages of its life. Then you should feed your dog amounts that allow it to maintain a weight corresponding to its weight on the growth curve.

Puppies and pregnant or lactating bitches need high-protein, high-calorie concentrated food. They should be fed two or three times daily. For each feeding provide only what they can consume in about ten minutes. Puppies require about twice the amount of food needed by adult dogs. Use of special puppy foods solves the problem of feeding schedules most conveniently. The amount to feed is usually specified on the puppy food package and depends chiefly on the dog's weight. Remember, toy breeds may be two pounds at maturity, while giant breeds may reach almost one hundred times that weight. With such a wide weight range, there are no simple rules that apply to all breeds.

Watch your puppy's progress and feed it accordingly. Puppies should grow well but be slightly thin, active, tough, and muscular, with shiny coats. It is not desirable to push them for rapid growth and get them roly-poly fat. Do not overfeed. Exercise, environmental temperature, a dog's metabolic rate, special physiological needs, and temperament all combine to determine food requirements.

After your puppy matures, in about twelve to sixteen months, keep its weight constant. Weigh the puppy monthly and increase or decrease the food as needed.

Feed an adult dog once daily—in the evening if you want it active during the day, and in the morning if you want an alert watchdog at night. Dogs, like people, get sleepy after eating. It is important to establish a sound feeding routine early and develop good habits. Resist those pleading brown eyes that ask you for one more snack.

Exercise

The need for physical activity varies greatly among breeds, and also among individual dogs. A toy terrier may get enough exercise from bouncing around an apartment, but a hunting hound needs a great deal of activity in order to work efficiently. Even confined pets get a surprising amount of exercise as they run around their pens or up and down trolley wires in response to outside distractions. If you have the space and time for two dogs, they will practically exercise themselves—wrestling and playing together and thus receiving both physical and emotional stimulation.

Whatever breed you have, try to provide regular exercise daily. Avoid strenuous weekend sessions with no work during the week. Do not feed your dog until one hour after exercise. If you plan long periods of strenuous work, such as hunting or long runs, give the dog rest stops for food and water several times during the day. Hard-working dogs require additional calories to supply energy. These can be provided by a combination of fat, proteins, and carbohydrates. For working dogs, daily requirements may increase to three or four times normal levels.

Some owners take their pets along when they jog or bike. If you do this, remember that your dog's bare footpads may be pounding a hard, hot pavement, and your pet may have to run hard to keep up. In general, most pets should not run more than a few miles in this manner unless a special training plan is formulated. At the other extreme, walking around the block for a toilet break is not much exercise for most breeds. Toy breeds are an exception.

Choosing a Veterinarian

When you take your new puppy to your veterinarian for its first physical examination, you will be told about vaccinations, parasites, feeding, behavior problems, and many other subjects that will enable you to understand the needs of your dog. Be sure to have this initial evaluation. It is important to establish a rapport with a veterinarian who knows you and your pet, and who can be an available, trusted advisor.

Before choosing a veterinarian, make sure that the office, clinic, or hospital is clean and well equipped. It should be conveniently located and open at hours that are reasonable for you. It should be covered by a twenty-four-hour emergency service. This is most important. Moreover, the staff should be friendly and enjoy caring for your pet. The veterinarian's personality should mesh with yours, and the charges should be acceptable to you. You and the veterinarian will act as a team to provide the health care your dog will need over the course of many years.

Vaccinations

The mystique of knowing which shot to have administered at what time is needlessly confusing. Puppies usually have natural protection against disease until they are weaned, and only then do they require vaccinations. At your first visit to the veterinarian, you will probably receive a vaccination schedule. To help you know what to expect, consult the schedule of required vaccinations included in this section.

When a puppy is born, it is vital that it nurse its mother during the first twenty-four hours to get the colostrum, or first milk. This milk contains special proteins and antibodies that can protect it against infectious diseases to which its mother is immune. If the bitch has been vaccinated against many diseases, the puppy will also be protected after ingesting the first milk for as long as fourteen to sixteen weeks. If the mother has a low level of resistance to a disease—or no resistance at all—the puppy will not be protected, or its protection will wane quickly in several weeks.

To reduce the risks of infectious diseases as much as possible, start vaccinations when your puppy is about six weeks old, repeat every two weeks until it is sixteen weeks old, and then give yearly booster shots. However, if you obtain a puppy that is about seven to eight weeks old (an ideal time for the puppy to be separated from its mother), vaccinations at eight, twelve, and sixteen weeks are usually adequate. A puppy purchased from a reputable dealer probably will have received some vaccinations already, depending on its age. If you have an older puppy, fewer injections will be needed.

It is crucial that at sixteen weeks or slightly later your puppy receive one vaccination for each major disease. These vaccinations are generally combined in two or three injections. Until your puppy has a fairly complete vaccination series, keep the dog relatively isolated so that it is not exposed to infection. Vaccinations are a great health bargain: Do not skimp on them or fail to keep them current. They are often packaged in combinations that help minimize both the cost and the number of injections necessary. It is particularly important that your dog receive booster vaccinations before boarding, attending dog shows, or beginning pregnancy.

Rabies

For public health reasons—animal and human health—it is the law in most areas to keep pets currently vaccinated against rabies. In many parts of the United States and Canada, rabies has become increasingly more common in wildlife, especially foxes, skunks, raccoons, and bats. Rabid animals act "funny": They may be especially affectionate or tame, when they should

be wild and furtive. Pets can be bitten by a rabid animal without their owners' knowing it. After several weeks or sometimes months of incubation, the bitten animal can develop rabies.

Rabies is a fatal disease in people and other warm-blooded animals. Therefore it is imperative that you do your part to control this disease by keeping your pet's rabies vaccination current. Many communities provide free rabies vaccination clinics. This is the only vaccine that requires a booster every third year. The injection must be given in the muscle of a rear leg and can occasionally produce temporary lameness, but that is a small matter. Rabies vaccines offer excellent protection from a devastating disease.

Distemper

This viral disease is a great killer of unvaccinated dogs. Sick dogs act as though they have a cold. They can develop pneumonia, diarrhea, and seizures. Vaccine protection is a highly effective preventative and must never be overlooked or even postponed.

Infectious Canine Hepatitis (Canine Adenovirus Type I)

Unrelated to human hepatitis, canine hepatitis usually causes only mild liver or blood-vessel disease in dogs. One side effect is the development of an opaque, blue-looking eye, involving a hardening of the cornea that results in temporary—or in the extreme, permanent—blindness. In rare cases, the systemic disease is severe and may be fatal. The vaccine is an effective preventative.

Respiratory Illnesses

Related to the hepatitis virus (adenovirus type I), adenovirus type II infection produces a cough and bronchitis. It is one cause of the contagious syndrome known as kennel cough, or infectious bronchitis. The vaccine for adenovirus type I protects against type II as well.

Two other infectious agents also often cause or contribute to kennel cough: a parainfluenza virus, for which a vaccine is available, and a bacterial infection caused by *Bordetella bronchiseptica*. The *Bordetella* bacteria normally live in the air passages of the lungs and, under stress, may precipitate disease. A vaccine for *Bordetella* infection can be given either by injection or in the form of nose drops. Usually a dog is given a combination vaccine for all three infections, which provides reasonably good but not infallible protection against kennel cough. If two or more of these infections occur simultaneously, a more severe respiratory illness results. But fortunately the disease, while troublesome, is generally self-limiting and not life-threatening.

Canine Leptospirosis
This disease is caused by a spirochete, or bacterial organism, that affects the liver and kidneys. It spreads through the urine of infected dogs or rats, and can be contracted from contaminated ponds. Symptoms of this disease are depression, lack of interest in food, high fever, and abdominal or back pain due to inflammation of the liver and kidneys. Canine leptospirosis can also affect people. The vaccine provides fairly effective prevention for six to twelve months.

Canine Parvovirus Infection
Although this infection is caused by a virus related to the cat distemper virus, it is not spread by cats. The virus causes severe diarrhea in dogs or a serious heart muscle disease that may be fatal in young puppies. Many cases respond favorably to vigorous early treatment. The vaccine is an effective preventative. If a pet becomes ill with this disease, food dishes as well as bedding and other articles used by the dog should be disinfected with a solution of one part chlorine bleach in thirty parts water.

All dogs require an annual revaccination for these diseases; for rabies, some states require revaccination every 3 years. A final injection at 20 weeks is sometimes recommended for parvovirus. The vaccine for hepatitis protects against canine adenovirus type I and II. In addition, the 3 vaccines for hepatitis, parainfluenza, and bordetella infections are necessary to protect against kennel cough.

Vaccination Schedule

	First	Second	Third
6–8 weeks			
Bordetella	●		
Distemper	●		
Hepatitis	●		
Parainfluenza	●		
Parvovirus	●		
10–12 weeks			
Bordetella		●	
Distemper		●	
Hepatitis		●	
Leptospirosis	●		
Parainfluenza		●	
Parvovirus		●	
12–16 weeks			
Rabies	●		
14–16 weeks			
Bordetella			●
Distemper			●
Hepatitis			●
Leptospirosis		●	
Parainfluenza			●
Parvovirus			●

Fleas and Other External Parasites

Dogs are susceptible to many external parasites that live on or are embedded in the surface of the skin. Fleas, lice, ticks, and mange mites are perhaps the most common pests. Most are easy to control with systematic treatment.

Fleas

The most difficult external parasites to control and probably the most common, fleas affect most dogs at some time in their lives. Fleas are especially troublesome where the climate is humid and temperate all year, such as in the southeastern United States and along the California coast. At high altitudes, in dry climates, and in areas where there is a long winter season, these parasites are more easily controlled.

Fleas are small, brown, rapidly moving jumping insects that spend a large part of their lives off the host. They will bite many host animals—dogs, cats, rodents, and even people—if dogs are not available. Fleas can live for over a year, and their eggs, found in cracks in the floor, in cool basements, or in sandy areas, may last even longer. Fleas often bite around the base of a pet's tail, but they may attack other areas of the body, too. The bite may cause an initial local reaction, but as your pet becomes sensitized to flea bites, a more generalized reaction may occur, causing a rash to appear on many parts of the skin. This reaction is called flea allergy dermatitis and is the bane of many sensitive dogs.

Controlling fleas requires a double-barreled attack: eliminating the fleas from your pet and your premises. Killing fleas on your dog demands persistence. Dips, powders, sprays, and collars—in order of decreasing effectiveness—must be used thoroughly and regularly. Flea collars are less effective than other control measures. In your attempt to control fleas, all animals in the household, especially cats, must be treated.

Eliminating fleas from your home, a dog house, and other places the dog commonly frequents is usually relatively easy and can be done with a commerical product. Only the most severe infestations require a professional exterminator. Many new long-acting insecticides can be obtained at farm and garden stores. One new type of product prevents immature fleas from developing, and another provides safe, long-term killing action against fleas that invade the living area. The combination is highly successful.

Dogs with flea allergies present a special dilemma. Some pets need veterinary care and additional treatment with cortisonelike drugs in order to get relief. Although dogs may be affected by other skin allergies caused by food or inhaled pollens, fleas are by far the most common cause of allergic skin disease.

Lice

These tiny parasites cause intense itching, but are easily controlled with flea dips or sprays repeated weekly for three or four applications. Look for dandrufflike eggs attached to the hair shafts and for adult lice on the surface of the skin.

Ticks

Common in woods, fields, and along sandy beaches, ticks attach themselves to the skin, especially around the ears and toes. Ticks can be removed with dips or can be picked off individually. Never use the tip of a hot cigarette to burn the tick.

The easiest way to remove this pest is to dab the tick with a generous quantity of alcohol for several minutes to stupefy it, and then pull it off gently with tweezers. Place the tick in a jar of alcohol to kill it. Most ticks attach themselves firmly by embedding their mouthparts in the dog's skin. If these pests are picked off with force, the mouthparts may remain embedded. Although this is not a major concern, it can be avoided by allowing time for the alcohol to act.

Mange Mites

Several different types of mites can afflict dogs. Some live in the ears or on the surface of the skin (otodectic mange and cheyletiella mange); others burrow into the skin (sarcoptic mange and demodectic mange). Surface mites and sarcoptic mange are contagious and cause intense itching. They are quite easily cured by insecticides. Usually each case needs to be treated several times, and because of the contagion, all animals in contact must also be treated. Some of these animal manges cause temporary skin problems in people, but these are contracted only by very intimate contact and are easily cured.

Demodectic mange is transmitted only during the puppy's first few days of life and does not itch. It may not appear until puppies are four months of age. Some cases are further complicated by skin infections. These cases tend to be hereditary and are resistant to treatment; affected animals should not be bred.

Intestinal Parasites

Worms, or intestinal parasites, can be serious problems for young puppies as well as for full-grown dogs. In warm, humid climates, they may be one of the major causes of dog diseases and death. Some worms affect dogs of all ages, and some can also be transmitted to people. Yet many dog owners are unduly concerned about worms and overworm their dogs. In most environments, these intestinal parasites are rarely a problem at all. Scare advertising about the need for monthly worming or about the terrible pain caused by worms is usually highly exaggerated.

Signs of Worms and Effective Control

Diarrhea and similar problems are the most common signs of the presence of worms. If you suspect that your dog has worms, it is best to consult your veterinarian. The veterinarian may want to examine a stool sample microscopically to make an accurate diagnosis and prescribe the correct drug. Some medications are effective only for certain parasites. If you use the wrong medication, there is no benefit. Moreover, worm remedies are poisonous and should not be given if unwarranted. If your dog is ill from something other than worms or in addition to these parasites, needless or even normal worming may be harmful.

The control of worms involves more than administering drugs. Obviously the best control is to prevent your dog from becoming infected. But sometimes this is impossible. For example, a puppy can become infected while nursing or even while still in its mother's uterus.

If a dog has worms, treatment requires breaking the parasite's life cycle. By definition, a parasite is an organism that lives on or in a host animal, which provides many or all of the parasite's needs. If those needs can be removed or reduced, or if the parasite can be attacked at some stage of its life when it is outside the host, control can be more effective and safer than when only worm medications are used.

Surveys of many areas of the United States show that more than half of all dogs have at least one kind of intestinal parasite. There are four major kinds that affect dogs: Roundworms most commonly affect young puppies; whipworms attack older dogs; and hookworms and tapeworms can pose problems to dogs of all ages.

Roundworms

Ascarids, or roundworms, can cause severe illness and even death in puppies. Sometimes they infect puppies before birth, but they can also be ingested after

Pilling a Dog
Holding pill between index and middle fingers, press down on lower jaw; place thumb of other hand behind large fang tooth and press up on roof of mouth. Push tablet far down dog's throat. Remove fingers, close mouth quickly; tap underside of chin.

birth. As a dog matures, it gradually develops a tolerance to roundworms, and can even live comfortably with a few parasites still inside its intestines. Roundworms lay eggs, which pass to the outside in the stool. When the eggs are eaten by another or the same dog, the infestation spreads. The eggs hatch and immature worms, or larvae, wander through the new host's body tissues. They eventually return to the intestines, where they develop into mature egg-producing worms; then the cycle is repeated.

Internally migrating worms cannot be contacted and killed by drugs given orally. This, together with repeated ingestion of eggs from the bitch's milk or the puppies' stools, is the reason that repeated doses of medications are needed. Better control will be possible when new drugs are developed that eliminate the parasites from all tissues in the body. Certain types of roundworms are a matter of public health concern because they may spread from dogs and cats to children. The larvae migrate into the children's tissues just as they do in the pets' bodies. Children can ingest the eggs, too. Parasite eggs can be consumed by children who eat sand or dirt from an animal's toilet area (the most frequent means of infection). Children's sandboxes should be covered when not in use to keep pets out. Children should not kiss pets or share food with them. With common sense sanitation, these concerns should be minimal.

Hookworms

Especially serious to puppies, hookworms suck blood from the wall of the intestine. Dogs affected with large numbers of these parasites can die of anemia from severe blood loss. These parasites are contracted through the bitch's milk, by ingestion of eggs, or they may penetrate the skin.
Control requires periodic worming of the dog and cleaning and treatment of infected soil to kill eggs and parasite larvae. Dirt, grass dog runs, or shady pens often harbor the stages of the worm that live outside the dog. Canine hookworms are almost never a menace to people. They can be troublesome in kennels or places where groups of dogs congregate or are housed together, because it is difficult to clean the premises effectively to prevent reinfection. Individual pets can almost always be successfully treated and permanently freed of hookworms.

Whipworms

This type of worm most commonly affects mature or older dogs, producing a peculiar type of intermittent diarrhea. Infection occurs through direct ingestion of parasite eggs, and the adult whipworms live in the dog's lower intestines. Because the eggs are very hard to kill outside the host, reinfection from contaminated soil is common. Although certain individual dogs seem to be more troubled by this parasite than others, treatment with drugs is usually successful. These parasites are not a public health hazard.

Tapeworms

Easily treated with medications, these parasites rarely cause severe damage. The head of a tapeworm attaches itself to the lining of the dog's intestine. Small segments of the worm containing eggs break off periodically and appear in the stool as small, flattened objects that look like rice.
To get rid of tapeworms, the heads must be removed by medication, and the tapeworm eggs must not be allowed to hatch. These eggs can complete the cycle only if they have a second host other than the dog, such as fleas, mice, rabbits, or other domestic animals. When the dog consumes the raw viscera of the second host, the life cycle is completed.

Giving Liquids
Put one dose of medicine in small bottle. Pull out lip at corner to form pocket. Pour in liquid, in small amounts; as patient swallows, add more medicine to pocket. Elevate nose only slightly to prevent liquid from entering air passages.

If you prevent your dog from eating the second host, tapeworms can be eliminated. Cooking food the dog eats effectively destroys all parasites. Direct ingestion of tapeworm segments by a dog will not cause infection.

One-celled Parasites

There are two types of one-celled parasites that can affect dogs: *Giardia* and *Coccidia*. *Giardia* are free-moving, single-celled parasites that infect dogs, beavers, and people. *Coccidia* affect many species of wild and domesticated animals. Both *Giardia* and *Coccidia* are transmitted by fecal contamination, which can occur by such means as drinking contaminated water from streams. Both of these parasites cause chronic diarrhea and can be detected only through laboratory tests.

How to Prevent and Control Worms

Prevention and control of intestinal parasites can be complex; multiple infections are common, so specific diagnosis by a veterinarian is essential. Usually this is best done by microscopic examination of a stool specimen. Many treatment measures can and should be taken at home. Most medications are pills or liquids given orally but a few can be added to your pet's food. The diagrams at the top of these pages will show you how to give your pet pills or liquid medication.

Steps to Control Parasitic Infection

1. Obtain a specific diagnosis and proper directions for treatment.
2. Use good sanitary practices:
a. Pick up and dispose of stool daily.
b. Never feed your pet on the ground. Use a clean dish.
c. Use parasite-inhibiting agents on the ground if pets are confined to small pens.
3. Control intermediate hosts to break the parasite's life cycle:
a. Keep your dog from eating raw food, such as mice, rabbits, or birds.
b. Control fleas and other insects with insecticides or regular spray programs.
4. Administer the correct drug at the proper intervals for as long as necessary to eliminate the worms.
5. Apply all of these measures. Used alone, no one control is entirely satisfactory.

Heartworm Disease

Unlike most other internal parasites that attack a dog's intestines, heartworms can severely affect the functioning of the heart and blood vessels. This is a common disease where mosquitoes abound. A mosquito that sucks blood from an infected animal can inject the developing larvae into the body of a healthy dog. Full-grown heartworms, four to six inches long, can live for many years in their host's heart.

The diagnosis of heartworm disease is complex, requiring blood tests and occasionally chest X-rays. Treatment is always difficult and entails risk. To prevent infection, minimize your dog's exposure to mosquitoes by keeping it in screened areas or by limiting outdoor activities at night or on dark days— times when mosquitoes are most active. In areas with many mosquitoes, your veterinarian will prescribe a drug that protects dogs from infection. In many regions prophylactic doses of diethylcarbamazine (DEC) must be given all year, but in other areas where mosquitoes are seasonal, treatment begins before the mosquitoes appear and continues until two months after the season ends. DEC cannot be administered if your dog already has heartworms. Failure to have a heartworm test performed before DEC is started may expose your pet to the risk of a severe reaction and even death.

If you live in a mosquito-infested area, take your dog for screening blood tests every six months to detect possible early infection. However, no matter where you

Muzzling Your Dog
With a generous length of bandage, cloth tape, or heavy cord, make a loop around dog's nose and mouth. Wrap bandage around again several times; secure by tying in a bow behind patient's ears.

live, your dog should be checked at least once a year for heartworms.

Gastric Torsion and Bloat

Bloat, like the similar gastric torsion, is a serious problem in large dogs with deep chests. It most commonly afflicts dogs that have eaten a large meal of dry food and then ingested a lot of water. To help prevent bloat, owners of predisposed breeds are advised to establish a routine of feeding their pets small meals of well-soaked food several times daily.

If bloat does develop, it usually starts within a short time of feeding, often within an hour. The dog's abdomen enlarges and there may be unproductive vomiting, restlessness, pawing at the mouth, and, if the abdomen swells enough, it may press on the diaphram and cause labored breathing. *Bloat is a dire emergency.* Day or night, a dog suffering from bloat requires immediate veterinary attention. Minutes can save a dog's life.

Pros and Cons of Neutering

Some pet owners are troubled by discussion of neutering dogs so that they cannot breed. Neutering means removing the reproductive glands, which does not affect the dog's health. Spaying the bitch involves removal of the ovaries and uterus; castrating the male removes the testicles.

Farm animals are often neutered so that they will gain weight more rapidly and become more placid. Dogs as well as cats usually have similar reactions, but not to the same degree. Neutering dogs can reduce the impulse to wander and fight, especially in males, making these dogs better house pets. However, such a behavior change occasionally may be detrimental to the performance of watchdogs, hunting dogs, and working breeds.

Spaying bitches prevents unwanted puppies and eliminates gatherings of ardent males around the bitch when she is in heat every four to eight months. (In most states, the license fee for spayed bitches is lower than the normal fee, to encourage spaying.) Generally, neutered dogs of both sexes are quieter, stay at home more, and are more attentive to their families, although occasionally spayed bitches become more active rather than tranquil.

Because neutered animals are calmer and less active, they have lower caloric needs. Too often owners overfeed their pets and the dogs get fat. With proper diet, however, this will not happen.

Neutering is, of course, an irreversible operation, making breeding impossible. If you decide to have your pet neutered, the operation should be done only when the dog is physically mature—has achieved its full height, weight, and muscle development. This time varies among breeds—from six to fifteen months—and may not coincide with sexual maturity. For example, some breeds are fully grown at twelve months, but have their first heat at eighteen to thirty months of age. In many parts of the country, there are too many unwanted puppies. Most authorities, including this writer, feel that this fact is a compelling reason to neuter. Many pet owners spay bitches; few castrate male dogs. Both should be done.

Basic First Aid

Every pet owner should be prepared for emergencies and learn what to do when basic first aid is needed. Injured animals are frightened and in pain. They may be uncooperative, attempt to run away and hide, or be so frantic that they attempt to bite or scratch even a beloved owner. Knowing how to handle the injured dog, muzzle it and wrap it in blankets, or provide other restraining measures can prevent further injury to the patient as well as to yourself. Timely action may be vitally important.

The most practical first-aid remedy is prevention: Keep your pet under control and away from sources of possible trouble. Freely wandering dogs are the most inclined to have problems. The most common accidents in approximate order of frequency include being hit by a car, bite wounds, cuts, heat stroke, injuries from foreign objects like fishhooks or thorns, poisoning (through chemicals or spoiled food), falls, or injuries as a result of cruelty.

Do you know what to do in an emergency? It is wise to have a book on pet first aid on hand and to be familiar with basic procedures before you need to use these skills. Always keep a simple first-aid kit for pets in your home. It should contain bandages, tape, scissors, materials for making a muzzle, and simple medications. These medications should include an antacid laxative such as milk of magnesia; hydrogen peroxide to induce vomiting; antibiotic ointments for the eyes and skin; an antidiarrheal medication such as milk of bismuth or a kaolin and pectin mixture; and mineral oil. Know the location of the nearest veterinary clinic or hospital. Most metropolitan areas have central emergency or out-of-hours veterinary centers to provide special facilities for injured animals.

The following practical first-aid information tells you what to do in the most common emergency situations until you can get your dog to a veterinarian.

Heat Stroke

When a pet is confined to a poorly ventilated car or a pen that is exposed to the summer sun, it may get heat stroke. The dog may become frantic, be unconscious, or groggy and gasping for breath. *Remove the dog from the overheated place at once and immediately wet it thoroughly with water.* Dip the dog in a pond, or use a water hose or whatever is handy to soak it all over. Rapid cooling

is vital. Then promptly transport the dog to a veterinary hospital for professional treatment.

Bleeding

Cuts on the feet or legs are common injuries, which occasionally can cause profuse bleeding. This almost always can be controlled by a firm pressure bandage. In an emergency, pull a clean sock on to the leg or wrap the cut area with a washcloth or layers of paper towels. Then wrap a bandage firmly over the sock or cloth. Start wrapping at the foot and continue up the leg in a spiral, going above the area of the cut. Seek veterinary aid for sutures or better bandaging. (See your first-aid manual for details.)

Fractures and Shock

If a dog falls from a great height or is hit by a car, it will probably have broken bones and may be in shock. Legs with broken bones that are allowed to flop around can produce more serious damage to vital blood vessels, nerves, or tendons in the area of the injury. To immobilize a leg fracture, wrap the leg in layers of towel or newspapers that are taped or wrapped with cord to hold them in place. Animals with severe injuries are always in shock. As part of the treatment for this condition they must be wrapped in towels or blankets to conserve heat— even in warm weather—and promptly taken to a veterinary hospital.

Transporting an Injured Dog

If a dog is small, grasp it by the skin of the neck and by the skin of the rump near the tail. Then gently slide it onto a blanket or into a cardboard box with the side folded down. Avoid bending the legs or backbone. Wrap blankets around the dog once it is in the box to keep it warm and make it comfortable. Then carefully lift the box into the car. If a dog is large, try to gently slide a blanket under it. Keep the backbone straight and pull the dog on the blanket along the ground so that it is moved with the legs trailing behind. For a large dog, you will need help in carefully lifting it and placing it inside the car, always keeping the back and legs as straight as possible. These measures are easy if the dog is unconscious and not difficult if the dog is groggy, or knows you well. If the dog is conscious, keep talking to it quietly to reassure it. Be careful in moving the patient so you do not get bitten. Unless the dog has trouble breathing, it is usually safest to apply a muzzle before moving it. If the dog is really obstreperous, it probably is not too seriously injured; just let it sit or lie in the car as it wishes as you go to the veterinary hospital.

Poisoning
Poisoning can result from toxic materials that contact the skin. Use lots of soap and water to remove them promptly and thoroughly. Do not use solvents that may themselves be toxic, such as turpentine, gasoline, or kerosene. Poisoning from ingested toxins should also be treated by prompt removal of the poison from the dog's system. Many dogs can be induced to vomit by administering one to two teaspoonsful of hydrogen peroxide orally every ten minutes for three doses. Medications such as Kaopectate should then be given to inhibit absorption of toxic material that may remain. In cases of suspected poisoning, always seek veterinary advice promptly.

Removing Fishhooks and Thorns
Deeply embedded thorns and fishhooks require veterinary help, since anesthesia will be necessary. If a fishhook is superficially embedded, try to push the hook through, then cut off the barbed end with cutting pliers and back the hook out. Thorns usually are so deeply embedded that they may be hard to find. If you can locate the thorn, remove it with tweezers and/or a sewing needle.

Puncture wounds are always infected, so treatment for this complication is necessary as well.

Further Recommendations
The health care suggestions in this section are only an introduction. See your veterinarian for a specific health plan for your dog and for recommendations of books that will provide more detailed information.

Key to Potential Health Problems

Preliminary Checks Before Purchase
For each breed account, the Potential Health Problems section mentions diseases and inherited problems that could affect that breed. Although most dogs are quite healthy, certain breeds are more prone than others to some kinds of illness. Before purchasing a dog, it is wise to learn whether your future pet is likely to be susceptible to any serious health difficulties.

Many ailments in dogs are not at all serious. Like people, dogs are subject to several troublesome but easily treatable maladies as well as health conditions that, while not completely curable, can be managed with medication. To help you evaluate the seriousness of a problem, the chart on the following pages lists common health problems veterinarians find in dogs and rates them according to four categories: treatable ailments, manageable conditions, problems that can be corrected with surgery, and serious problems.

Key to Potential Health Problems

	Treatable Ailments	Manageable Conditions	Corrected with Surgery	Serious Problems
Bone Problems				
Arthritis		●		
Back problems		●		●
Bone tumors				●
Congenital bone defects				●
Craniomandibular osteopathy				●
Deterioration of ball of hip		●		●
Fractures			●	
Gait ataxia or gait abnormalities				●
Hip dysplasia				●
Digestive and Related Disorders				
Bloat or gastric torsion				●
Congenital kidney disease				●
Colitis				●
Diarrhea		●		●
Digestive complaints		●		
Esophogeal problems				●
Eye Problems				
Cataracts, usually in old dogs		●		●
Collie eye				●
Congenital eye defects				●
Corneal ulcers	●			
Distichiasis			●	
Eyelid abnormalities			●	
Entropion			●	
Glaucoma, usually in old dogs				●

	Treatable Ailments	Manageable Conditions	Corrected with Surgery	Serious Problems
Herniated disc	●			●
Hypertrophic osteodystrophy				●
Invertebral disc disease	●			●
Metabolic bone disease				●
Osteochondritis desiccans				●
Progressive spinal cord disorder				●
Slipped stifle			●	
Vertebral osteochondrosis				●
Wobbler's syndrome				●
Liver disorder (copper toxiosis)				●
Perineal hernias		●		
Inguinal hernias			●	
Stones: bladder, kidney, or urinary	●			●
Swallowing disorders				●
Renal disease				●
Keratoconjunctivitis	●			●
Lens luxation			●	●
Persistent pupillary membrane		●		
Progressive retinal atrophy (PRA)				●
Prolapse of eyeball	●			●
Retinal dysplasia				●
Tear deficiency				●
Tear duct abnormalities				●

	Treatable Ailments	Manageable Conditions	Corrected with Surgery	Serious Problems
Circulatory Problems				
Anemia		●		
Bleeding tendencies or hemophilia				●
Congenital heart problems				●
Hormonal, Metabolic, and Neurological Problems				
Cushing's disease		●		●
Diabetes		●		●
Hypoglycemia or low blood sugar		●		
Hypothyroid		●		
Skin Diseases				
Acanthosis nigricans				●
Allergic skin disease	●			
Bacterial skin disease	●	●		
Blue Doberman syndrome		●		●
Cysts			●	
Demodectic mange				●
Fold dermititis	●			
Hair follicle tumors			●	
Hormonal skin disease		●		
Respiratory Problems				
Chronic respiratory disease		●		
Collapsed trachea			●	●
Hypoplasia of larynx			●	●
Other Health Concerns				
Cleft palate or lips			●	●
Dwarfism		●		●

	Treatable Ailments	Manageable Conditions	Corrected with Surgery	Serious Problems
Gray Collie syndrome				●
Von Willebrand's disease				●
Progressive neurological disorder				●
Rage syndrome				●
Scottie cramp		●		●
Hot spots	●			
Immune mediated skin disease				●
Mast cell tumors				●
Pattern baldness (affects appearance only)				
Pododermatitis				●
Psychological skin disease		●		
Seborrheic skin disorders		●		●
Skin acne	●			
Zinc responsive skin disease	●	●		
Laryngeal disease				●
Laryngeal paralysis				●
Respiratory infections	●			
Epilepsy		●		●
Hydrocephalus, or open fontanelle				●

Raising a Puppy

A Demanding Job

No one can deny the joy of having a puppy around the house, but it is not necessarily the right experience for everyone. Puppyhood is a brief moment in a dog's life, and for that short time a great deal of care and sacrifice are required. If you decide to raise a puppy rather than adopt a mature pet, here are some of the things you should consider.

Choosing the Right Dog

Remember that in as little as twelve to fourteen weeks, a puppy is coasting through adolescence and solidly on its way to adulthood. It is the adult dog that you will live with for ten to fifteen years. So it is wise to try to overlook cuteness as a factor, and decide what kind of dog you want to spend the next decade with. Read the essays in this book entitled How to Select a Breed Suited to Your Life-style, and Purebred or Random-bred? Learn about purebreds, or choose a dog of mixed heritage.

Bringing Your Puppy Home

When you have made a choice, don't expect to bring a newborn puppy home; puppies should not be separated from their mothers until they are about eight weeks old. Considerable expertise is required in the proper handling of newborn puppies, so deal only with a breeder that you can trust. This is the only way you can be assured that the animal will receive adequate socialization in its early days. Puppies without that early exposure to people often grow to be problem dogs.

When the puppy is turned over to you, it is essential that you continue its socialization. No longer completely helpless, the puppy is now a creature full of lively curiosity with great potential for learning from humans. Take advantage of it.

The home atmosphere you create— through your care or carelessness—will play a large role in shaping your pet's emotional stability. When your puppy arrives home, keep in mind that the animal has experienced stress in its separation from its mother and littermates as well as its entry into a new environment. Do all you can to reduce the anxiety the puppy is experiencing, which means keeping family members from exhausting the newcomer with over-attentiveness.

You can help your dog adjust to its new environment by treating it with affection and consistency. You should not strike your pet, raise your voice, or express undue anger.

Be especially mindful of the puppy during its first few nights with you. You may be tempted to have the dog sleep in the same room with you, but be forewarned that allowing it to do so is likely to set a pattern.

Caring for Your Puppy

Puppies require a special diet. Ask your breeder if your dog has become accustomed to a certain type of food before buying one of the many perfectly acceptable commercial pet foods designed for puppies. Avoid the temptation to feed your dog milk, meat, or table scraps, which interfere with its digestion and foster behavior problems, such as begging.

One of the first responsibilities of ownership is to bring your puppy to a veterinarian for an examination. The dog must be immunized against such illnesses as rabies, parvovirus, and distemper, and must also be checked for heartworms. The schedule of vaccines in the section Health Care will give you a detailed account of what is necessary.

The chances are very good that your dog will one day lose its way home. In order to be sure that your dog is returned, attach a personal identification tag with your name, address, and telephone number on its collar. Some dog owners wisely tattoo their dogs with an identifying symbol, such as a social security number, and list the symbol with a national dog registry. Such tattooing is painless, and by having your dog thus marked you will improve the chances of its being returned. (One recommended agency is the American Dog Registry, P. O. Box 262, Mount Prospect, Illinois 60056.) It is also advisable to keep up-to-date photographs of your dog on hand for identification.

Housebreaking

The first task you will face in training your puppy is housebreaking. This can be accomplished most easily by establishing a fixed, daily routine. Let your puppy know it can depend on you: Feed it at the same time every day and take it out at regular and frequent intervals—first thing in the morning, after the dog eats, drinks, and plays, and at bedtime.

Watch for behavior that may indicate that the puppy needs to go out. When your puppy goes in the right place, show it that you are proud. If an accident does happen, as it is bound to, act reasonably. Striking the animal will make the dog fearful without making it clear what it has done wrong. Sticking the dog's nose in its mess will only confuse the animal; it wasn't the nose that caused the problem. If you see your pet in the process of dirtying, interrupt the dog immediately, indicate that you are displeased, and direct the pup to the correct place. If the dog leaves a mess, deodorize the area after cleaning it to insure that your pet does not use the same spot again. (For more detailed information, read the essay on Obedience Training and Problem Solving.)

A Place of Its Own

As a den animal, your dog instinctively desires the security provided by a small place of its own; a wooden crate, either store bought or homemade, can adequately serve your pet's needs at home. The crate must be well ventilated and roomy enough for the dog to stand up and lie down comfortably, but it need not be much larger. Encourage your dog to seek comfort in his box by feeding it there and by leaving a water dish inside. Put a blanket or some carpeting in the crate, and keep it clean. Once acquainted with its little place, a dog will use the crate and even yearn for it.

Do not try to force things along by shoving your puppy inside. That will frighten the dog and, in the long run, undermine its training. Of course, don't leave your pet in its crate for too long. Every dog, though, should have its own safe place.

Disciplining Your Puppy

The basis of most successful training is reward. Use lots of praise when your puppy pleases you or obviously tries to. Give it an occasional treat; pet it; let love work for you. If you must discipline the dog physically (and chances are that at some time you will), take your pet by the scruff of the neck and shake the animal in imitation of maternal behavior. In dog language, this means "Cut it out!"

You should also have some understanding of the canine social instincts of dominance and submission, which determine an ironclad hierarchy within the dog pack. If you want your dog to obey you, you must become its leader. Discipline can be taught and your puppy will welcome it, if you impress upon the animal early and often that you are absolutely the Number One dog. You are the center of its world, and don't ever let the puppy forget it. When you require the dog's attention, do not let him ignore you. But there is no need to provoke or challenge your dog unnecessarily.

Finally, bring the puppy along slowly with patience and devotion. Remember that it needs companionship, which should not be difficult to provide—in fact, it is a positive joy. Play games with your dog, but keep in mind that you are teaching behavioral patterns all the while. Tug-of-war games are a bad idea because they encourage your pet to fight against you. Get a ball and roll it around with the dog. Be sure that your own children and their friends don't handle the puppy too much, and protect it from larger, mature dogs. Puppies are often unaware of the deference they must show to other animals, and they can be injured. Above all, enjoy your dog's puppyhood for as long as it lasts—and make it easy for your puppy to do the same.

Grooming and Routine Care

More Than Cosmetics

Far too many people look upon grooming as a way to make their dogs look "nice," a minor chore to suit their own egos and reputation. While it is certainly true that a well-groomed dog is cleaner in the house and a boost to the image of the owner, much more is at stake. Grooming is a matter of health just as much as it is a matter of looks. Outlined below, step by step, are the things you should attend to when grooming your dog.

Ears

It is not difficult to tell when a dog's ears need cleaning. They look and smell dirty. It really is as simple as that. The average dog should have its ears checked once a week. Dogs with "long leather" —pendulous ears like those of a Basset Hound—should be checked every other day. Doing this takes no more than a few seconds and is not something for which you have to make a schedule. Because long, flopped-over ears allow less air circulation than upstanding or "prick" ears, they are far more likely to become infected. Long before that happens, the problem can be detected.

Fortunately, the canine ear canal takes a rather sharp bend and does not provide a clear avenue to the eardrum, which is extremely sensitive. An ordinary cotton swab can be used without danger of doing damage. With a swab dipped in lukewarm, soapy water, you can clean any accumulation that may have occurred because of temporary neglect. Cotton, another swab, or an old piece of terrycloth, dipped in baby oil or soapy lukewarm water, can be used to clean the external ear flap, whether it is upright or floppy. If the ears appear red or if the dog is in obvious pain, your veterinarian can supply ointments or drops that will correct or fend off real infections that can spell trouble and even become chronic. In very large dogs, such as Bloodhounds, an index finger wrapped in a soapy cloth will do the work of a cotton-tipped swab.

Routine Inspections

Dogs inevitably feel better when their ears are clean, but few dogs like having their ears attended to. You can expect them to twist their heads, kick with their hind legs, and even complain a bit, but you should know your dog well enough to sense the difference between slight annoyance and real pain. If you have any doubts, ask your veterinarian or a professional dog groomer to show you how to clean the dog's ears.

Cleaning ears is not, you must remember, a casual or occasional task. It should be a quick, regular check to make certain things are not getting out of hand. In time, your dog will come to expect it, even if it never grows to love it. If your dog is very shy, it may mean its ears are tender. In a sense, the less your dog likes having its ears checked, the more it needs this precaution.

Nails

Unless a dog runs and walks constantly on a very hard, rough surface, it is almost certain its nails will grow too long. When this happens, it not only spoils the dog's movement but also causes it discomfort and even pain. Nails must be trimmed back regularly; doing so will encourage the dog not to splay its toes. Splayed toes are generally a sign of improperly maintained nails.

All dogs hate having their nails trimmed. It may not hurt them, but they are sure it is going to—in fact, many dogs apparently believe the procedure is life-threatening. You have to bite the bullet and ignore your dog's misgivings. Try to be encouraging and reassuring, and apply no more restraint than is necessary—but cut those nails. How well your dog eventually learns to tolerate the procedure depends in large measure on how well you do it earlier in its career. A dog's toenails have a vein and a nerve; if you draw blood, your dog will be unlikely to trust you for a long time to come—not when its feet are involved.

If you have not had experience clipping a dog's nails, have a veterinarian or professional handler or groomer show you how it is done. If the nails are light in color, you will be able to see the vein and thus know where the nerve is as well. If you miss one, you miss the other. In fact, you can come to within a tiny fraction of an inch of both and cause your dog no more pain than trimming your own fingernails occasions.

Recommended Tools

The best type of nail trimmer is the guillotine type, which holds the tip of the nail in a slot while you squeeze the implement. A sharp, replaceable blade slips up and cuts the tip away. Do not take large pieces of the nail off at once; instead, take the tip off first and then, turning the clipper at an angle, gently trim the nail back as far as you can go. You really should be able to condition your dog to the procedure; if you have an extremely excitable dog, you may have to go as far as having your veterinarian tranquilize your pet while a staff groomer trims the nails for you. It seldom is necessary to take such drastic steps, but no dog may be considered safely and properly groomed if it is walking around like a fourteenth-century Chinese mandarin.

Teeth

Very few dog owners become involved in canine tooth care except insofar as they anticipate problems and supply the right food. Soft canned foods—the so-called moist foods—do little toward oral hygiene or tooth care in pets. Dry food is far better for your dog's mouth, even though you may moisten this food with a little warm water and add some cottage cheese, scrambled eggs, or a tablespoon of canned food for aroma and taste. But it is better yet for tooth care to give your dog a treat of a tough, dry biscuit; the kind that come in the shape of a bone are fine. These treats can be purchased in bulk from animal-food suppliers in twenty-five pound boxes at a small fraction of the price you would pay in a grocery store.

Because of their body chemistry, toy dogs may have tooth trouble; this is something your veterinarian should be consulted about early in an animal's life. If you wait too long, all your veterinarian can do is remove loose teeth, and this is not the best kind of care. Some veterinarians recommend "brushing" your dog's teeth with a rough cloth; it is a good idea to have that discussion as soon as you get your puppy. You may find plaque building up, and its removal requires scaling after the dog has been suitably tranquilized—very few dogs will tolerate scaling while they are awake. The better part of tooth care in the grooming process will be done in the veterinary clinic, not in your home. You can, though, head off trouble with proper diet and good, tough, chewy biscuits. A diet that is all soft and mushy will lead to trouble.

Skin

If your dog's skin is not healthy, there is nothing on this earth you can do to make its coat gleam. Dry skin means constant itching, scratching, raw "hot spots," and a scraggly-looking coat.

It is important, first, to get rid of external parasites. While skin does reflect the general health of your dog, it also reflects how many critters are living in its fur, out of sight. Ticks and fleas must go; the use of chemical dips, sprays, and powders is advisable. Your veterinarian can prescribe the right solutions for your dog, depending on its age and the kind of coat it has. Remember, parasites can reinfest your dog fast; to kill fleas, ticks, flea eggs, you must spray and dust cracks in the floor, areas where the dog sleeps, and fabrics your pet may rest on. Use the best products available, and keep your dog as free of external parasites as possible. During tick season, check your dog every single evening and remove all ticks. There is no such thing as a flea season; some dogs, particularly indoor dogs, can have them throughout the year..

During the winter months, many animals have dry skin because their owners' homes are overheated. Dry skin is usually easy to deal with; adding anywhere from a few drops to a teaspoonful of salad oil (depending on the size of your dog) to the dog's food will keep the skin soft and supple. There are also special oils made for a dog's dry skin. Veterinary dermatology has come a long way in the last twenty years; if your pet is having skin problems, it is easy to attend to it before it gets out of hand. Only when the skin is soft and healthy can you expect your dog to have a good coat.

Coat

Basic coat care can consist of simple maintenance or fine-tuned grooming. If you have a Schnauzer (of any size), a Poodle, a Bichon Frise, or any other breed that requires trimming, plucking, or cutting, you are going to need help, at least initially. The best idea of all is to have your dog seen to several times a year by a professional, although some owners do learn to take care of elaborate coats. If you do decide to give it a go, get some beginning instruction and be sure to buy the proper equipment.

Bathing Procedures

First, the bath. Some dogs, such as the Old English Sheepdog, the rough Collie, and other breeds with off-standing coats, are seldom bathed unless it is absolutely essential—if they begin to smell bad or

if they get into a mess of oil or briars. Even then, briars or stickers can often be worked or cut out, but there are times when the coat has to be softened and cleaned. Start by putting a nonskid mat in the tub: Dogs hate to slip. Use a good dog shampoo on the body and use human baby shampoo on the head. Always put eye drops into your dog's eyes before a bath to avoid eye irritation. (You can get drops from your veterinarian or use mineral oil.) It is much kinder to your dog to use baby shampoo on its head, in case some lather should get into sensitive areas. Shampoo in the eye is as rough on a dog as it is on you.

A dog's bath water should be only lukewarm, a little cooler perhaps than you might at first think quite right. It should never approach being hot. The very first step, after you put in the eye drops, is to soak and lather all the way around your dog's neck. A wide band of lather worked right down to the skin will deter fleas from heading toward your dog's head for safety. Isolate the pests down on the body and give them their due. Use a mobile shower spray head or a plastic pitcher to soak the dog's coat, and lather up according to the instructions that come with the dog shampoo you use. Work the lather through the coat again and again, and then rinse thoroughly. Lather up again, repeat the entire process, and rinse and rinse and rinse. When you are absolutely certain that you have rinsed far more than should be necessary, rinse some more. Don't leave soap on the skin or you will invite itchy spots and constant scratching. Towel your dog dry and keep it in a warm place. If you have a heavy-coated dog, such as a Bearded Collie, you will want to use a hair dryer while you brush the coat into shape. By now, of course, you should know just what kind of coat trimming you should be giving the dog.

Undercoats

A good many breeds, including the northern, Spitz-type dogs—Siberian Huskies, Keeshonden, Alaskan Malamutes, Samoyeds, and the others—have tremendously heavy undercoats. To loosen and remove undercoat fur (before your dog sheds), use a rake—a toothed band of steel with leather handles at both ends. Form the band into the loop and go to work, out-of-doors. It is not at all unusual to get three or four pillowcases full of undercoat hair in several spring workouts. (There are even places that will spin this dog wool and knit sweaters and scarves for you.) If you do not rake the undercoat loose, you will be driven mad all summer and early fall—because your dog will shed that coat instead. One way or another, the undercoat is going to come out.

Virtually all dogs (except Poodles, which don't shed at all, and a few breeds that tend to shed rather little) need some raking after the cold months have passed. Shorthaired dogs, such as Boston Terriers, Beagles, and Pugs, require very little in the way of raking; but with the heavy double-coated breeds you can predict how much housework you will do all summer by how much raking you do in the spring. Do not attempt to rake a dog indoors. It will take weeks for you to get all the dog hair settled and vacuumed up. What is more, if you do the heavy coat care outside in the spring, birds will use the hair to line their nests.

Dry Shampooing

Some dogs, as we noted above, do not really need to bathe. If there is not some grand emergency that mandates a bath, dry shampoos are best. These are powders, available in pet shops, supermarkets, and at your veterinarian's office, that are brushed through the coat, leaving it clean and neat. Read the instructions carefully and take the manufacturer's advice. Bathing off-standing coats more often than is really required will break the coat down and leave it limp and unimpressive.

Short-coated dogs need relatively little care between baths. A brush or even a very rough old face-cloth or towel may be all the equipment you need. Briskly rubbing the coat with the grain will usually be enough; you are really doing little more than dusting the dog. Brisk rubbing also stimulates the dog's skin and gets out bits and pieces of debris. If your dog has been swimming in salt water, you will want to rinse it thoroughly with fresh water to prevent the salts from building up on the skin, which can lead to all kinds of dermatological complications.

Elaborately coated dogs need daily brushing. Depending on the breed, the coat style, the dog's age, and its recent activities, this may take five minutes or half an hour. Far too many people buy themselves a fancy-coated dog and are then distraught when their animal fails to look like a model. If you do not know how to give your breed the care and attention it needs, ask a professional groomer to teach you or attend a grooming school or evening class. If you can't do this, have someone else do it for you. If learning to care for the dog is too expensive or inconvenient, select another breed. You can no more ignore a dog's skin and coat than you can your own scalp and hair. Coat-care requirements are collectively a major point in selecting the right dog for you.

Dogs and Skunks

One final point about bathing. If you live in or visit the countryside, remember the skunk. Skunks are generally not keen on dogs, and are quick to spray dogs with their musk. Dogs are no happier about such encounters than you are. If your dog comes home smelling of skunk, here is what to do:

Change into clothes you can discard. You are going to have to. Nothing will enable you to salvage clothing that has been worn while de-skunking a dog. Do everything possible to do the job out-of-doors: De-skunking a bathroom isn't exactly a joy, either. If you try to attend to this in the basement, the skunk smell will work its way up through your whole house. If you try it in an apartment, your landlord may break your lease.

Put your dog in a metal or plastic tub that you have purchased for the occasion and open four or five large cans of tomato juice. The amount of juice you use, obviously, depends on the size of dog you have to de-skunk. Work the undiluted tomato juice again and again through the areas of the dog's coat that have been hit. Keep it up until your hands ache. If your dog complains, remind him of what it could be like to be sent to a foster home. After you have really thoroughly saturated your dog with tomato juice all the way to the last square inch of skin, rinse the dog in tepid water.

Shampoo the dog at least three times, preferably with a heavy-duty bar of yellow laundry soap. Then rinse thoroughly for the last time, towel your pet dry with towels you can afford to throw away (a step strongly advised) and bathe yourself. Every time it gets wet, your dog will probably smell at least a little like a skunk.

If you live in an area where skunks are common, it is a good idea to have the de-skunking material on hand. The same procedure works on children.

Keeping a dog healthy, happy, and handsome is not very time-consuming. It is, though, humane, and it can be fun. Above all, it is good for the dog and offers you and your pet a chance to interact in a positive way.

Grooming Accessories

A Range of Utensils

The kind of brush you will want to use when grooming your pet will depend, of course, on the length and style of the dog's coat and how tangled and matted the hair has become. Outlined below are several of the different kinds of tools that you may find helpful.

Pin Brush

This looks like an ordinary hairbrush—oval, with a handle at one end. The bristles are fairly widely spaced, imbedded in a rubber cushion, and may be made of metal or a stiff synthetic material. A pin brush is a must for show dogs, as it removes only dead hairs.

Natural Bristle Brush

Like a hairbrush, this kind has closely spaced natural bristles. These brushes are usually oval, with or without a handle. Natural bristle brushes are very good for shorthaired dogs, such as the Basenji, and most harsh-coated breeds.

Slicker Brush

This style of brush has a long handle at one end attached to a rectangle of bristles, made either of soft, flexible wire or stiffer wire. Slicker brushes are used for the heavy-duty brushing of heavily matted or longhaired, densely coated dogs; the soft-wire style is also excellent for grooming delicate coats for the show ring.

Hound Glove

Many of the shorthaired dogs—sporting dogs and hounds in particular—do not need lengthy work-outs with a long-bristled brush, requiring only a rubdown with a hound glove instead. This is a mitt that has a roughened surface of horsehair or nylon at the palm; some styles may have soft-wire bristles. A brisk rubdown will remove dirt and massage the dog's skin.

Half-fine, Half-coarse Comb

Resembling a pocket comb, this is good either for roughing out major tangles or putting finishing touches on a dog that has been fully groomed.

Mat Comb

This device is intended to remove the heaviest mats from the coats of longhaired dogs. It has thick, widely spaced bars that are worked through the mat, from the skin outward.

Rake

This looks like a miniature garden rake, with a fairly long handle and one or two rows of widely spaced teeth. It may be made of metal or wood. A rake will help with the messier tangles of longhaired dogs.

Curry Comb

The kind used for dogs, like that for horses, consists of several concentric ovals of pliable, nubbed plastic. This kind of comb is best for smooth-coated dogs.

Poodle Clips

Puppy Clip

In this clip, the dog has a long coat with a pompon at the base of the tail. The look is created by shaving the face, throat, feet, and the base of the tail only.

Sporting Clip

In this clip, the dog's coat is trimmed to no longer than one inch, revealing the outline of the body. The only places that are shaved are the face, feet, throat, and base of the tail.

English Saddle

This clip is created by shaving the face, throat, feet, upper forelegs, base of tail, a spot on the flanks, and bands on the hind legs. The dog then has a full coat on the front portion, a pompon on the tail, and puffs of hair on the forelegs and hind legs.

Continental Clip

This style resembles the English Saddle, but the hindquarters are shaved entirely, as are the upper hind legs. There is an optional pompon on the hips, and pompons at the ankles.

Obedience Training and Problem Solving

A Dual Responsibility

A well-behaved dog is not the result of wishful thinking. Good behavior is the product of teaching your dog to understand what is expected, what behavior will or will not be tolerated. The dog is only as good as its owner. And you are the person responsible to teach the dog in a way that it can understand what is expected.

The Basics of Training

Obedience training is like insurance: You may be sorry you didn't get it before you needed it. Training is necessary and beneficial for a dog; it is a must for the owner.

Behind almost every behavioral difficulty dog owners encounter there lies a problem in communication. Obedience training teaches an owner how to communicate with his dog.

There are two ways to educate your dog: either by training at home or by enrolling your pet and yourself in obedience classes taught by a professional. For many breeds, home training is satisfactory as long as the owner is a patient and capable educator. Using a standard obedience-training guide and working systematically with your dog is likely to produce good results.

Formal schooling, the other option, is the more certain method for success; it may be used for any breed and is especially recommended for large dogs and breeds that tend to have independent and willful temperaments. While a professional can train a dog at any age, it is best to begin schooling at eight months. In several weeks, your dog will learn such basic commands as Sit, Lie Down, Stay, and Come.

Many people still think that poor behavior may be corrected by hitting and yelling. Abuse, however, is not training; it is just abuse. Introducing pain and intimidation into a learning situation only retards learning, because a dog cannot understand what is being taught when it is fearful of being hurt. Although owners often correct their dogs out of anger, doing so is likely to inflict more damage than the original crime. Put yourself in the dog's place: Think about living with someone who comes home and starts to yell, hit you, or tell you what a horrible creature you are, while you have no understanding of why you are being punished. This is the case with many dogs and owners. If these owners invested the time in obedience training, life would be far more pleasant for both partners in this relationship.

Talking to Your Dog

Training your dog with verbal commands not only teaches it what you expect but teaches you what your dog's limitations are. We tend to judge dogs by human standards, rather than according to their way of thinking. But dogs are remarkable creatures whose intelligence is amazing—once you realize that they do not think like people. Obedience work will show you how to communicate on a level your dog understands.

There are many situations in life where a dog is not able to decide what the appropriate behavior is. Physically controlling many dogs is nearly impossible and often dangerous; the only way to be able to direct your dog's behavior is by verbal commands. Training can prevent or cure almost any problem a dog owner encounters. The ability to give your dog a direction will make it a pleasant companion and ensure that your walks together will be pleasurable excursions.

Meaning What You Say

A common mistake many people make is to repeat a command. Since a dog's hearing is roughly sixteen times keener than ours, it is clearly not a hearing problem that makes for ill-behaved dogs.

They just aren't responding. Bear in mind that constantly changing terms or commands is very confusing for a dog. There are hundreds of ways of expressing an idea in our language; thus "Come here"; "Get over here"; "Sit"; "Sit down"; "Go lie down"; "Stop"; and "Get out of there" can all be different ways of saying the same thing to a dog. But the unreliability, the inconsistency, of these commands makes it difficult for a dog to respond appropriately. Little wonder that many dogs don't respond at all.

It is also true that, with dogs, it is not just what you say that counts, but how you say it. People who speak too softly may sound like they are issuing a complaint instead of a command. Yet it is very difficult to realize this unless you are getting feedback from someone who knows how to use his voice properly. Basic obedience training makes it possible for you to control your dog with a word. Instead of telling your dog that it is wrong, you will be able to give it an indication of what you want. It is always easier to work in a positive direction, whether you are dealing with people or dogs. And remember—one of a dog's chief joys in life is pleasing its owner. Through obedience training, you will learn how to use your voice and to keep it at a reasonable volume. You will learn that your constant repetition of commands has taught your dog not to respond to you, because you are not willing to enforce what you say when you say it.

Body Language and Praise

Obedience training will also teach you the importance of body language—how to move. Proper movement will make it much easier for your dog to understand where you are going so it can follow or stay when it is supposed to.

Another essential tool that you will learn to use is praise, the importance of which is hard for most people to understand.

But lavishing positive acknowledgment on a dog for being good is one of the most effective ways of teaching it to be a happy companion and good canine citizen.

The Benefits of Training

Basic obedience training will enhance the relationship between you and your dog in a variety of ways. If you start training early, behavior problems will not develop. Training will enable your dog to understand what you expect from it and to consistently follow your wishes. The expense, aggravation, and incessant nuisance of having an unruly animal will be corrected or avoided altogether.

One of the biggest advantages of training is that it instills in your dog the confidence that comes from being with a loving, approving, and reliable owner. Some of the most insecure and shy dogs will blossom with the new-found confidence that training gives them.

A dog has a need to be able to work for you. If you develop that working relationship through training, you will find that the relationship you and your pet establish is the one everyone looks for from their dog. Through training you make your dog a devoted, trusting, and loyal friend. But the decision is yours, not your dog's. If you want a dog that is a pleasure to live with, a pride to own, and the love of your life, train it.

One last point: Training your dog is also an excellent way to make new friends. Dogs are one interest that people throughout the world have in common. The understanding of another creature, the sensitivity, and the fun that training give to a person can bring out some of the more positive traits in the human character.

Solving Behavioral Problems

There are several problems that dog owners will be likely to face as they learn to live with their pets. The simplest of these—such as learning to persuade your dog to walk calmly by your side, or to come when called—are addressed by basic obedience training. But there are other problems that arise which will be far more likely to have a harmful effect on your relationship with your dog; these include failure of the dog to be housebroken; aggressive or overprotective behavior; and destructiveness.

Each of these problems requires a fair amount of patience and hard work to overcome. As in basic obedience training, the solutions to these difficulties lie in being able to communicate effectively with your dog, so that it can learn what kind of behavior makes you happy—not just that it is sometimes a very bad dog.

Housebreaking Your Dog

Dealing with any behavioral problems can be frustrating, but it is housebreaking difficulties that seem to provoke the strongest response of anger. Remember, first of all, that a dog's housebreaking problems can be the result of ill health. If your dog has internal parasites, mistakes will be unavoidable; the only way that you can be sure that your dog does not have parasites is to take a stool sample to your veterinarian. Additionally, bitches sometimes suffer from a low-grade urinary tract infection that can result in spot wetting. Many veterinarians believe that such an infection should not cause spot wetting; nonetheless, clearing up the infection also usually clears up the problem.

The moral is that if you are suddenly confronted with unpleasant surprises from your four-footed friend, be sure to have the veterinarian check its health. Now let us turn to specific types of housebreaking problems and why they occur. As was noted before, many owners try to correct a dog when they are angry and frustrated, usually resorting to physical discipline to make a point. The first reaction most people have to a dog's

accident is one of well-focused rage. The offender is disciplined with shouts and a firm hand, or is dragged to the scene of the crime to have its face rubbed in its mistake. Now these actions can make you feel better, but ultimately this type of discipline leads to more mistakes. Most dogs are not capable of remembering an offense; and even if they could remember, the memory evaporates in the face of an owner's anger. In fear, dogs concentrate on survival, not on the mess. To solve the problem, look at why the dog is doing this, not at what it did. When does your dog make a mistake? Many dogs have accidents only when they have been left on their own. If this happens, it is not cause to feel persecuted by your dog—there is a big difference between spite and nerves. When you are gone and there is no one around to let the dog out, it becomes nervous. But you can take a number of precautions to ensure that you return to a dry, odor-free house. You must provide your dog with adequate opportunities to relieve himself in the approved manner. Most dogs need to be walked at least three times each day, and no dog can be left alone for more than eight to ten hours. Before you let your dog know that you are angry, examine your conscience and be sure you are being fair.

Don't become so caught up in the training that you overlook the most important courtesy of a dog owner: You must never allow your dog to foul a sidewalk or another person's yard or lawn. Many cities and towns now have laws making it the responsibility of an owner to clean up after a dog. A lack of consideration in this regard will earn you and your dog no friends, and may get you in hot water with the law.

The Confinement Technique

The use of the confinement technique is an absolute must for housebreaking, because most dogs will not mess where they must stay unless they are forced to. Nonetheless, there is a right and wrong way to limit your dog's space. Do not close a dog in a room with the door shut; it will not like it and will, accordingly, let you know. Using a tension bar gate or a crate is the best way to limit your dog's access to the house. This kind of confinement has a calming effect on dogs, and it prevents a dog from pacing (which can cause an accident).

Every time you return to your dog, greet it in a positive tone. You need not be happy about finding a mess, but biting your lip will help you get over your initial burst of anger. Practice leaving your dog for a few minutes at a time; gradually work up to five, ten, fifteen, and then thirty minutes, until the dog is sure you are returning to it. Continue the training with your dog for one to three weeks, gradually giving it access to larger parts of the house. (During the training, it is critical that the dog be confined whenever it cannot be supervised.) In a very short time, the dog will be housetrained.

Marking Territory

Many male dogs insist upon leaving their scent—i.e. urinating—throughout a house to mark their territory. In many small breeds, the leg-lifting routine can go unnoticed until the finish on your furniture is spoiled. Some dogs do this to reassure themselves that it's their turf and to let the other dogs, neighbors, and family members know this as well.

One of the first steps to stopping this behavior is to have your dog neutered. To many owners, performing this procedure may seem cruel, even barbarous. Nonetheless, neutering is effective, has medical benefits, and makes a dog a better pet and companion. (In addition, neutering obviously eliminates the risk that your dog will be responsible for a litter of hapless, unwanted puppies.)

Neutering does not have the effect of a frontal lobotomy; the dog's personality is not destroyed by it. What neutering will do is remove the dog's aggressive need to mark his territory. Bear in mind that aggressiveness and protectiveness are different; altering your dog will not remove his instinct to protect you.

Nor will neutering make a dog fat. If your friend is becoming too well padded, reduce or change his diet and get out and exercise him. The latter will be good for both of you.

There are times when a dog will mark its territory whether the owner is at home or not. When you are out, confine the dog. When at home, keep the dog on a leash with you to break his pattern of behavior. Trying constantly to watch the dog usually will not work, but keeping it next to you will.

What to Do When Accidents Happen

If you should find a mistake, clean it up first. Then go and get the dog, take it to the spot, and have it lie down. Doing this is not a punishment, but a subtle way of letting the dog know that it is going to be spending time there; when it knows this, it will be convinced that it is an unsatisfactory place to relieve itself. A good technique for dealing with some offenders is the balloon cure. Take a balloon, inflate it, and then shake it at the dog menacingly and say "What is this?" in a stern voice. As the dog starts to back away, take a pin and pop the terrible thing. Doing this establishes the balloon as a dreaded object; taping a balloon wherever a dog is hiking its leg should cure it fast. Remember that this technique must be used with obedience training and confinement.

Cleaning a dirty area properly is important because most dogs are inclined to repeat their mistakes if they are reminded of them. Cleaning the area with an odor neutralizer works the best; products such as Nilodor, Hygia, or others are very effective. To remove stains, Four Paws or Dog-Tex are reliable products and include odor neutralizers in the solution; you can double up by adding concentrated odor neutralizers to the stain remover. Club soda is a great standby if you run out of the stain removers.

In summary, take the following steps to cure housebreaking problems: Give your dog a medical check-up; clean the dirtied area properly; confine the dog with a crate or tension bar gate; use balloons when applicable; and supervise the dog when you are at home. If you catch your dog in the act, use your voice to convey —thoroughly but gently—your utter disgust and disbelief at its deed. But remember that hitting your dog and yelling at it will not change this behavior; training it properly, with positive steps, will.

Good Dogs, Bad Dogs

Dogs differ in personality just as people do. The fact that you have lived with and trained one dog or even twenty dogs may not give you the experience or knowledge to correct the problems that you are having with the dog you currently own.

In order to correct any behavioral problem you and your dog are experiencing, the first step is to understand why the dog is behaving the way it is. Ignoring the underlying reasons for the problem will lead to confusion for both owner and owned. Often, a cycle of negative correction is established in an attempt to change the dog's behavior. Then correcting the dog becomes an exercise in frustration; the problem remains and usually grows worse. The important question you should be asking yourself is why the dog is behaving in such a way and what the two of you can do to correct it.

In the best dog–owner relationships, it is clear that dog and owner are on the same team, not opposing ones. It is vital that you believe that the dog is not doing anything to hurt you, but is acting and reacting according to its environment, genetic make-up, and the care it is receiving from you. If there is a problem with your dog, it is more than likely that there is a problem with the way you are currently handling your pet, even though your intentions are golden.

Redirecting Your Dog's Natural Instincts

While instincts help a dog survive in the wild, they often do not help a dog adjust to the world of man without the owner's guidance. All dogs have an innate desire to achieve the top rank in their social structure—to dominate other members of the pack, whether that pack consists of canines or humans. If you do not establish yourself as the superior member of the pack, the relationship between you and your dog will be one of constant competition. Your dog's position in your household can be established through obedience training. When you issue a command and the dog obeys, the dog learns that listening to you will make life much easier for you both.

Another instinct that is very strong in a dog is the "fight or flight" response to certain situations. If a dog is threatened or frightened, its first reaction will be either to fight or to run. If you cannot control your dog with your voice, you are asking for trouble. Your dog may bite someone because it couldn't or wouldn't take direction from you; or it may run under the wheels of a car because it was not taught to look to you for direction. In either case, the basic problem is the same—lack of training. Such tragedies are predictable, preventable, and cannot be called accidents.

To illustrate how behavior problems arise and how they can be solved, it may be helpful to consider a case history. This is the story of Princess, a Doberman

Pinscher bitch, whose family could not correct the dog's aggression and overprotectiveness.

Princess is grossly overweight and aggressive with both strangers and family. At the age of two years, she had become not just the reigning dog, but the terror of the house. She begged, she growled, and had recently added biting to her repertoire. Her family tolerated her behavior until Princess bit the grandmother. At this point, they decided something must be done about the dog's behavior. They called in a professional dog trainer.

Friend or Foe?

When the trainer arrived at the house, Princess was waiting, her ivories showing. She began to size him up, trying to decide whether to bite, threaten, or run and hide.

The reactions of the family members—the grandmother, mother, and two children—varied: The mother was concerned about the trainer's physical well-being, and she attempted to restrain the dog. The grandmother thought that all was fine, but the boys knew that Princess could be dangerous and were waiting for a disaster. Princess was receiving a lot of confusing signals; the message she understood was that everyone was upset and that the new person in the house was the cause.

It was very clear that any attempt to restrain the dog now would cause another biting incident. To defuse the tension in the air, the boys were sent into the next room and instructed to call Princess, loudly and enthusiastically. This they did, and it was apparent by the dog's immediate response she was happy to have an excuse to resolve the fight-or-flight dilemma and remove herself from a confusing situation. The discussion turned to Princess' background and the circumstances of the biting incident. It appeared that a game

of tug-of-war had got out of hand. To put an end to it, the grandmother picked up a toy and threw it at the dog, and the dog responded by redirecting her aggression toward the woman. After the bite, Princess settled down; the family concluded that she was a dog to be feared if she did not have her own way.

The family did not know that the game of tug-of-war encourages aggression—and is in fact used to train attack dogs. Playing tug-of-war with your dog can lead to chewing and aggression problems. It is much better to choose a game of fetch, which does not promote aggressive behavior.

Princess had grown too large to play tug-of-war safely. But it was the game of her puppyhood, and naturally she could not know that the game had become dangerous to the family. Furthermore, it was not just the game that had encouraged Princess' aggression, but also the family's lack of consistency and direction.

The Importance of Socialization

One reason for Princess' negative attitude toward people was that she had never been socialized as a puppy. There is a critical, sixteen-week period in a puppy's life that is an imprinting period. Many puppies that are not exposed to strange noises, objects, and people never adjust to the world properly. Such dogs are limited in their reactions to basic instincts for survival.

Princess' case was not unusual, as she had never been exposed to anything or anyone outside the house. Verbal control had not been established, so Princess could not be given instructions she could understand; the signals her owners gave were confusing and alarming at best. The dog was forced to guess if a particular person was friend or foe. Princess was not capable of realizing that her family was upset with her, not with the person coming into the house. Her aggression toward the family was the result of their lack of control; the dog was convinced that she was the boss.

Correcting Aggression Through Training

The first step in clearing up the problem was to lay a foundation that both the family and dog could work from—namely, obedience training. Princess was soon taught some basic commands, and this training let her know who was the boss in the house. Princess realized that she would now be told what to do and told only once. All commands would be enforced—through correction, consistency, and lavish praise. Hitting the dog was prohibited, since it didn't work and Princess was not hesitant to challenge this type of discipline. But by the tone of voice and use of a leash, she learned what was expected of her.

When strangers or friends came to the door, the family used laughter to reduce the usual tension. This technique worked well with Princess, allowing her to relax and not maintain the role of guard dog, which she was inclined to take far too seriously.

Life is becoming simpler for Princess. She can now depend on her owners to make the decision as to who is friend or foe. When someone approaches the house she still warns her people that someone is there, but now she is praised for doing her job and for responding to the command given by one of the family. Barking at people or threatening them without due cause is strictly forbidden. Not that Princess doesn't have bad thoughts occasionally, but her reactions are no longer feared or ignored. The commands are the tools that enable the family to tell the dog what her behavior should and will be.

Correct Your Dog Before It Is Too Late

If your dog is too aggressive, the problem will not go away on its own.

Rationalizing or making excuses for your dog's unwarranted aggression will pave the way for a tragedy. You are the only one that can correct your dog's behavior. If you are uncomfortable with your pet's responses to people or other dogs, consult a professional dog trainer or behaviorist for the proper guidance. Make a point of socializing and training your dog when it is a puppy; socialization is especially important, and should take place early, during the sixteen-week imprinting period of a puppy's life.

Group classes are inexpensive and offer both training and socialization. Such an investment will yield untold benefits.

Chewing and Destructiveness

There is no question that the damage dogs do by chewing belongings and furniture is costly and upsetting. Learning to control this behavior in your dog will save you much aggravation, money, and heartache.

There are a number of reasons why dogs chew; the most common causes are puppyhood teething, bordeom, lack of exercise, and separation anxiety.

As puppies, many dogs learn to fill their time with destructive activities. But owners often ask for this destruction by allowing a puppy free access to the house; just like an unsupervised two-year-old child, a puppy left to its own devices will be a terror. Once a dog learns to chew your belongings, you can be in for years of an expensive habit. Thus prevention, not correction, is the best course to take.

The only way you can prevent a dog or puppy from getting into trouble is by confining it, either with a tension bar gate or a crate. (As many disbelieving owners have learned, a dog can chew right through a closed door.) When using a tension bar gate, a good place to keep a dog is the bathroom, which can be dog-proofed easily. Dogs have a need to chew, so make sure that you give them appropriate articles to chew—rawhide sticks and dog toys are your best bet. Never give your dog something of your own; distinguishing between old and new is not in its power.

Some dogs cannot have rawhides because they swallow them almost whole or get an upset stomach from them. Beware also of certain plastic toys, which can be indigestible or harmful.

How to Deal With Chewing Problems

If you find your dog or puppy chewing on something it shouldn't, substitute the proper article. Doing this with little fanfare and a lot of praise will encourage good habits. Remember that, as with housebreaking, it is important not to react in anger. If you return home to find your new shoes shredded, bear in mind that puppies have short memories; the chances are slim that a puppy will associate the dim memory of its misdeed with your rage. Correction after the act is useless in stopping a dog from being destructive; in fact, it usually increases the chewing problem.

Separation anxiety is often the reason for a dog's destructiveness. If you suspect this is the cause, leave the dog or pup for short periods of time only, starting with a few minutes and gradually working into longer time periods. Do not make a production of leaving, but always make your return a happy event.

Leaving a radio on when you are out helps reduce chewing because a dog will not feel completely alone. When left alone, some dogs like to sleep or be near a piece of their owner's clothing; the scent reassures the dog of the owner's eventual return.

Aids for Correction

There are several products made to deter chewing; one of these is Bitter Apple, which you can apply to most objects except finished wood. On wood you can use alum, which you can get at a drug store. Mix the alum with water to form a paste and coat the area being chewed.

Some dogs become especially fond of chewing a few prohibited articles. One way to cure this is by using shake cans—empty soda cans with a handful of pennies inside. Tie three or four shake cans to the article in question and place the cans out of view on a table or shelf; when the dog takes the bait, the cans come tumbling down. After a couple of ambushes, the startled dog decides to stick to its own toys.

Some dogs will chew walls and wallboard; this behavior is usually the result of a calcium deficiency, which can be cured by adding some dolomite to your dog's food. If you are unsure how much calcium to give your dog, consult your veterinarian; too high a dose can cause medical problems.

Dogs do get cabin fever, and the only way to stop a pent-up pooch from chewing is by giving it regular exercise. If your dog wants a good long run, use forty or fifty feet of rope tied to its collar. It is wise to remember that providing your pet with adequate exercise will help to avoid many behavior problems. Exercise is crucial in the happy development of any dog's personality.

The Dog Registries

A Standard of Perfection

There are two principal purebred, all-breed dog registries in the United States. The largest and oldest is the American Kennel Club, founded in 1884, which registers 129 breeds and about one million dogs each year. The United Kennel Club, founded in 1898, registers 85 breeds and about 225,000 dogs annually.

Both registries strive to maintain the high quality of their breeds by establishing a set of guidelines, or a standard of perfection, for each breed. (In this book, the Ideal Appearance section of each breed account is based on these standards.)

Through its registry, each organization certifies the legitimacy of a dog's background—that is, its pedigree. However, the pedigree does not assure show quality, which can only be judged by performance in shows or field and obedience trials.

American Kennel Club

An independent, nonprofit organization, the American Kennel Club is comprised of over 425 autonomous breed clubs, whose representatives elect directors and decide upon breed rules that will be enforced by the board of directors. The board determines whether a new breed of dog should be added to the breeds currently recognized, and sets rules regarding registration, certification of judges, and the sanctioning of dog shows, field trials, and obedience events. Every recognized breed is judged in competition at dog shows against a standard agreed upon by the appropriate breed club and the AKC board. The standards are published annually, and it is those standards that the registry seeks to protect through registration requirements, representation at approved dog shows, and field competitions. The AKC has its headquarters at 51 Madison Avenue, New York, New York 10010, and publishes the magazine *Pure-Bred Dogs/American Kennel Gazette.* All of the breeds registered by the American Kennel Club are included in this guide.

United Kennel Club

A privately owned corporation, the United Kennel Club works with affiliated national breed organizations. Although the club registers many of the same breeds as the AKC, the UKC places stronger emphasis on the working or hunting qualities of its breeds. Included in this guide are ten breeds that are recognized only by the UKC. The organization publishes three magazines: *Bloodlines,* featuring most UKC breeds; *Coonhound Bloodlines,* which is devoted to the six coonhound breeds; and *Hunting Retriever,* which focuses on retrievers. The UKC has its headquarters at 100 East Kilgore Road, Kalamazoo, Michigan 49001.

Registering Your Dog

Purebred Background Required

In order for a puppy to be registered with either the American Kennel Club or the United Kennel Club, the puppy's parents—the dam and sire—must both already be registered with that club. Soon after the whelping, which must take place in the United States, a breeder applies to register the entire litter.

If a breeder registers with AKC, he or she will be sent a litter kit containing partially completed application forms for each of the individual puppies. When a puppy is purchased, the breeder completes the section of the application relating to the puppy's breed, sex, and color; its date of birth; the registered names of the dog's sire and dam; the breeder's name; the date of the transfer; and the name and address of the new owner.

If a litter is registered with UKC, the breeder must complete all background information on a litter application before the puppy registration certificates are sent. Each puppy is then assigned its own number. If a dog is inbred (the product of the mating of a brother and sister, mother and son, or father and daughter), a registration certificate from the UKC will also include this information.

Your Part of the Application

When you take your puppy home, you will need to complete the application form by adding the preferred name for your dog. (The AKC requires two choices for a name. The UKC requires a name that is made up of at least two words, but which does not contain more than twenty-two letters.) In a matter of weeks, provided the appropriate application fees are paid, the registry will furnish a registration certificate. If the ownership changes again, a supplement to the form can be filed.

All registration information remains on file in the registry computer. This filing system makes it possible for an owner to prove a dog's origins; it also enables the registry to calculate the number of dogs registered each year, and to compute the popularity of each breed.

Why Register Your Dog?

Club registration adds to your dog's value because it enables you to trace the dog's ancestry. Lineage is very important: Genetic factors can be a major determinant both of a dog's behavior and its health.

A reliable breeder can be counted on to supply you with all the background material about your dog that you need to properly evaluate its pedigree. At the time of purchase, make sure you are given full identifying information. Do not accept a promise of later identification.

Showing Your Dog

A Standard of Excellence

The terms "pet quality" and "show quality" are often heard by prospective owners of purebred dogs, but it is not always clear what these terms mean. In effect, a show-quality dog is one that conforms very closely to the breed's standard of excellence. Such a dog has a chance to earn points, win major shows, and eventually be designated as a champion of its breed.

A pet-quality dog may be as bright and certainly as likable as a show animal, but it has some variation in its appearance or conformation that pretty well rules out its becoming a star of the show ring. This fact in no way detracts from the animal as a lifelong friend and companion, nor does it make it any better as a friend to your children.

How Dog Shows Work

To become a champion, a dog must earn fifteen points and win at least two major shows, under two different judges. (Points are awarded on the basis of the number of competitors over which a winner is selected; the system varies from region to region and breed to breed.) A major show is one that awards three or more points to a winning dog.

Newcomers to dog shows—those animals not yet champions—show in a variety of classes (puppy, novice, bred-by-exhibitor, American bred, and open classes) against dogs of the same sex and breed. As these dogs progress, they may eventually win Best-of-Breed and move up to compete against other class winners in a group.

There are now seven groups: Sporting, Non-Sporting, Working, Hound, Terrier, Toy, and Herding. The Best-of-Breed for every breed in one group compete not against each other directly but against the published standard of excellence for their breed. The dog in the group that is judged to most closely match that standard wins the group. At the end of the day you will then have only seven dogs left—the group winners. They compete once more against their own standards; one dog wins Best-in-Show—and that is very high praise indeed.

You can, then, think of a dog show as a pyramid. You start with anywhere from a few hundred to several thousand dogs, and by the end you have one animal left.

Growing Enthusiasm

Not terribly long ago, showing a dog was considered an elite affair, one that people of moderate means seldom bothered with. That has changed remarkably in the last thirty or forty years, and today many more people are displaying an interest in showing. You do need a good dog and you do need a means of handling the dog in the ring. Many people use professional handlers, who will charge you $50.00 or more a show; for that fee they will prepare your dog for the ring, take it to the show, and bring it home again—perhaps with some ribbons.

More and more people show their own dogs, and even if these owners are less skilled than the hired handlers, they have a splendid time—and their dogs seem to love it, too. Some owners are more interested in results than in the process. These people often campaign— they send their dogs on the road, in the care of professionals, for months at a time. Generally it is far less expensive to show your own dog and drive it to and from the shows yourself.

If you have selected a dog with an elaborate coat (such as a Poodle, Old English Sheepdog, or rough Collie), you are going to have to learn how to get that coat into its full glory, because the appearance of the coat counts for a great deal with such dogs.

Knowing Your Judges

Judging beauty, style, and perfection in a dog are of course subjective; most people who show their dogs know this and watch the bulletins carefully. Keeping up in this way, they know which judges favor their kind of dog and at which shows those judges are officiating. Some officials are known to prefer one sex, while other judges will not seriously consider a dog being handled by anyone but a professional handler. Still other judges prefer larger or smaller examples of a given breed. When it comes to the show ring, choosing your judge is second only in importance to selecting your dog.

Obedience Competition

Most dog shows of significance also include obedience competitions, which are growing in importance. There, conformation does not really matter. For certain breeds, interested owners can also participate in field trials. Both the American Kennel Club and the United Kennel Club publish excellent magazines as well as pamphlets and information sheets that will keep you up to date. People interested in the spirit of the shows but reluctant to test their dogs against truly stiff competition can enter match shows. No championship points are awarded, but ribbons and trophies are doled out by the station wagon load, and lots of fun is had by all.

There is no way of predicting how much money it will cost you to show or "finish" your dog—that is, take it all the way to the championship. The expense depends on many things, including the breed and quality of the animal and whether you are going to show it yourself. Some people finish a dog for as little as $250, but others may spend $25,000.

Why Show Your Dog?

The most obvious purpose of a dog show is to distinguish, through open, public competition, the dogs that are the best examples of their breeds. These winners are bred to continue their line and keep the breed itself moving ever closer to the ideal of perfection.

In fact, though, dog shows are a bit of a circus, where all the participants can gossip, compare dogs, and share their enthusiasm. Like other sporting and competitive events, dog shows have their own code of sportsmanlike behavior. In the main, good manners should prevail; distracting entrants, currying favor with judges, complaining about a judge's decision, or any other rude or unsportsmanlike conduct is distinctly unwelcome. Do not come to a dog show with your own dog unless you are showing that day.

Even if you are not a serious competitor, remember that some people spend a lot of time and money on these events; winning or at least competing well is of enormous importance to them. You are expected to show the respect that is due them and the sport.

The best way to decide if you really want to show a dog is to spend some Saturdays and Sundays at dog shows. Talk to people, see what they do and how they do it. Make an appointment with a professional handler or breeder to get advice on whether or not you will be wasting your time and money.

The dog show is an international sport, and there is no reason why you can't participate. A car or van will be helpful, but otherwise—if your dog does not have an elaborate coat—preparation is minimal. If you decide to make a go for it at Madison Square Garden, the stakes and the investment go up, but most shows are less serious affairs.

Showing a dog is, by the way, a fine family activity. Children who are showing the family dog seldom find time to get into trouble, and there are junior showmanship classes where the youngster's performance as a handler is judged. For the fun of it, at least, showing your dog is something you should consider.

Illustrated Glossary

The drawings shown in this table illustrate some of the most common terms used in describing the breeds in this guide.

Ears	Bat ears

Rose ears

Hanging ears

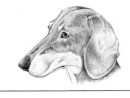

Skull	Bumpy skull

Muzzle	Short muzzle

Prick ears

Semi-prick ears

Button ears

Drop ears

Domed skull

Upward-tipped muzzle

Tails

Rat tail

Saber tail

Docked tail

Stance

Out at elbows

Moderately angulated
hindquarters

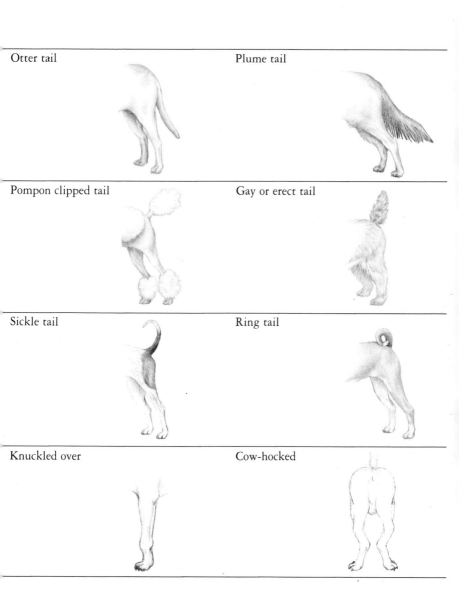

Otter tail

Plume tail

Pompon clipped tail

Gay or erect tail

Sickle tail

Ring tail

Knuckled over

Cow-hocked

Dogs and Owners

This list provides the names of all the dogs photographed for this guide, along with the names of the dogs' owners. "Ch." before a dog's name indicates that it is a champion; "PR" designates a special UKC bloodline called Purple Ribbon.

---

1 Miniature Dachshund
Ch. Farr's Wee Augustus Aimée, ML
Owned by Leah Farr-Williams

2 Pekingese
Ch. Muhlin Magician of Wyn-D-Hill
Owned by Mary McCracken

3 Yorkshire Terrier
Ch. Mayfair Barban Verik
Owned by Barbara Wolferman

4 Silky Terrier
Ch. Admiral Nelson's Blue Rebel
Owned by Gloria Setmayer

5 Papillon
Ch. Janra's Fauconneau De Luci
Owned by Lois L. Horan

6 Maltese
Fable-Kapthan Rockin' Robin
Owned by Liz Morgan, Cathy
Budenbender, and Kathy DiGiacomo

7 Japanese Chin
Ch. Ut-Chu vem Haus Sonnenschein
Owned by Willy and Ursula Hill

8 Tibetan Spaniel
Tashi Bajah Konda
Owned by Fredric P. Terman

9 Prince Charles English Toy Spaniel
Ch. Luary Mercury
Owned by Mary L. Hoagland

10 Blenheim English Toy Spaniel
Luary Valcan
Owned by Mary L. Hoagland

11 King Charles English Toy Spaniel
Green Yale Mac-A-Million
Owned by Nancy and David Byram Jr.

12 Ruby English Toy Spaniel
Ch. Nanda's Red Dragon
Owned by Dr. and Mrs. Morton
Schwimmer

13 Brussels Griffon
Treyacre's Ike of Demi-Jo
Owned by Gardner F. Sheridan

14 Affenpinscher
Deer Run's Eric the Red
Owned by J. Tobin Jackson

15 Toy Poodle
Marweg Tres Tacky
Owned by Mary Ann B. Giles

16 Pomeranian
Ch. The Pine's Hells a Poppin
Owned by Gloria Setmayer

17 Long Coat Chihuahua
Dickerson's Sioux City Soe
Owned by Louis Colacurto

18 Smooth Coat Chihuahua
Crest-Haven Rose Cuervo of Oz
Owned by M. L. J. Orlik

19 Toy Fox Terrier
Ch. PR Singleton's Tarzan's Jane
Owned by Jeri Singleton

20 Miniature Pinscher
Ch. Radel's Rainier Filius Regis
Owned by Rose J. Radel

21 Smooth Dachshund
Ch. Sandword Magpie
Owned by Herbert L. Peters

22 Longhaired Dachshund
Ch. Bayard la Joliette
Owned by Leah Farr Williams

23 Wirehaired Dachshund
Ch. Solo's Seafarer W.
Owned by Patti Nelson

24 Dandie Dinmont Terrier
Wincidell's Promise to Keep
Owned by Laura Greene and Henry
Kauffman

25 Miniature Poodle
Ch. Merene's Silver Calypso CDX
Owned by Irene Meitzler

26 Bichon Frise
Petit Four Ultra Violet
Owned by Judith L. Hilmer

27 Lhasa Apso
Ch. Anbara-Rimar Mary Puppins
Owned by Barbara Wood

Many of these dogs are also featured in Coat Types, the Key to the Color Plates, and in the black-and-white show poses of each breed account.

The Dalmatian photographed for The Dog's Anatomy, on pages 24–25, is owned by Janet Ashbey.

The illustrations of Poodle clips on page 293 are reproduced from *The Complete Dog Book,* by permission of the American Kennel Club.

---

28 Shih Tzu
Ch. Lou Wan Rebel Rouser
Owned by Lou and Wanda Gee, Emily Gunning, and Dolly Wheeler

29 Norfolk Terrier
Castlepoint Jeroboam
Owned by Mrs. Mary Stevens Baird

30 Norwich Terrier
Ch. Stoney Meadow's Betsy Rose
Owned by Mrs. W. P. Wear and Patricia Whiteside

31 Australian Terrier
Ch. Ha Su's Raucas Caucas O'Wattle
Owned by Susan Semegram and Beth McCraken

32 Cairn Terrier
Ch. Shin Pond Tradition
Owned by Mrs. Laura De Vincent

33 West Highland White Terrier
Ch. Dawns Up N Adam
Owned by Dawn L. Martin

34 Sealyham Terrier
Ch. Goodspice Sesame Hobbit Hill
Owned by Margery Good, Marion Strodtheck, and Thomas Farrell

35 Skye Terrier
Ch. Besdam Evita
Owned by Ernest and Barbara Koseff

36 Scottish Terrier
Royal Scott's Brindle Boy CDX
Owned by Blanche L. Everett and Dawn L. Martin

37 Miniature Schnauzer
Spring-Along Night Rider
Owned by Mary E. Spring

38 Wire Fox Terrier
Ch. Tallyho Tyrone
Owned by Eva Sasovetz

39 Lakeland Terrier
Kilfel Pointe of Vu
Owned by Patricia Peters

40 Smooth Fox Terrier
Ch. Foxden Warspite
Owned by Foxden Kennels

41 Border Terrier
Ch. Farmway Cherrywren
Owned by Hazel and Jennifer Wichman

42 Pug
Ch. Laughing Water's Bronco
Owned by Carroll and Toni Harrold

43 Beagle
Ch. Jo-Mar's Repeat Performance
Owned by Marcia A. Foy

44 Beagle
Ch. Pin Oak's Mello Maverick "Hooper"
Owned by J. Ralph Alderfer

45 English Cocker Spaniel
Carry-On Kerry Ceili, UDT, WDX
Owned by Emily McDermott

46 Cocker Spaniel
Ch. Saucon Valley's Rocket Fire
Owned by Helen and Rudi Rayner

47 Cocker Spaniel
Ch. Daybreak's Bottoms Up
Owned by Bettie A. Burnett

48 Cocker Spaniel
Ch. Pineshadow's Black Prince
Owned by Bettie A. Burnett

49 Shetland Sheepdog
Brandymen's Precious and Few
Owned by Connie Fiedler

50 Schipperke
Valkyra Mazeltov
Owned by Diane L. Jackson and Carol L. Schnur

51 Toy Manchester Terrier
Ch. Golden Scoop Abbigail Aurora
Owned by Gladys and Earl Weikel

52 Italian Greyhound
Ch. Tudor's Ferrari Navi Blu
Owned by Nancy Tubb

53 Basset Hound
Ch. Charton's Racketeer
Owned by Mrs. Tontan McHale

54 Clumber Spaniel
Ch. Crosswind's Ian of Rivendell
Owned by Ricky Blackman

55 Pembroke Welsh Corgi
Terenelf's Paddy Hopscotch
Owned by Lois E. Kay

56 Cardigan Welsh Corgi
Ch. Aragorn's Out of the Blue CD
Owned by Steve and Marieann Gladstone

57 Bulldog
Bounty's Arrogant Mutineer
Owned by Roberta Arnold

58 French Bulldog
Ch. Kyle's Mon Ami
Owned by F. Behr

59 Boston Terrier
It's Mister Chips Again
Owned by J. T. Les

60 American Staffordshire Terrier
Mydelle's Centerfold
Owned by Leslie Nelinson

61 Staffordshire Bull Terrier
Ch. Dauntless Brindle Doll ("Dolly")
Owned by John D. Recca

62 American Pit Bull Terrier
Mydelle's Independence
Owned by Leslie Nelinson

63 Bull Terrier
Ch. Brunswick Jet Rangu
Owned by Linda Frederick

64 Bull Terrier
Ch. Banbury Bendetta of Bedrock
Owned by Jay and Mary Remer and
W. E. Mackay-Smith

65 Basenji
Ch. Djakoba's Solo Spotshot
Owned by Tom and Judy Matunas

66 Manchester Terrier
Ch. Marlyn's Good Vibes Sunkist
Owned by Carl Adiletti

67 Pharaoh Hound
Crescent Moon's Kato Zak Ro
Owned by Kim H. Cooke

68 Whippet
Ch. Ondega's Sedgewick
Owned by Kathy Lieblich

69 Plott Hound
PR Everson's Renegade Eagle
Owned by Larry L. Everson

70 Bluetick Coonhound
Coon Creek Blue Ranger II
Owned by Weslie Blue

71 English Coonhound
William's Hardrock II
Owned by Michael Seets

72 Redbone Coonhound
Pel-Mel's Moonliten Junior
Owned by Jesse L. Melton and Brian K.
Pell

73 Harrier
Pixshire Fame
Owned by Robert Paust

74 Treeing Walker Coonhound
Ch. Table Rock Mundo III
Owned by Raymond Lasseter, Jr.

75 English Foxhound
Ch. Plum Run Wagner
Owned by Suzy A. Reingold and
Richard L. Reynolds

76 American Foxhound
Ch. Sportin' Life Trail Blazer
Owned by Sue A. Lackey

77 Dalmatian
Ch. Sugarfrost High Fashion
Owned by Janet Ashbey

78 Brittany
Ch. Jen Mar's Time After Time
Owned by Mary Ann Breininger

79 English Springer Spaniel
Willowbank's Loon, CMD
Owned by Patty Hauer

80 Welsh Springer Spaniel
Ch. Statesmen's Charming Kismet CD
Owned by Richard A. Rohrbacher

81 Sussex Spaniel
Ch. Eryn B. Harviestoun Lexxfield
Owned by August E. Wieland

82 Field Spaniel
Ch. Pin Oak's Midnight Arrogance
Owned by Helga Alderfer

83 American Water Spaniel
Ch. Wildemoor's Nisha Hanne CD
Owned by Dr. Sheldon and Barbara
Dubinett

84 Tibetan Terrier
Ch. Taichen's Tsampa
Owned by Paula A. Hutchinson

85 Bearded Collie
Ch. Bendale Special Lady CD
Owned by Michele Ritter

86 Puli
Ch. Wallbanger Kedves Szuka
Owned by Carolyn S. Nusbickel

87 Standard Poodle
Gorgi's Joval Starting Over
Owned by Debra Berglond

88 Portuguese Water Dog
Ch. Spin Drift Genoa CDX
Owned by H. Edward Whitney

89 Bedlington Terrier
Ch. Willow Wind's Satin Doll
Owned by Elaine T. Haskett

90 Wirehaired Pointing Griffon
Cherry Valley's Spring Mist
Owned by Linda Williams

91 Standard Schnauzer
Ch. Farm Hill's Zoe
Owned by Carol Thordsen

92 Soft-Coated Wheaten Terrier
Ch. Shandalee Write on Lacey!
Owned by Sue Goldberg

93 Kerry Blue Terrier
Ch. Elbrley's Trefoil Demon
Owned by Carol Postley

94 Welsh Terrier
Ch. Sutop's Classy Lass
Owned by Sue Weiss

95 Airedale Terrier
Ch. Piccadilly's Irish Coffee
Owned by Bonnie B. Moyher

96 Irish Terrier
Ch. Rockledge Encore O'Aberdovey
Owned by Sally Critchlow

97 Australian Shepherd
Ch. Liberty Yankee's Meg (I)
Owned by Patricia F. Clark, Liberty
Kennel

98 English Shepherd
Danfred's E.T.
Owned by Diana L. Karr

99 Border Collie
Wood Glen's Erin v. Fortora Cox
Owned by Julie J. Forsyth

100 Australian Cattle Dog
Ch. Red Jester's Blue Jazz
Owned by Carol Selzle Petruzzo

101 Norwegian Elkhound
Ch. Nyker TNT Silver Buccaneer
Owned by Mrs. Polly Nickerson

102 Keeshond
Ch. Ruttkay Sahnsirai of Min-Mac
Owned by Joan D. Hoffman

103 American Eskimo
Pada's Fight-O, Jr.
Owned by Frank Morlock

104 Samoyed
Ch. Norwood's White Magic
Owned by Chuck and Lorraine Waldes

105 Belgian Tervuren
Pepite de Chateau Blanc CD
Owned by Phoebe R. Wolff

106 Belgian Sheepdog
Ch. Breines Mensch CD
Owned by Estelle Breines

107 Belgian Malinois
Ch. Croc Blanc's Victoire Zool
Owned by Mary Bowell

108 Siberian Husky
Ch. Innisfree's Ms Cinnar
Owned by Dick Dalakian

109 Old English Sheepdog
Ch. Moptop's Crystal Clear
Owned by Susan L. McLaughlin

110 Otter Hound
Ch. Birchdell's Ragmop of Sunwood
Owned by Elizabeth Muthard

111 Chow Chow
Ch. Dusten's Kid Shelleen
Owned by Cindy Attinello

112 Briard
Ch. Phydeaux Take the Money N Run
Owned by Terry Miller

113 Bouvier des Flandres
Ch. Chien d'Argent du Plateau CD
Owned by Lucille Gill

114 Giant Schnauzer
Appawillow's Chevalier CD
Owned by Karen Palmer

115 German Wirehaired Pointer
Ch. Jerelin's Chin-E-Chin-Chin, CD
Owned by Linda H. Krepak

116 German Short-haired Pointer
Ch. Shill Rest's Invincible Tank
Owned by David R. Zehner

117 Pointer
Ch. Marjetta's National Acclaim
Owned by Michael Zollo

118 Black and Tan Coonhound
Ch. Silver Ridge Caro
Owned by Eleanor A. Keefe

119 Weimaraner
Gental Hand's Crystal Ann
Owned by Joseph V. Maffeo Jr.

120 Vizsla
Ch. Brylynn's Viking Valkyrie
Owned by Florence Knudsen

121 Rhodesian Ridgeback
Calico Ridge Rocky Mt. High
Owned by Kathleen Kolp

122 Labrador Retriever
Tobrelle's Mocha Chunky Nut, UDT
Owned by Donna P. Barto

123 Labrador Retriever
Halfway Broadreach Galaxy
Owned by Kendall Herr

124 Labrador Retriever
Rocky Acre's Bay of Baffin
Owned by Mary Lynn Moser

125 Golden Retriever
Ch. Cumming's Chip of Gold
Owned by Mrs. Mary W. Cummings

126 Flat-Coated Retriever
Ch. Quillquest Eros, CD, WC
Owned by Gillian Impey

127 Chesapeake Bay Retriever
Ch. Eastern Waters' Break O'Day, CD
Owned by Daniel Horn

128 Curly-Coated Retriever
Ch. Karakul Echoes of Freedom, CDX
Owned by Doris and Brad Hodges

129 Irish Water Spaniel
Uates of Lishabrogue, TD, WC
Owned by Elissa J. Kirkegard

130 Gordon Setter
Ch. Brunswick's Britt of Kalon
Owned by Joan L. Worthington

131 Irish Setter
Kindelan's Finnigans Rainbow, CDX
Owned by Karen Hertzog

132 English Setter
Anjo's Dusty Road
Owned by Andy and Joanne Mistler

133 Afghan Hound
Ch. Shamalar's Fuzzbuster
Owned by Gail S. Dobrowolski

134 Saluki
Ch. Desiderota Symatar of El-Roh
Owned by Harry E. Stiles and Lee
Walker Jr.

135 Greyhound
Eldon's Parti Girl
Owned by Mary Trubek

136 Ibizan Hound
Conamor Isla Del Sol
Owned by Deidra Lawrence

137 **Doberman Pinscher**
Ch. Telstar's Rachel of Bel-Greg
Owned by Jane N. Benfield

138 **Boxer**
Beaufront's First Edition
Owned by Mrs. Billie McFadden

139 **Alaskan Malamute**
Kahoon's Arctic Quinn
Owned by Scott Shive

140 **German Shepherd**
Guy Von Der WestFestend
Owned by Thomas Walsh

141 **Smooth Collie**
My Friend's Gray Agate
Owned by Heidi Myers

142 **Smooth Collie**
Ch. My Friend's Whodunnit
Owned by Heidi Myers

143 **Rough Collie**
Ch. Hi-Crest Knock On Wood
Owned by Joseph Reno

144 **Bernese Mountain Dog**
Ch. Palmer's Astarte von Ursa, CD
Owned by Gail Palmer

145 **Komondor**
Ch. Summithill Gillian, CD
Owned by John Landis

146 **Irish Wolfhound**
Ch. Powerscourt Tom Dooley, M.D.
Owned by Mrs. Thomas Powers

147 **Borzoi**
Ch. Majenkir Wotan of Foxcroft
Owned by Angela and David San Paolo

148 **Scottish Deerhound**
Ch. Gayleward's Checkmate
Owned by Maryann Yuran

149 **Great Dane**
Fadania's Harlequin Romance
Owned by Clydette J. Lobach

150 **Great Dane**
Coventry's Golden Grand Duke
Owned by Robert and Ruth M. Cyr

151 **Akita**
Ch. Tobe's Abrakadabra
Owned by Beverly A. Bonadonna

152 **Rottweiler**
Noblehaus Decathlon Pete
Owned by Barbara J. Morris

153 **Bullmastiff**
Bo Duke of Mountain View
Owned by Marjorie Saylor

154 **Mastiff**
Deer Run Fawn
Owned by J. Tobin Jackson

155 **Shorthaired Saint Bernard**
Ch. Schnitzer's Kunstwerk, CD
Owned by Robert L. Harris

156 **Longhaired Saint Bernard**
Eiba's Simeon von Mallen
Owned by Brandon Baker

157 **Bloodhound**
Ch. Serendipity's Nick Chopper
Owned by Kenneth Sexton

158 **Newfoundland**
Ch. Pouch Cove Gref of Newton-Ark
Owned by David A. Helming

159 **Kuvasz**
Ch. Lofranco's General MacSuibhne
Owned by Herbert V. Sweeney

160 **Great Pyrenees**
Ch. Galesway May Be So, CD
Owned by Gale B. Armstrong

Cover
Cairn Terrier
Owned by Mrs. Laura DeVincent

Index

Numbers in boldface type refer to color plates. Numbers in italics refer to pages.

Chanticleer Staff

Publisher: Paul Steiner
Editor-in-Chief: Gudrun Buettner
Executive Editor: Susan Costello
Managing Editor: Jane Opper
Project Editor: Ann Whitman
Production Manager: Helga Lose
Art Director: Carol Nehring
Art Associate: Ayn Svoboda
Drawings: Robert Villani

Design: Massimo Vignelli